Nadya Williams

Christians Reading Classics

An Introduction to GRECO-ROMAN CLASSICS from Homer to Boethius

ZONDERVAN ACADEMIC

Christians Reading Classics

Published by Zondervan, 3950 Sparks Drive SE, Suite 101, Grand Rapids, MI 49546, USA. Zondervan is a registered trademark of The Zondervan Corporation, L.L.C., a wholly owned subsidiary of HarperCollins Christian Publishing, Inc.

Requests for information should be addressed to customercare@harpercollins.com.

Zondervan titles may be purchased in bulk for educational, business, fundraising, or sales promotional use. For information, please email SpecialMarkets@Zondervan.com.

ISBN 978-0-310-17107-2 (softcover)
ISBN 978-0-310-17108-9 (ebook)
ISBN 978-0-310-18160-6 (audio)

HarperCollins Publishers, Macken House, 39/40 Mayor Street Upper, Dublin 1, D01 C9W8, Ireland (https://www.harpercollins.com)

Cover design: Micah Kandros Design
Cover image: Shutterstock
Interior design: Denise Froehlich

Printed in the United States of America

25 26 27 28 29 LBC 5 4 3 2 1

"Nadya Williams is my trusted teacher of the classical world. For Christians who long to know the world that preceded and paralleled their Scriptures, her introduction should be the primary resource. She is a devoted Christian and engaging writer who makes the classical era sing for contemporary readers!"

—Jessica Hooten Wilson, Fletcher Jones Chair of Great Books, Pepperdine University

"Nadya Williams is a discerning guide to the Greco-Roman classics, showing us not just *that* Christians should read these authors but *how* they should do so. She appreciatively and critically calls attention to the unresolved tensions and shortcomings in classical works yet highlights the proleptic glimpses of the gospel these works provide. Neophytes and seasoned readers alike will find great riches in the Egyptian gold that Williams recovers in this delightful book."

—Jeff Bilbro, Professor of English, Grove City College and editor-in-chief, Front Porch Republic

"Many classical Christian schools help children sail smoothly but leave parents swirling between the Scylla of embarrassing ignorance and the Charybdis of preachy didacticism. Nadya Williams gives those without classical education the right amount of background to address intelligent questions to inquiring minds."

—Dr. Marvin Olasky, *Christianity Today* executive editor for news and global

"Every follower of Jesus Christ who is considering reading ancient Greek or Roman literature should explore this wise, learned, and faithful book. *Christians Reading Classics* educates, edifies, and entertains. Nadya Williams is the faithful guide I have been waiting for; I needed this book more than I knew."

—Timothy Larsen, McManis Professor of Christian Thought, Wheaton College

"What a gift Nadya Williams has given us! This is not only a masterful introduction to the Greek and Roman classics but also a compelling account of how Christianity wrestled with, challenged, and ultimately fulfilled the deepest longings of the classical world. Believers and skeptics alike will be enriched by this remarkable book—I wish I had read it twenty years ago!"

—Dr. John Dickson, author, historian, Jean Kvamme Distinguished Professor of Biblical Studies and Public Christianity, Wheaton College

"Hospitable and beautifully written, this book reminds us why ancient texts still speak to the soul. Nadya Williams offers not just a guide but a kind of spiritual friendship across time."

—Sarah-Jane Murray, PhD, Professor of Great Texts, Baylor University, founder of The Greats Story Lab

"Nadya Williams brilliantly offers a fresh perspective on Greco-Roman classics through a Christian lens. With insightful analysis and practical guidance, she reveals how these works can spark joy, deepen biblical understanding, and foster virtue, just as they did for early believers like Augustine. I recommend this book for anyone seeking to enrich their faith through the wisdom of antiquity."

—Soren Schwab, Vice President of Partnerships, Classic Learning Test

To Dan. Omnia vincit amor.

Contents

Part IV: Heroes and Role Models

Part V: Virtues and Vices in the Age of Anxiety

ca. 2100 BC
The *Epic of Gilgamesh*

ca. 750 BC
Iliad (attributed to Homer)

ca. 725 BC
Odyssey (attributed to Homer)

ca. 700 BC
Hesiod, *Theogony* and *Works and Days*

ca. 518–446 BC
Pindar

ca. 530s–470s BC
Phrynichus

ca. 545/4–456/5 BC
Aeschylus

ca. 397–322 BC
Aeschines

ca. 390–325/4 BC
Lycurgus

384–322 BC
Aristotle

384–322 BC
Demosthenes

Mid-4th c. BC
Aeneas Tacticus,
to Survive Under

239–169 B
Quintus Enni

234–149 B
Cato the Eld

2100 800 700 600 500 400 300

ca. 650 BC
Semonides of Amorgos

ca. 630–570 BC
Sappho

ca. 480–420s BC
Herodotus

ca. 496/5–406 BC
Sophocles

ca. 480s–407/6 BC
Euripides

ca. 450s–386 BC
Aristophanes

ca. 469–399 BC
Hippocrates

ca. 460–400 BC
Thucydides

ca. 459/8–380 BC
Lysias

ca. 429–347 BC
Plato

ca. 420s BC
Old Oligarch,
The Constitution of the Athenians

ca. 430s–360s BCE
Xenophon

1. Some of these dates are disputed. Most of the dates used in this timeline are from the *Oxford Classical Dictionary* (Oxford University Press, 1999).

ca. 110–24 BC
Cornelius Nepos

106–43 BC
Marcus Tullius Cicero

102–43 BC
Quintus Tullius Cicero

100–44 BC
Gaius Julius Caesar

ca. 86–35 BC
Gaius Sallustius
Crispus (Sallust)

ca. 84–54 BC
Gaius Valerius
Catullus

Early 1st c. AD
Apicius

Mid-1st c. AD
Pamphila

AD 27–66
Gaius Petronius
Arbiter

Mid-late 2nd c. AD
Artemidorus,
Oneirocritica
(*The Interpretation
of Dreams*)

AD 121–180
Marcus Aurelius

AD 124–170s
Apuleius

AD 160–240
Tertullian

ca. AD 182–203
Perpetua

ca. AD 204–270
Plotinus

ca. AD 210–258
Cyprian

ca. AD 480–524
Anicius Manlius
Severinus Boethius

ca. AD 484–585
Cassiodorus

65–8 BC
Horace

59 BC–AD 17
Livy

ca. 55–19 BC
Tibullus

ca. 54–16 BC
Propertius

43 BC–AD 17/18
Publius Ovidius Naso
(Ovid)

Late 1st c. BC
Sulpicia

AD 56–118
Publius Cornelius
Tacitus

ca. AD 69–120s
Gaius Suetonius
Tranquillus

ca. AD 46–120s
Plutarch

ca. AD 125–180s
Lucian

Mid-4th c. AD
Faltonia Betitia Proba

AD 348–413
Prudentius

AD 354–430
Augustine

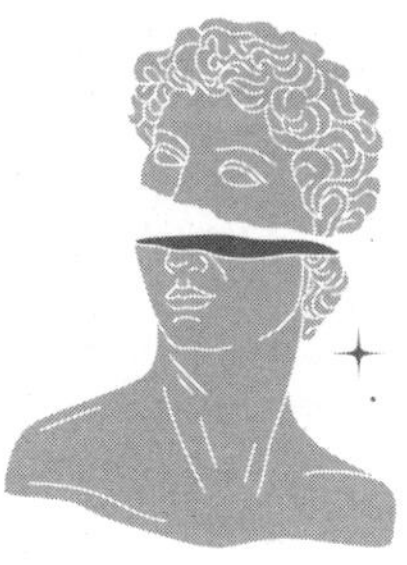

Introduction

Why Should Christians Read the Greco-Roman Classics?

> St. Augustine defines virtue as *ordo amoris*, the ordinate condition of the affections in which every object is accorded that kind of degree of love which is appropriate to it. Aristotle says that the aim of education is to make the pupil like and dislike what he ought.[1]

Can Christians Read Greco-Roman Pagans for Spiritual Formation?

This book's goal is simple: to encourage Christians to read the Greco-Roman classics as Christians and to equip them to do so productively by providing a thematic and chronological introduction to key authors in all periods of Greco-Roman literature, from Homer to Boethius.

We begin with a question that may appear scandalous at first glance: Can Christians today read the great classics of Greco-Roman pagan literature for spiritual formation and growth in the virtues? This book seeks to show that yes, we can. Indeed, we will see examples of Christian readers in the Late Roman Empire, like Augustine and Boethius, who did just this.

1. C. S. Lewis, *The Abolition of Man* (HarperOne, 2001), 16.

But this goal does require reading differently than you are, perhaps, used to doing.

In other words, this is a book about reading the Greco-Roman classics *as Christians*—the why, the how, and, to a lesser extent, the when. Thankfully, this exercise, equal parts intellectual and spiritual, is timely; the past few years have seen the appearance of several excellent defenses of liberal arts education for Christians.[2] Other books have focused more specifically on the value of literature in nourishing our minds and souls—developing the practice of reading not just the Bible but all that we read for spiritual formation.[3] These encouragements, in a world of excess information available at our fingertips, are more necessary than ever.[4]

Just as our bodies are what we eat, so our minds are what we consume.[5] But books on reading for spiritual formation have focused largely on medieval and modern literature, involving antiquity only peripherally. Even though we are continually exhorted to "read old books," those who urge this generally mean something much more recent than Greco-Roman antiquity. Thus, many books and authors that have inspired Christians for nearly two millennia are now less read than ever, falling victim to our increasingly less educated culture and (alas) church. This too, I contend, is part of the scandal of the evangelical mind.[6]

With the exception, perhaps, of a few epics and maybe some dialogues

---

2. See Jeffrey Bilbro, Jessica Hooten Wilson, and David Henreckson, eds., *The Liberating Arts: Why We Need Liberal Arts Education* (Plough, 2023); Jeffry C. Davis and Philip G. Ryken, eds., *Liberal Arts and the Christian Life* (Crossway, 2012); and Alex Sosler, *Learning to Love: Christian Higher Education as Pilgrimage* (Falls City Press, 2023).
3. See Zena Hitz, *Lost in Thought: The Hidden Pleasures of an Intellectual Life* (Princeton University Press, 2020); Jennifer L. Holberg, *Nourishing Narratives: The Power of Story to Shape Our Faith* (IVP Academic, 2023); Alan Jacobs, *The Pleasures of Reading in an Age of Distraction* (Oxford University Press, 2011); Alan Jacobs, *Breaking Bread with the Dead: A Reader's Guide to a More Tranquil Mind* (Penguin Books, 2020); Christina Bieber Lake, *Beyond the Story: American Literary Fiction and the Limits of Materialism* (University of Notre Dame Press, 2019); Roosevelt Montás, *Rescuing Socrates: How the Great Books Changed My Life and Why They Matter for a New Generation* (Princeton University Press, 2021); Karen Swallow Prior, *On Reading Well: Finding the Good Life Through Great Books* (Brazos Press, 2018); Jessica Hooten Wilson, *The Scandal of Holiness: Renewing Your Imagination in the Company of Literary Saints* (Brazos Press, 2022); and Jessica Hooten Wilson, *Reading for the Love of God: How to Read as a Spiritual Practice* (Brazos Press, 2023).
4. Jeffrey Bilbro, *Reading the Times: A Literary and Theological Inquiry into the News* (IVP Academic, 2021).
5. This is a central premise for Lanta Davis in her book *Becoming by Beholding: The Power of the Imagination in Spiritual Formation* (Baker Academic, 2024).
6. Mark Noll, *The Scandal of the Evangelical Mind* (Eerdmans, 2022).

of Plato, most Christians today feel that the literature of the ancient world is irrelevant for them as Christians. This philosophy is also reflected in the absence of classics programs from the vast majority of CCCU (Council for Christian Colleges & Universities) schools. Even Great Books or classical education reading lists habitually leave out large swaths of Greco-Roman literature. Admittedly, it is difficult to blame these programs that are trying to cover a broad range of texts. And yet something is lost in this approach. What are we consequently missing? One avid lifelong reader's story can help us begin to understand.

The little boy opened his eyes, shaking off remnants of sleep and the vivid dreams that invaded night after night. Seared in his memory were the images of mythical beasts and mythological quests, along with the stories of gods and monsters. Leaping at him from the pages of the books into which he has been escaping for years since he could reliably read on his own, these tales filled his mind while awake and haunted his dreams while asleep. He loved them so. But they also terrified him, filling him with dread and, perhaps, longing for something he could not describe. He knew at a certain level that these stories were not true—yet they seemed so real in his mind and they inspired his imagination like nothing else could.

Motivated by his love of mythology and the fantastical world, this boy would grow up to become a distinguished scholar of medieval literature. Then, following his dramatic conversion to Christianity at age thirty-two, he became one of the most famous Christian thinkers of the twentieth century: C. S. Lewis.

Decades later, writing of his childhood obsession with ancient Greek, Roman, and Norse mythology and literature, which shaped his mind and soul, Lewis would simultaneously share the story of his remarkable and all-consuming coming to Christ. In his conversion memoir *Surprised by Joy*, Lewis reflects on the contrast between the truth of the gospel, which brought a striking degree of previously unknown joy and peace into his life, and the lies of the mythological tales, which only instilled in him alarm and distress. Later, Lewis recognized that these stories contained hints of the questions that would bring him to Christ while acknowledging that he did not have a full framework for understanding these tales as a child.[7] In

7. C. S. Lewis, *Surprised by Joy: The Shape of My Early Life* (HarperOne, 2017).

the end, however, this contrast between the pagan stories and the truth of the gospel made the joy of knowing God truly come alive, make sense, and fill him with delight. In other words, reading the pagans strengthened C. S. Lewis's Christian faith.

Too often, the genre of apologetics literature emphasizes very modern logical arguments for the veracity of the Bible and the claims of Christianity.[8] Lewis certainly proposed logical arguments in his most famous work of apologetics, *Mere Christianity*.[9] And yet *Surprised by Joy* is also a work of apologetics, even if of a different sort—apologetics through the reading of the ancient world and its myths. This makes Lewis's remarkable conversion story as ancient as it is modern. Let me explain.

Almost two thousand years ago, as Christianity was first beginning to spread in the ancient Mediterranean world, the gospel came to believers who had also grown up hearing and reading the pagan myths. They saw these stories everywhere in their world, which was saturated with pagan gods in literature, public and private art, coins, and more. I imagine that these new converts, like Lewis, exulted joyfully in encountering Jesus and learning of God's love for all of sinful humanity when they contrasted this hope against the stark cruelty of the pagan worldview that comes through so clearly in these myths. And yet they too could see hints of truth and spiritual longings for salvation in pagan books and myths.

So why should Christians read the Greco-Roman pagan classics? As C. S. Lewis's example shows, the "why" in this question is inseparable from the "how": Christians should read the Greco-Roman classics while remembering their own identity in Christ and seeing the pre-Christian antiquity in dialogue with this identity. In other words, this means reading these texts as the earliest Christians did—to the extent that we can, at least.

When we look at the world around us as believers, this changes everything, including how we read fiction and nonfiction from over two thousand years ago. Instead of mocking the sorrow of unlikeable characters, we are moved with compassion for them; instead of decrying injustices as mere

8. See, for example, Josh McDowell, *Evidence That Demands a Verdict: Life-Changing Truth for a Skeptical World* (Thomas Nelson, 2017), and Lee Strobel, *The Case for Christ: A Journalist's Personal Investigation of the Evidence for Jesus* (Zondervan, 2016).

9. This book makes multiple references to the concept of genre. The best modern overview of the genres and how they work for Christian readers is Andrew Judd, *Modern Genre Theory* (Zondervan Academic, 2024).

affairs of this world, we see them in a cosmic light as part of the fallenness of creation; and instead of idolizing the great powers of the past, we see God's plans for them along with all nations past, present, and future. These insights contribute to what is known as "common grace"—the recognition that some shared aspects of God's goodness and mercy are gifts common to all of humanity, including unbelievers. With all this in mind, we can see more clearly three related reasons for reading the pagan classics for our spiritual formation as Christians: reading to be surprised by joy, reading to understand the world of the Bible and the earliest Christians, and reading for character formation. What do I mean by this?

First, reading the classics as Christians can strengthen our faith and teach us to cherish the story of the Bible with joy—just as it did for C. S. Lewis. In this process, we will learn to appreciate the beauty of the Greco-Roman classics more as we see a longing for spiritual truths that many ancient writers displayed; for example, they frequently asked difficult questions about the nature of the human soul. In other words, reading the classics while thinking about the Bible will enrich our understanding of both.

Second, reading the texts that the earliest Christians read is one of the best ways for us to grow in our understanding of the early converts and believers—our brothers and sisters in Christ. Reading is always a historical, theological, and cultural exercise. It also calls us to appreciate great art. We simply forget this truth all too often when reading familiar things. And yet reading in light of eternity is also a historical exercise—which is why historical writers are an integral part of this book's coverage.

Finally, after millennia of readers using these texts for character formation, both in antiquity and beyond, surely we can safely admit that we also need to do this kind of reading. Of course, we do need to recognize that these virtues, as presented in the pagan texts, do not reflect the complete picture that is only fully visible to those equipped with gospel eyes. Still, we will see that reading for character formation is a goal that the Greco-Roman authors already had in mind. This was, indeed, one of the chief aims of literature in the ancient world, no less than offering entertainment.

The cliché that we are what we eat extends readily to our reading practices. Our minds and hearts and souls are shaped by what we consume—by reading, listening, and watching. And, so, I invite you to taste and see the beauty in ancient Greco-Roman literature. I especially invite you to consider how this beauty is perfected when we read it with gospel eyes.

An Invitation to Explore

If you are reading this book, chances are that you already find one or more of these arguments for why Christians should read the Greco-Roman classics compelling. Yet you still may feel reluctant to go ahead and check out all the Plutarch or Aristophanes volumes off the shelves at your next visit to the local public library. I can understand this reluctance. Few want to admit this openly in polite company, but Greek and Roman texts often exemplify to many modern readers the definition that Mark Twain gave for the Great Books: Many people feel better once they have read Homer than to be in the process of slogging through Homer.[10] Ancient epics or tragedies or historical narratives just might not feel like reading for joy. If this is you, please feel no shame in admitting this. I hope that reading this book will change your mind.

Unfortunately, many readers who approach these ancient texts for the first time might never have encountered similar literature before. Reading something so far removed from us by time and cultural barriers requires a guide, which I hope this book will prove to be. For instance, humor of the sort that permeates ancient comedy is difficult to understand without knowing some historical and cultural background. Just think how difficult it is to understand a political or cultural joke from twenty years ago, much less two thousand years ago! And then, of course, there are all these strange gods and their stories (for some less familiar names and terms, the glossary at the back of this book can be your good friend). What does all this mean anyway, and how do we approach this kind of reading as Christians? With this umbrella question in mind, each chapter in this book offers you a brief orientation for one particular author, whose work is representative of a larger tradition. Ultimately, I do not claim to provide all the answers, nor do we

---

10. Mark Twain, "Disappearance of Literature," address at the dinner of the Nineteenth Century Club at Sherry's, New York, November 20, 1900, https://www.originalsources.com/Document.aspx?DocID=TIZG36QPLEMQUYI&H=1. I have adapted the definition to fit this book's context; Twain's original words were "[A classic is] something that everybody wants to have read and nobody wants to read."

cover all possible ancient writers. Rather, I invite you to explore, think, and enjoy—with an eye to reading more on your own as you find authors you would like to explore in greater detail.

Perhaps you are a high school or college student of the Great Books or are enrolled in a classical education program in a traditional schooling or homeschooling environment. You may be a lifelong learner and have previously read many or all of the books considered in this volume, but perhaps have not considered how you might read them specifically as a Christian. Maybe you are an educator—whether at a public or private school or as a homeschooler—who would like to teach the classics to your students. Maybe you have tried reading Greco-Roman literature before but have found yourself lost and confused or just bored. Or perhaps you would like to experience what C. S. Lewis did—you would like to be surprised by joy all over again through reading the classics. Whatever your particular reason is, I hope to provide you with training wheels so you can read Greco-Roman literature more comfortably on your own going forward.

This book proceeds mostly chronologically for two main reasons. First, this allows us to get oriented in time. After all, the literature we examine, if we approach it chronologically, really does reflect ancient history, because all people are the product of their time and place even though the human experience in many ways is timeless. Texts, like the people who first produced them and read them, do not exist in a vacuum. While all of us can profit from these texts, we will benefit even more if we understand the original context better. And, second, ancient readers were aware of which texts came earlier or later. Accordingly, understanding how to read the classics as their ancient readers did requires an awareness of this chronology. This will also help us to see more clearly the influence of ideas over time: Who influenced whom? Some answers will emerge naturally.

At the same time, I also group the selected authors into thematic categories that will help us see consistent themes in these texts over time. Part I, "Longing for Eternity," focuses on the theme of eternity in the earliest Greek literature. While the Greeks were unaware of the Christian values, we will see the longing for eternity present in their imagination, reminding us that this is an in-built human impulse that should point us to God. And so we will look at this theme in the epics of Homer and the shorter poems of Hesiod; in the Odes of Pindar, commissioned to celebrate the victories of the greatest athletes of his day; and in the quest for writing eternal—or, at least, timeless—history that historians like Herodotus and Thucydides undertook.

In Part II, "The Formation of Virtuous Citizens," we turn to the question of citizenship and the struggle between the individual and the state. Whose desires take precedence? All citizens wish to protect their own interests and those of their families, and yet the success of the state requires individuals to sometimes sacrifice their own desires for its benefit. Ultimately, as we will see, this type of struggle, so foundational to political discourse, reflects an even greater cosmic conflict: our desire to be the masters of our own universe rather than relinquish this power to God.

Building on this concept of the struggle between the individual and the state, we turn in Part III to "Words of Power and Power of Words." Our own world is brimming with words, some of them powerful. And yet our society offers less formal rhetorical training than possibly any previous society in world history. In this section, we consider the ancient world's emphasis on empowering one's words to the maximum degree possible in the work of legal and political speechwriters, writers of manuals and handbooks, and, finally, love poets.

In Part IV, "Heroes and Role Models," we turn to the subject of character formation that is present in ancient literature from Homer onward. Ancient writers and their audiences took this aspect of literature and storytelling for granted: Stories were meant to convey moral lessons and shape the character of their audiences. Who are the best role models? What makes someone a good or bad role model? In this section, we consider how Roman historians, epic poets, and biographers approached these questions and explore how this motivation to form readers shaped their own thinking about the importance of their work. In this process, we will see that certain virtues have a timeless aspect to them, even though the endemic cruelty of the ancient pagan world did not respect all persons.

In Part V, "Virtues and Vices in the Age of Anxiety," we consider what happens when the lessons and values of all previous literature are challenged by the troubles of the age of Late Antiquity. When things fall apart all around us, to what—or to whom—do we hold fast? In this last section of the book, as we consider voices from the turbulent final centuries of the classical world, we examine both pagan responses to the crises through which they were living and several Christian responses to these crises.

The latter—especially Augustine, Prudentius, and Boethius—display a remarkable familiarity with pagan literature of previous ages, reinforcing to us the overall lesson of this book: When we read as Christians, we can discern God in all that is beautiful in this world, including the literature of pagan thinkers who yearned for God but never knew him.

Join me on this time-traveling adventure. We begin—where else?—in the Greek Bronze Age, the world of the Homeric epics, a time of power-hungry demigods and the greatest war in the Greek imagination.

A Brief Note on Translations

Perhaps one of the most common questions I get from readers has to do with what translation to use for a Classical work. This is remarkably difficult to answer. For many texts I discuss in this book, many translations exist and have their merits. In particular, there are probably more translations of the Homeric epics than any other Greek text—and several more are in progress, even as of this writing. So, while I will recommend some translations for the texts I discuss in this book, these are just suggestions and are meant to be a starting point—not the ultimate or exclusive endorsement of any one translation over all others. In reality, there are so many good translations, and choosing one is a subjective decision. It's kind of like with the Bible: Everyone has a favorite version.

So, how might you select a translation of an ancient book? Select one that you find the most readable. Ideally, look at sample pages from a translation on Amazon or another online platform so you can get a sense of the style. Since your goal is to read literature for joy, find a translation that gives you joy.

In the long term, it is even better to learn Greek and Latin. But that's not essential to be able to appreciate the texts discussed in this book, just as not everyone has time and energy to go forth and learn Hebrew and Greek to enjoy the Bible in the original languages.

In fact, while I have a PhD in classics (Greek and Latin), you see that in this book I am quoting from other scholars' translations rather than providing you with my own. Why? Because my tendency is to translate literally—but that is not literary. In other words, gifted translators, especially those who translate poetry, are able to translate not simply word-for-word (which I can do) but also offer you the feel of the ancient text in another language (which I cannot do well).

So, when it comes to translations, please rest assured that we live in the age of an embarrassment of riches! Last but not least, I should mention the incredible resource of the Loeb Classical Library. Loeb books are distinctively colored—green volumes for Greek texts and red for Latin. They contain on facing pages the original Greek or Latin text and the English translation. This makes them an ideal resource for someone who knows some Greek or Latin and wants to be able to easily read the work while occasionally referencing the original language.

PART

Longing for Eternity

CHAPTER

Homer and Glory Before the Foundation of the World

Rage—Goddess, sing the rage of Peleus' son Achilles,
murderous, doomed, that cost the Achaeans countless losses,
hurling down to the House of Death so many sturdy souls,
great fighters' souls, but made their bodies carrion,
feasts for the dogs and birds,
and the will of Zeus was moving toward its end.[1]

Dreaming of Eternity

Early in my time living in Georgia, now almost a decade and a half ago, I walked out of the house and into the garage to get something. I stopped cold when I saw a rattlesnake inches from my bare foot. Immediately I grabbed a shovel leaning against the wall close by and killed the snake. To this day, I am still not entirely sure how I did this, as my arms operated entirely of their own accord in those few seconds without consulting my panicked brain.

One of the strongest human impulses is our sense of self-preservation. In times of danger, a built-in fight-or-flight instinct kicks in, not because of anything we have been taught but because of how we just *are*. We are wired to love our life and wish to preserve it. More than that, though, the earliest known texts of human civilizations around the world show

1. Homer, *Iliad*, trans. Robert Fagles (Penguin Classics, 1998), 1.1–5.

that this same impulse of self-preservation has also led people to dream of immortality—the dream of never dying but living forever, eternally. This dream undergirds the entire genre of ancient heroic epic poetry.

After the death of his best friend, King Gilgamesh, the hero of the Mesopotamian *Epic of Gilgamesh*, is confronted with the reality that he too will die. Determined to defeat even death, he goes on a quest beyond the bounds of the known world, earnestly hoping to learn the secret of immortality. Alas, he fails. Two-thirds god and one-third mortal (yeah, Mesopotamian math makes no sense—sorry!), he still dies a man's death. Foiled in their quests for immortality, heroes like Gilgamesh learn instead to settle for the next best prize. They reason that living forever is not the only kind of immortality that exists. The glory that the greatest heroes win through commemoration in epic compositions offers another way to become immortal. The ancient Greeks knew this well.

Sometime in the Late Bronze Age, following the mysterious and catastrophic destruction of the city of Troy in Asia Minor ca. 1100 BC, but well before there was a Greek alphabet for writing down literature (or, really, anything else), itinerant bards in Greek-speaking lands began weaving beautiful stories together for the delight of their audiences. How do we know, you might (and should) ask? Because their tales survived to get written down later—possibly in Athens in the sixth century BC. Close analysis of the language, style, and historical details in these epics—the *Iliad* and the *Odyssey*—shows that they were composed orally over the course of centuries and they do not represent the fruit of one man's labors. Yet the people of antiquity readily attributed these works to Homer, a blind bard who perhaps never existed. Recited at festivals and gatherings, large and small, these epics were the bestsellers of literature before there was such a thing as either bestsellers or literature. Their popularity reminds us of the desire we all have for entertainment, especially entertainment through good—or, one could even say, epic—stories.

We forget sometimes that life without television or the internet or even a smartphone can indeed involve plenty of such entertainment, which is delivered live rather than onscreen. Composed in formulaic epic language, the epics consisted of lines and phrases and entire sections that—before they were written down and "fixed" in a particular version—could be strung together like beads on a custom-made necklace. Composed earlier, the *Iliad* deals with the Trojan War itself, focusing on a sequence of events in the tenth and final year of the greatest war in Greek mythology. The *Odyssey*, composed slightly later, focuses on the decade-long struggle of Odysseus, one of the heroes of that war, to get home after the war's end.

Bards were known as *demiourgoi*—public workers in the best sense of the term. They were professionals who practiced a craft essential for human flourishing, akin to other *demiourgoi* such as physicians. And, like physicians, bards traveled around, bringing entertainment for a few evenings wherever they went—although we see from the evidence of the Homeric epics themselves that wealthy nobles also employed their own bards. No two performances could ever be alike before the epics were written down. But the overall feelings and desires they reflected were the same. These were action-packed stories about heroes, war, love, family, and sacrifice. Most of all, the epics were about an instinctive desire that people in all time periods of history have felt: the desire for undying glory that would give the greatest warriors an immortality of sorts. The Homeric epics made this glory possible by celebrating the deeds of heroes—just as the *Epic of Gilgamesh* did for its own protagonist.

Craving the immortality that is made possible by glory, the original listeners did not know a key truth that we possess: that God "chose us in [Jesus] before the creation of the world to be holy and blameless in his sight. In love he predestined us for adoption to sonship through Jesus Christ, in accordance with his pleasure and will—to the praise of his glorious grace, which he has freely given us in the One he loves."[2] We desire to be eternal creatures because we ourselves have been created by the only one who is eternal. Although we are children of dust with frail bodies, we also possess immortal souls that long for eternity. Eternity with God is each true believer's reward. Yet manmade and man-perpetuated glory is an empty kind of immortality. It reflects a true and good desire, but it fails to see that desire's ultimate fulfillment for the soul.

Reading the Homeric epics as Christians, we can see a God-shaped void—a yearning for something greater than what the Greek bards and their audiences could ever see here on earth—even in those heroes of the

---

2. Ephesians 1:4–6.

pagan world and in the gods, who (in the Greeks' imagination) populated the landscape all around them.

The *Iliad*: The Wrath and Glory of Achilles

By the time the *Iliad* opens, the Trojan War, the bitter siege of Troy by the combined army of the Greeks, is in its tenth year. It may seem deeply frustrating and confusing for the modern reader to be dropped into this tale mid-action. What is this war, anyway? Why does everyone assume it needs no introduction? Our confusion is a reminder that most of us did not grow up hearing these myths regularly, as the ancient audiences did. Furthermore, reading the epics in silence is a far cry from the dramatic performances the original audiences enjoyed. Nevertheless, we do see hints and flashbacks to earlier events, including the cause of the war, scattered throughout the epic.

The war started because of a beauty contest gone wrong. At the wedding of the mortal king Peleus and the immortal sea nymph Thetis, an uninvited and angry guest drops off a gift that keeps on giving. This guest is Eris, the goddess of discord, and the reasons for not inviting her to a wedding are, perhaps, self-explanatory: Would *you* invite discord to your wedding? Alas, she "crashes" the wedding by throwing a golden apple inscribed "to the most beautiful" in front of three powerful goddesses: Hera, Athena, and Aphrodite. Each of the three wants the apple, and so the contest is on. We see here at play the anthropomorphic—humanlike—nature and desires of the gods. Like people, the gods are capricious, vengeful, and cruel. But they are also immortal, which means they can do anything they wish to mortals, who are justifiably afraid of them. Always.

The three goddesses appoint Paris, a prince of Troy, to serve as the neutral party in judging the beauty contest. Yet even after going to the trouble of finding a seemingly neutral judge, each goddess in turn offers him spectacular bribes. At the end, Paris accepts the bribe that Aphrodite offers: to give him the most beautiful woman in the world as his wife. Paris declares Aphrodite the winner of the contest and gives her the golden apple; then Aphrodite fulfills her end of the bargain. There is a problem with this last part, however—a sort of fine print to the original bargain that neither Paris nor Aphrodite seemed (or cared) to consider. The most beautiful woman in the world, Helen, is already married—to Menelaus, king of Sparta.

No matter. Aphrodite helps Paris kidnap Helen from her husband and bring her to Troy. A number of mythological retellings of this myth in later Greek literature suggest that Helen was quite happy to go, while others are less sure. But the consequence of the kidnapping, in any case, is certain. The Greeks, under the leadership of Menelaus's more powerful brother, King Agamemnon of Mycenae, gather an army and launch a massive fleet, whose size later earns Helen the nickname "the face that launched a thousand ships."

Although Agamemnon is the commander-in-chief of the Greek army, the son of Peleus and Thetis—the couple at whose wedding things first went so awfully awry—becomes known in the Trojan War as "the Best of the Achaeans," the greatest of all Greek heroes. ("Achaeans" is one of the terms used to describe the Greeks in the epic.) His name is Achilles, and the opening line of the *Iliad* reveals a curious truth: This poem is about his wrath.

> Rage—Goddess, sing the rage of Peleus' son Achilles,
> murderous, doomed, that cost the Achaeans countless losses,
> hurling down to the House of Death so many sturdy souls,
> great fighters' souls, but made their bodies carrion,
> feasts for the dogs and birds,
> and the will of Zeus was moving toward its end.
> Begin, Muse, when the two first broke and clashed,
> Agamemnon lord of men and brilliant Achilles.
>
> What god drove them to fight with such a fury?
> Apollo the son of Zeus and Leto.[3]

War, this opening states matter-of-factly, means death and destruction. Readers both in antiquity and today often focus so closely on the idea of heroes and heroism to the point of abstraction that they overlook this basic fact. But the *Iliad* is remarkably frank about the calamity of war, even while celebrating the heroes' exploits. There is an irreconcilable conflict of interests, at least among the Greek heroes: The aim of going to war technically is to win the war (and win Helen back). And yet each individual Greek

3. Homer, *Iliad*, 1.1–10.

hero sees the war in very self-centered terms: Every hero's main goal is to be recognized as "the Best of the Achaeans," squeezing the maximum glory he could possibly gain to thereby achieve immortality in future song. The conflict between Agamemnon and Achilles, to which the opening of the epic refers ("when the two first broke and clashed"), is an example of this phenomenon at work.

In the first book of the *Iliad*, Agamemnon insults Chryses, the priest of Apollo in a region near Troy. During one of their raids, the Greeks had captured his daughter, Chryseis, who became a special prize for Agamemnon. Chryses asks for her return. When Agamemnon refuses, the priest calls upon Apollo's help and the entire army learns to its chagrin why it is not a good idea to upset the god of (among other things) the plague!

A murderous plague from Apollo is no joking matter—especially when the plague is killing soldiers during a war and threatening to defeat the attacking army off the battlefield. Agamemnon ultimately has no choice but to give back Chryseis to her father. If things ended here, there would be no *Iliad*. But, of course, Agamemnon does not stop at this point. Upset with Achilles, who was the one who had encouraged him to return his prize to end the plague, Agamemnon takes away Achilles's prize, the captive girl Briseis. Achilles, in turn, announces his own great resignation, 1100 BC style: He will sit out of the war, benching himself in his camp until he gets a good and proper apology. As you might imagine, Agamemnon refuses to play this game. This is the quarrel to which the opening verses of the *Iliad* are referring. Achilles's wrath—the rage that is the very first word of the epic in Greek—is his rage in response to this insult from Agamemnon.

This opening episode is key for our understanding of the Greek heroic code. It shows how honor-driven and externally bestowed this heroic code is. Essentially, honor is something that others think someone has—or not. Chryseis and Briseis are pawns who demonstrate this nature of honor in the Homeric world. These women are no ordinary captives. Rather, each of them is designated a *geras*, a special prize of valor. They are portable trophies whose presence in a hero's tent shows his own special status. To be a great hero meant, after all, receiving public recognition by others—including through special honor prizes. This means that the removal of a *geras* visibly degraded one's honor and prestige as a warrior. Think of it as the stripping away of a medal from a winner after the competition—this person suffers even greater dishonor than if he had never won the prize to begin with. It is no wonder, therefore, that Agamemnon did not want to give back his own prize and that he took away Achilles's prize when he returned Chryseis to her father.

The externally governed nature of this heroic code—that one is only a great hero if this person is recognized by others and has accumulated great prizes of honor, including prizes that are real people!—is a warning to us as we consider how aspects of such a code appeal to our own desires even today. Each of us wants to be declared good—as God once spoke when he created Adam. In fact, we would like to be declared "the Best," and we would like this coronation to come unconditionally from absolutely everyone around. But our worth and any declaration of goodness, excellence, and ultimately righteousness is to be found in God alone, not in other people's view of us. The suffering of the heroes in the *Iliad* and in other ancient epics, where heroes do all they can to be declared "the Best," is an important warning of what happens if we place our value in others' opinion of us. It reminds us of the empty promises of this kind of glory—it cannot satisfy.

The story of Achilles highlights the emptiness of the Greek heroic code. For most of the epic after his initial quarrel with Agamemnon, Achilles keeps his promise and stays out of the fight, only returning at last after his best friend Patroclus is killed. The poem, chock-full of very graphic and bloody violence and so many duels of heroes ending with the death of one or both of them, finally ends with a Greco-Trojan truce so the opposing forces can bury their dead. We are left with a poignant image of the futility of war. "Is this really all?" we cannot help but wonder as we read or hear of the numberless funeral pyres of the dead on both sides. Yes, if you seek glory through war—yes, this is all that there is.

While Achilles does not die in the *Iliad*, he knows at the end that his own death is drawing nigh. In the Homeric epics, he is satisfied with the choice he has made—given the choice between living a long life in obscurity and dying young in glory, he chooses the latter fate. Some later Greek writers, however, were not so sure that anyone could be truly happy with such a choice. Writing in the mid-second century AD, the satirist Lucian includes Achilles among the many notables in his *Dialogues of the Dead*. And there Achilles remarks mournfully that it would be better to be a lowly man still alive than to be the king of the dead. Perhaps Ecclesiastes offers the most sobering answer to Achilles and the values of the Greek heroic code:

"Meaningless! Meaningless!"
says the Teacher.
"Utterly meaningless!
Everything is meaningless."

What do people gain from all their labors
at which they toil under the sun?
Generations come and generations go,
but the earth remains forever.[4]

Ultimately, eternity only gains meaning if spent with the one who is eternal. True, Achilles's glory has lasted. Three thousand years later, you also know who he is because of the *Iliad*. And yet this is all meaningless apart from God. What has Achilles gained from his labors, his decade-long and despairing toil under the blazing sun and the ruthless winters of Troy? Nothing but an early death. And earthly glory.

Penelope and Odysseus's Happy Ending

While the Homeric epics largely revolve around the heroes, women connected to these men in various ways are also part of the story. Many of them are clearly victims of the war—like Chryseis and Briseis, the kidnapped and enslaved women from the towns around Troy. But one woman in particular is presented as an example of virtue: Penelope, Odysseus's wife, who stayed home for twenty years waiting faithfully for his return.

Penelope, though, is no passive housewife. In her, we meet someone who is strategically minded and able to plot several moves ahead—she really is the ideal wife for Odysseus, who is best known for his craftiness. Most of all, her labors at home in

4. Ecclesiastes 1:2–4.

Odysseus's absence enable him to get a happy ending after his initially rough homecoming. As you read the *Odyssey*, pay attention to Penelope and the model of feminine virtue that she presents in a world primarily focused on men.

On January 1, 2018, the internet persona Bronze Age Pervert self-published a book on the value of Homeric values for the modern man. Aptly named *Bronze Age Mindset*, it took off like wildfire, building its author an X following of over 190,000 as of this writing.[5] The author's description of his book on Goodreads includes the following explanation of his argument and aims:

> The contents are pure dynamite. He explains that you live in ant farm [*sic*]. That you are observed by the lords of lies, ritually probed. Ancient man had something you have lost: confidence in his instincts and strength, knowledge in his blood. BAP shows how the Bronze Age mindset can set you free from this Iron Prison and help you embark on the path of power. He talks about life, biology, hormones. He gives many examples from history, both ancient and modern. He shows the secrets of the detrimental robots, how they hide and fabricate. He helps you escape gynocracy and ascend to fresh mountain air.[6]

While the Bronze Age Pervert is the best-known example of someone misreading Homer to get at what he considers the primordial masculine virtues, he is not alone. Of course, as noted earlier, the *Iliad* is a remarkably violent poem, which should caution us against wholesale emulation of its heroes. Additionally, readers looking for the most masculine of virtues from ancient Greek and Roman epics invariably tend to overlook one: the manly virtue of tenderness. Overlooking this virtue in the heroes amounts

5. See Rosie Gray, "How Bronze Age Pervert Built an Online Following and Injected Anti-Democracy, Pro-Men Ideas into the GOP," *Politico*, July 16, 2023, https://www.politico.com/news/magazine/2023/07/16/bronze-age-pervert-masculinity-00105427, and Graeme Wood, "How Bronze Age Pervert Charmed the Far Right," *The Atlantic*, August 3, 2023, https://www.theatlantic.com/magazine/archive/2023/09/bronze-age-pervert-costin-alamariu/674762/.
6. Goodreads, "Bronze Age Mindset," January 1, 2018, https://www.goodreads.com/en/book/show/40388177.

to cherry-picking material from the epics—proof-texting, if you will—focusing only on battle sequences while ignoring the considerable swathes of text that show heroes in more peaceful settings, where their nature as heroes and exemplars is still clearly recognized.

Strikingly, the virtues on display off the battlefield have nothing to do with displays of brute strength—just as we do not walk around flexing our muscles for no reason at all outside the gym. Or, at least, most people don't. The overwhelmingly narrow definition of masculine virtues in Homer by some modern readers that merely relates them to strength is, indeed, modern and not ancient. It is more frat boy heroic cosplay than Achilles. It is more Bronze Age Pervert and less actual Homer. Let us consider here in brief just two examples of heroic tenderness which remind us that bravery and brute strength do not alone a Homeric hero make.

Throughout the *Iliad*, Odysseus singles himself out by his preeminent craftiness. Indeed, his masterful subterfuge ultimately wins the war against Troy. Odysseus is the inventor of the Trojan Horse scheme—long before this became a computer virus, this was the trick that involved building a hollow wooden horse, filling it up with armed warriors, and sending it to Troy as a peace offering. The Trojans fell for the trick and brought the horse inside the city. That same night Troy fell to the Greek warriors hiding inside the horse, who opened the city gates to the rest of the army waiting outside.

But Odysseus's craftiness is not the only virtue that puts him above all other heroes. Rather, in a world where all other heroes bravely introduce themselves as sons of their fathers, reciting genealogies proudly going back to the gods, Odysseus repeatedly introduces himself as the father of Telemachus. Telemachus was just a baby when Odysseus left for Troy. He was no famous hero and had not accomplished anything. And yet Telemachus was the most important, identity-defining feature in Odysseus's vision of himself, an anchor he held fast to in hope for a future after the war. Telemachus was the one of whom his father, as all proud fathers we know, bragged in every conversation. There is admittedly much to dislike about Odysseus in the Homeric epics; he is a liar, an ever-scheming opportunist, and a serial adulterer to boot. Indeed, in later Greek tragedy he is uniformly portrayed as a villain, and Dante will take up this depiction in the *Inferno*. But Odysseus's rejection of the typical Homeric genealogies to rejoice, instead, in being a father to a dear son gives us a surprising glimpse of tenderness, otherwise unseen in this hero.

Here is one more example. In Book 6 of the *Iliad*, during a lull in the fight, the greatest Trojan hero, Hector, goes home to see his wife and son. Remember that they have all been living in a city under siege for nearly ten years. Yet even in this difficult situation people get married, families are formed, and children are born. The baby son of Hector and Andromache is not yet a year old. When Hector walks into the room with his war helmet on, its decorative crest swaying gloriously but ominously, the frightened baby bursts into tears. In that moment, Hector removes the helmet to show his baby his real face and to comfort him.

This episode didn't mean much to me when I first read it as a high schooler. But now that I read it with the eyes of a parent, this brings to my mind memories of my youngest daughter, who was the quintessential "rabbit" for the first three years of her life, terrified of every loud or sudden noise, large animals, and anything that looked new and unfamiliar. A war helmet with a towering crest would have certainly set her crying, too. So what did her father do whenever she cried in fear, as she did multiple times each day—over the distant bark of a dog, the sound of a hand dryer in a public restroom, or the noise of a leaf blower from the neighbor across the street? He picked her up and held her tenderly, showing her that he would always offer safety for her in her times of fear.

The tenderness of mothers in all societies is taken for granted. Mothers have, after all, carried their children for nine months and have nourished them with their own bodies first within and then outside the womb. By contrast, the tenderness of fathers, the loving emotion of the heroes who otherwise mercilessly kill on the battlefield, is a remarkable picture of something transcendent and beautiful. It is a reminder that war is not the natural state of affairs but the result of the fallenness of creation. What God made good, we have twisted, all for nothing—as many of Homer's heroes seemed to realize even though they felt trapped in the glory-seeking machine.

In our society also, some become overly obsessed with a hypermasculine idea of heroes—which the Bronze Age Pervert takes to a new extreme. But it is particularly problematic when we also project this same muscle-inflated ideal to God. In the process, we overlook God's remarkable tenderness to us, his beloved adopted children. In the early Christian catacombs, where believers gathered in secret, a popular art motif emerged: the Good Shepherd. In these simple wall paintings, done by believers taking refuge and with limited means, Jesus also looks humble and lowly, dressed in poor shepherd's clothing as he tenderly carries a lamb on his shoulders. The same eternal God who created the universe and formed the stars, was—and still is—showing love and tender care for the needy—us.

Eternity

The concept of eternity in the minds of ancient epic heroes is deeply self-centered: It is all about the hero receiving the glory that, he believes, is his due. In this way, each hero, while mortal, conceives of himself as achieving at least a small portion of godlike immortality. But we also see much sadness in the heroes' lives as they abandon all possibility of earthly happiness for their heroic quests. Achilles's obsession with immortality through glory ultimately turns out to be an obsession with his own death. For example, in the final book of the *Odyssey* the ghosts of Agamemnon and Achilles encounter each other in the underworld. Knowing him all too well, Agamemnon describes Achilles's funeral in elaborate and sumptuous detail.

In the end, the Greek heroic code, with its tunnel-visioned focus on the hero's greatness, is utterly empty of any lasting significance. Achilles's delight in listening to Agamemnon's riveting account of his funeral obsequies confirms that this kind of glory is ephemeral. Achilles, not knowing the immortal God and his promises, settled for a dim shadow of something he could feel but never knew or experienced. On the other hand, if we recognize our identity as eternal beings endowed with eternal souls, we gain a different view of our life in the here and now. Our brief time in this mortal coil is a gift to cherish and treasure. It is not a time to spend hunting for immortality or questing for the eternity of our own creation. This is something that even Gilgamesh realized at the end, but the pagan heroes never fully knew the *telos* of mortal time. Ultimately, we must redeem our time for the glory of our Creator.

This has implications for the epics we construct in our minds and in our imaginations—epics with ourselves as the heroes. There is a reason, after all, that modern superhero cartoons appeal so powerfully even to young children. We all want to be our own superheroes—cape optional.

This impulse can be good and true and beautiful—but only if we direct it to serve the world rather than our own selfish desires and only if we give God the glory. Ultimately, the language of the Homeric epics, as theologian Dennis R. MacDonald argues, equipped the writers of the Gospels to do just this—to tell the greatest epic ever told, the story of Jesus.[7]

Recommendations for Further Reading

Epic of Gilgamesh. Translated by N. K. Sandars. Penguin Books, 2006.

Homer, *Iliad*. Translated by Robert Fagles. Penguin Books, 1998.

Homer, *Iliad*. Translated by Emily Wilson. Norton, 2024.

Homer, *Odyssey*. Translated by Robert Fagles. Penguin Books, 1999.

Homer, *Odyssey*. Translated by Daniel Mendelsohn. University of Chicago Press, 2025.

Lombardo, Stanley. *The Essential Homer*. Hackett, 2000.

Questions for Discussion and Reflection

1. Have you ever had an encounter with danger that left you thinking about your mortality? How did you react?
2. Which character(s) in the Homeric epics do you relate to the most? Why do you think this is the case?
3. How does the knowledge of Jesus and his promises change or complete your understanding of the stories of the Homeric epics?

7. See Dennis R. MacDonald, *The Homeric Epics and the Gospel of Mark* (Yale University Press, 2000); *The Gospels and Homer: Imitations of Greek Epic in Mark and Luke-Acts* (Rowman & Littlefield, 2014); and *Luke and Vergil: Imitations of Classical Greek Literature* (Rowman & Littlefield, 2014).

CHAPTER

Hesiod and the Quest for the Meaning of Life

I begin my song with the Helikonian Muses whose domain
is Helikon, the great god-haunted mountain;
their soft feet move in a dance that rings
the violet-dark spring and the altar of mighty Zeus.[1]

Oh Homer, Where Art Thou?

About three centuries after Odysseus finally made it home from Troy and the last of the heroes of the Trojan War slept in uneasy peace with their ancestors, a more ordinary man, whom we simply know as Hesiod, began weaving his own epic yet significantly less heroic poems.

The son of a hard-working small farmer, Hesiod also lived a farmer's life in a little village within the shadow of Mount Helicon, known in his days as the haunt of the Muses, the goddesses of poetry, music, and the arts. The agricultural life was intense and its responsibilities heavy. Furthermore, strife with his backstabbing brother over the inheritance from their father plagued Hesiod for years. As a result, although he lived close to the sea, he had only once in his entire life left his village and boarded a ship. He tells of that experience with pride:

1. Hesiod, *Theogony*, in *Hesiod: Theogony, Works and Days, Shield*, trans. Apostolos N. Athanassakis, 2nd ed. (Johns Hopkins University Press, 2004), vv. 1–4.

I never sailed the open seas on a boat,
except when I went to Euboea from Aulis, where once
the Achaeans weathered a grim storm and then with a great
host
from holy Greece sailed over to Troy, land of fair women.
There I crossed over to Chalkis for the prizes
in honor of wise Amphidamas, the many prizes proclaimed in
advance
by his magnanimous sons. And I claim that there
I was the victor in a song contest and won an eared tripod,
which I dedicated to the Helikonian Muses,
where they first taught me mastery of flowing song.[2]

Hesiod's account of the memorable sole sea voyage of his life offers us several key hints about the poet himself and what he hoped to offer his similarly hardscrabble audiences.

First and foremost, Hesiod's world and imagination were saturated with Homer. In referencing his travels to Euboea, he mentions Aulis, from which the Greek army once set out to the war in Troy. Second and related, no less than the Homeric heroes, Hesiod too felt a desire to be the best in his craft. He certainly saw his victory in this poetic contest as the greatest achievement of his life. The reality of sailing to this contest—a war among the poets—from the same harbor as the Greeks once sailed from to war against Troy, was not lost on Hesiod. He was a warrior of a different sort, also embarking on a dangerous adventure. He persevered and won—and did not need a full decade to get home, for the favor of the goddesses was with him every step of the way.

All this ultimately brings us to the third point. Hesiod's dedication of his prize to the Muses, the goddesses of poetry, acknowledges the same reality that permeates the Homeric epics. This world of the early Greeks was saturated with the pagan gods, whose favor meant success and whose disfavor meant destruction. Indeed, as Hesiod tells us at the beginning of his *Theogony*, the Muses first came to him as he was pastoring his sheep

2. Hesiod, *Works and Days*, in *Hesiod: Theogony, Works and Days, Shield*, trans. Apostolos N. Athanassakis, 2nd ed. (Johns Hopkins University Press, 2004), vv. 650–59.

and called him to the task of composing poetry. Just as God in the Old Testament calls prophets, so the Muses in ancient pagan societies also call poets, who are prophets of a different sort. The Muses breathed the gift of song into a mere shepherd and asked him—quite rudely to boot—to bring the glory to them and to the rest of the gods with his words. Since Hesiod won the poetic contest with this poem, the task brought glory to him as well.

Hesiod took his calling seriously. His poetic vocation became for him parallel to the calling of mythological heroes to go forth and found a new city or the calling of Homeric epic heroes to perform extraordinary feats on the battlefield. After all, these tasks were also the work of gods acting through men, and divine inspiration was the key to their success:

> Blessed is the man
> whom the Muses love; sweet song flows from his mouth.
> A man may have some fresh grief over which to mourn,
> and sorrow may have left him no more tears, but if a singer,
> a servant of the Muses, sings the glories of ancient men
> and hymns the blessed gods who dwell on Olympos,
> the heavy-hearted man soon shakes off his dark mood, and
> oblivion
> sooths his grief, for this gift of the gods diverts his mind.[3]

Hesiod's two most significant poems to survive are *Theogony*, which tells of the birth and origins of the Greek gods, and *Works and Days*, a meditation on the struggles of the agricultural life. Hesiod composed both poems in the dactylic hexameter epic meter—the exact same poetic meter and style as Homer. And yet these are not epics of the same variety, even if they also use epic language. These are, rather, didactic poems—works that aimed to teach their audience about the topic at hand. Still, the seemingly mundane lessons Hesiod offers are thoroughly Homeric. They teach about the timeless human yearning for glory and eternity in a world filled with death, destruction, and despair. One might note parallels to the Psalms—also composed so often by those in tears and sorrow. The parallel, though,

3. Hesiod, *Theogony*, vv. 96–103.

stops there, as the pagan gods, unlike God, cannot take away sorrow. All the praise of them in hymns and other poetry only grants "oblivion"—forgetfulness, akin to what one might get from drunkenness or sleep.

It matters not whether there was ever a poet named Homer. No trace of any real man's personality comes through in Homeric epics—the focus is all on gods and heroes. But there was a real man called Hesiod, and he includes enough personal elements in his poetry to remind us of his embodiment. He may have been inspired by the Muses, but he was still thoroughly mortal—and he was open about what a bummer that reality could be like. And yet, in the poverty and discouragement of everyday life, Hesiod's inclusion of himself and his life story in his poetry reminded his audiences of something else that was revolutionary: They too, everyday farmers and shepherds, could be humbler heroes of their own stories. Sure, they are a lower sort of heroes than Homer's, but they are still worthy of poetry.

In other words, as Hesiod shows, feats worthy of poetry did not end with the Trojan War. Even a life of farming and generally mundane hardship—no *Iliad* this!—could be the stuff of an epic—a shorter and humbler one, but an epic nevertheless.

Another Genesis: Ancient Greek Visions of Creation

In the beginning, as Hesiod says, divinely inspired by the Muses to know this information to which no other mortal has direct access, there was Chaos. Next came Gaia, the primordial goddess of the Earth, who proceeds to give birth to Ouranos, the sky. Together, Ouranos and Gaia give birth to a new generation of gods, including the hundred-armed monsters and the twelve Titans.

However, there is strife from the beginning, as the children of Ouranos and Gaia hate their father. The feeling is mutual; Ouranos hates his offspring too, and keeps hiding the various monsters within Gaia, who is groaning in pain from their weight. At last, the most enterprising of this next generation, Kronos, the Titan of time, takes the lead in the violent overthrow of Ouranos—first castrating him with a sickle. Kronos does not get to rest easy, however, as the cycle repeats itself with the next generation. Anticipating his own overthrow by one of his children, Kronos devours each baby god or goddess that is born to him and his wife Rhea. At last, however, Rhea tricks him: When the youngest god, Zeus, is born, she gives Kronos a swaddled large stone to swallow instead of the child.

This is not the first nor the last time in Greek mythology that the gods trick each other. After all, the pagan gods are not omniscient like God. Their knowledge is always limited. And so, in another trick due to a potion, Kronos regurgitates his offspring (and the swaddled tricky rock). None of the disgorged gods are the worse for wear, but they are understandably not happy with Pa. Thus, the next round of divine revolution is imminent. In that next round of fighting among the gods, Zeus and his siblings do manage to defeat the older generation of gods and inaugurate their own reign over Mount Olympus. Yet more chopping is in order first, as Kronos's children dismember the body of the Titan of time—the only way to sort of kill an immortal god who is, technically, unkillable. And yet the pieces still remain out there, somewhere, forever. Just like with time and, of course, eternity, they can never be destroyed.

Sprinkled amidst these dramatic battles of generations of gods against each other are the genealogical accounts—who begat whom. We are familiar, of course, with the Bible's "begats," but our bewilderment—and, let's be honest, occasional boredom—at these accounts makes it difficult for us to appreciate their significance. In the ancient world, however, these genealogies were a way to measure eternity and encapsulate it. The gods' genealogies mattered for this purpose, but so did those of mortals. A sliver of eternity, even for men, could be measured in these lineages. Mortals may be dead now, but they lived. Furthermore, their lives have led to the continuation of other lives. Gods and mortals in the Greek worldview are not so different in this obsession with lineage. We are reminded of this every time two heroes encounter each other in a duel on the Homeric battlefield: They introduce themselves by dutifully reciting their respective genealogies to each other before they fight.

The spectacular nature of *Theogony*'s genealogical accounts and stories of the gods shows two important truths that are significant for understanding the early Greek imagination. First, eternal life belongs to the gods alone. And, second—and even more important—this life does not bring them joy. Petty in their treatment of each other and of the human race, suspicious of everyone, and ever power-hungry, the gods live a miserable eternity that seems more curse than blessing. For some, we learn, the eternal curse is just that. Just think of Atlas, whom Hesiod mentions in passing, holding the heavy weight of the world on his shoulders forever. What kind of eternal life is this?

And then there is Prometheus.

Arguably none of the gods in Greek mythology had a softer spot for humankind in his heart than Prometheus. A Titan—a member of the same older generation of gods as Kronos—he was always an object of Zeus's suspicion. As Hesiod tells us, after one transgression too many, he took on Zeus's full wrath for his assistance to humans. His punishment? He was chained to a rock in (the Greeks believed) the Caucasus Mountains. There, all day, every day, an eagle—the sacred bird of Zeus—picked at his liver, eating it one tiny pecked-out bite by bite. At night, Prometheus received a break, just long enough for his liver to grow back, and in the morning the savage punishment would resume anew.

The tale of Prometheus presages Jesus at more than a surface level: Here is the one god in all of Greek mythology who truly chose to suffer on behalf of frail humans. This is the closest, indeed, that we ever get in pagan mythology to something remotely akin to substitutionary atonement. All other gods repeatedly treat human beings as their playthings to be toyed with and disposed of as needed, with no pity or mercy. Tales of rape of mortal women by the gods keep surfacing in *Theogony* so casually that if we do not stop long enough to process these brief asides and lists, we might miss these stories for the horrific violence against personhood that they represent. But Prometheus, we see, is different. Helping people through such actions as stealing fire for them from Zeus costs him something—the joy of having an immortal life. As a god, Prometheus cannot be killed. But he can most certainly suffer, and Zeus makes sure that he does.

Such stories of the suffering of the gods present a rather unpleasant vision of eternity. It clashes with that Homeric dream—that desire to live forever that the heroes chased in vain. But then, such is the limit of human vision and human imagination. Left to our own devices, as Hesiod's stories about the gods remind us, we could never imagine a God who would choose to be chained, like Prometheus, and suffer in a horrible way, all to save humankind. Such self-sacrifice, after all, requires an anthropology unlike any seen in Greek mythology—a view that human beings are precious. But the point is, we never see such a philosophy or such a view of humanity in *Theogony* or, really, anywhere in Greek mythology.

We repeatedly see the judgment over anyone's preciousness or lack thereof as wholly subjective: A god may or may not like a particular human. Likewise, people may or may not like other people. There is no absolute moral stance over the value of anyone's life. The result, as Hesiod matter-of-factly shows in his didactic epic poem *Works and Days*, is the simple reality of human life as suffering from birth to death. Indeed, we find in this process that there is only one difference between gods and men. Gods may suffer all day long, as Prometheus did, but they never die. People, however, suffer all day long, all their lives, and then they die. If they're lucky, however, they will have descendants, who will continue that story in their own suffering lives.

Works and Days: From Here to Eternity?

Hesiod ends the divinely focused *Theogony* with a few final genealogical observations concerning the births of some of the heroes of the Trojan War, including Achilles and Aeneas. In contrast, *Works and Days* sticks mostly to the human rather than divine experience. The story it tells can be seen as the product of another chronological age: a time later than the heroes of Troy. Just as *Theogony* told of the generations of the gods, so *Works and Days* presents the mortals' side of existence. It is a life, Hesiod emphasizes, that is filled with curses: family strife and enmity, the misery of marriage, and a sense of the pointlessness of existence. Year after year, the works and the days will repeat. Actually, they do not repeat precisely. With each repetition, things only get worse.

One of *Works and Days*'s most striking episodes is the sequence of the generations of man:

> There was, at first, a golden age:
> At first the immortals who dwell on Olympos
> Created a golden race of mortal men.
> That was when Kronos was king of the sky,
> And they lived like gods, carefree in their hearts,
> Shielded from pain and misery. Helpless old age

Did not exist, and with limbs of unsagging vigor
They enjoyed the delights of feasts, out of evil's reach.
A sleeplike death subdued them, and every good thing was theirs;
The barley-giving earth asked for no toil to bring forth
A rich and plentiful harvest. They knew no constraint
And lived in peace and abundance as lords of their lands,
Rich in flocks and dear to the blessed gods.[4]

This first age, we learn, was truly blessed. Indeed, the humans of the golden age seem to have been better off than the gods themselves, as we recall the strife and misery that had been a feature of the gods' lives from their creation. Incidentally, we learn that these humans overlapped with the age of Kronos as "king of the sky."

Once that age all died out, however—and Hesiod doesn't tell the reasons why—the gods made a second, worse race: the silver age of humanity. Because this second race disrespected the gods, Zeus (now in charge of Olympus) destroyed it. He himself made the third race—of bronze. Bent on violence and destruction, this race of humanity destroyed itself, and Zeus then made the race of heroes. These heroes, Hesiod tells us, fought the great mythological wars, especially against Troy, but were consequently wiped off the face of the earth. This brings us at last to Hesiod's own age. Unfortunately, as he notes, it is the worst age of all—the age of iron, wracked by persistent and systemic injustice and misery. He sadly asserts that it would have been better not to have been born than to live in this age of unjust and unlawful oathbreakers.

Hesiod knows this well from personal experience, as he gradually reveals over the course of the poem. His brother Perses had cheated him out of his inheritance from their father. Tied up in courts for years and years, Hesiod futilely kept trying to get the inheritance back. This miscarriage of justice has pursued Hesiod all the days of his life, making him bitter and angry. He vacillates between the certainty that Zeus will always punish such oathbreakers as his brother and will restore justice and the belief that no consequences are forthcoming for the unjust until Zeus one day destroys this present evil generation, just as he had done with the ones that preceded

4. Hesiod, *Works and Days*, vv. 110–21.

it. But then, as the pattern of existence has shown, if the gods create another generation, it will be even worse.

Still, one has no choice but to live out his or her lot. Perhaps one can at least be glad that it's not eternal. And so, in the meanwhile, even in this horrible and unjust age one must go through the works on the designated days and seasons. Spring demands planting, while summer and fall bring a harvest—if all goes well. At least, sometimes it does. It is hard work, to be sure, but such is life in this age of iron. In addition to these seasons of works of the land, one must not forget the seasons of life. At some point, a young man must find a wife and start a family. It is a misery of another sort, Hesiod admits: The hard work of marriage is just like the labor that is involved in the life of farming. It is yet another curse of this iron age, but one must bear it. So, it continues—each new morning, new season, and new year. You suffer injustice, you mourn that suffering, and you work and work and work—until you die, probably mourning at that last moment how unfair both life and death are.

Reading Hesiod, one is struck by the theme of despair that runs through his poetry, connecting both *Theogony* and *Works and Days*. Life is hard for both gods and humans, although it is certainly harder for the latter, on average—unless you are Atlas or Prometheus. The pagan gods, we see though Hesiod's own eyes, could not even provide a happy existence for themselves, much less for the mortals they created. It is an endless cycle. No one in the Greek imagination is going to come out of it well.

In the midst of this misery and despair, it is striking to reflect about the idea that every new morning brings a renewal of blessings rather than curses. Such is the promise God gives us repeatedly, responding to the kind of pagan despair that Hesiod exemplifies. Lamentations 3:22–24 is an especially poignant example of this. It is a passage many know because of the hymn "Great Is Thy Faithfulness," whose refrain comes to my mind so readily in time of trouble, great and small:

> Great is Thy faithfulness!
> Great is Thy faithfulness!
> Morning by morning new mercies I see:
> All I have needed Thy hand hath provided—
> Great is Thy faithfulness, Lord, unto me!

Because of God's faithfulness to sinful humanity, each morning reveals new mercies of God's love to us. "I remain confident of this: I will see the goodness of the Lord in the land of the living," David proclaims in a psalm in the midst of his own hardship.[5]

We are no Atlas or Prometheus. But we are no Hesiod, either. Despair and hardship have been people's companions since the earliest days. Our own days right now are filled with suffering—if not our own, then that of other people we know, near or far. But we know that such suffering does not hold the final word; God does. The days and years repeat, and so do the seasonal works and family obligations, but the cycle of our year is not Hesiod's. Why? Because we know how the story ends. Christ's sacrifice for humanity, unlike that of Prometheus, has ransomed our lives. This gives our lives meaning for times of both joy and suffering. Furthermore, we are freed from despair over the evils and injustices of this world and from fear over the death that will surely be our mortal bodies' lot.

The Cup of Nestor

Sometime in the eighth century BC in the Greek trading colony of Pithekoussai, located on a small island off the coast of Italy, someone attended a nice dinner party. He defaced one of his host's drinking cups by scratching a silly ditty on it: "I am the cup of Nestor, well-suited for drinking. Whoever drinks from it, straightaway the desire of beautifully crowned Aphrodite will overtake him."[1]

This is maybe not the deepest message, but it is an obvious reference to the *Iliad*, where there is an elderly hero, Nestor, who does happen to have a legendary golden drinking cup.

Most significantly, this is one of the earliest (and some have said the earliest) known texts written in the Greek alphabet,

1. The translation is mine.

5. Psalm 27:13.

then in its infancy, only recently adopted from the Phoenician alphabet. It is striking to consider that one of the earliest texts written in this brand-new alphabet was not a work of literature or anything lofty, but a graffito referring to a work of literature—a silly poem about a Homeric hero.

Around 1000 BC on the island of Euboea, where Hesiod traveled for the poetic contest that he won with his *Theogony*, a middle-aged man was buried. We do not know who he was, and yet his burial tells a powerful story about his life and dreams. He was cremated, and his ashes were placed in a much older bronze bowl. Weapons were placed next to him. Buried nearby, but not cremated, were his companions on his journey out of this life: four horses, ceremonially slaughtered, and a young woman, decked out with gold jewelry.[6] Ever since this burial was discovered, scholars have been asking questions about it. Who is this man? Why was he buried in such an unusual manner? Who is the woman buried with him? Was she connected to him in life? Did she die a natural death, or was she killed as part of his funeral proceedings in order to accompany him in death? What's the deal with the horses, anyway?

We cannot answer all of these questions, but we can formulate a partial answer. Our answer key, it turns out, lies in Homer. This man's burial, which seems so strange, replicates closely the descriptions of heroic burials in the Homeric poems. Indeed, as I mentioned earlier, when the ghost of Agamemnon catches up with the ghost of Achilles in *Odyssey* 24, Agamemnon shares with Achilles all the details of his funeral. His description looks very similar to the account of Patroclus's burial in *Iliad* 23. It also resembles the burial of the unknown hero of Euboea. Perhaps this man, having heard the heroic epics in life and eager for the glory of heroes to be his own lot, decided that even if he did not live a Homeric hero's life, at least he could be buried as one. And yet, driving home the point of the insignificance of man's vain dreams of glory, we do not even know this man's name.

The Euboean man's obsession with his own burial echoes that of

6. For an overview of this heroon (hero shrine) at Lefkandi, see "Archaeologies of the Greek Past—Lefkandi," Joukowsky Institute for Archaeology & the Ancient World, accessed March 6, 2025, https://www.brown.edu/Departments/Joukowsky_Institute/courses/greekpast/4729.html.

Achilles, but the desires of both men raise an important question: Does our life's meaning lie in our death and burial? As Christians, we know that our story does not end there. For after death and burial comes the resurrection. The Bible promises repeatedly that just as the Son of God promised—and spectacularly achieved, to the amazement of the earliest witnesses—we too will rise with him some day. Our quest for eternity, therefore, looks infinitely more hopeful and joyful than that of Homeric heroes or their wanna-be imitators, like the self-staged nameless hero of Euboea.

Yet the strife for glory did not stop with Hesiod or his iron age contemporaries. In antiquity, as today, the realm of athletics provided yet another opportunity for those craving immortal glory to achieve it—not on the battlefield of Troy, and not on the farmlands in the shadows of Mount Helicon, but in the greatest athletic contests of the age. Good business acumen led one poet, Pindar, to capitalize on the Homeric urges of the athletic competitors of his age. For a handsome fee, Pindar composed commensurately handsome odes celebrating the heroism of the victors. We turn next to his visions of glory and immortality through athletic victories and the writing of poetry about them.

Recommendations for Further Reading

Hesiod, *Theogony, Works and Days, Shield.* Translated by Apostolos N. Athanassakis. Johns Hopkins University Press, 2004 (second edition) and 2022 (third edition).

Hesiod, *Theogony and Works and Days.* Translated by M. L. West. Oxford University Press, 2009.

Questions for Discussion and Reflection

1. What does Hesiod think about glory and eternity, and how does his vision differ from the Homeric epics?
2. What do we learn from the Lefkandi burial on Euboea? What

do you think the man was thinking when he designed such a burial for himself?

3. What is the meaning of your life? How do you know that this meaning is true? If you were to find a time machine and go visit Hesiod for a day, what would you like to tell him in response to his reflections about life?

CHAPTER

Pindar and Seeking Eternal Glory Through Athletics

> Kylon plotted a dictatorship and I wonder why they dedicated a bronze to him. My reasoning is he was physically very beautiful and quite well known for winning a two-lap race in the Olympic games.[1]

The Quest for Immortality at the Stadium

Chances are, if you talk to many a little boy (or if you ever were a little boy yourself) and ask him what he would like to be when he grows up, the answers will include famous athletes in one or more of his favorite sports. To be honest, I am not a sports afficionado myself so I will not mention any athletes here, but you can go ahead and take a minute right now to rattle off the names of your own personal heroes and perhaps even their best stats in their respective sports. It's okay—it is therapeutic. Most of all, it is true: Perhaps the closest that our society comes to having its own Homeric heroes is in the realm of athletics.

Heroes in our world today are made and unmade in front of thousands of fans watching any given game in person at a stadium or on television or livestream from home. The most dedicated of fans know stats about players going back nearly a century and get excited about those moments when it seems

1. Pausanias, *Guide to Greece*, vol. 1: *Central Greece*, trans. Peter Levi (Penguin Classics, 1979), 79.

that someone is about to break an old record and set a new one. Furthermore, famous athletes themselves reap the financial and reputational benefits from their successes on the field. They become advertisers of products, especially athletic gear. They write books—and are the subject of books—they make cameo appearances in movies, and more. Their glory, for a time, is secure.

But here's the surprising thing. The quest for immortality at the stadium is nothing new. In the early fifth century BC, a talented poet made a name—and likely quite a nice nest egg—for himself by writing poems that celebrated the greatest athletic victors of his day. His name was Pindar, and he became the go-to poet of the age for patrons of athletics all over Greece, who paid him handsomely. Millennia later, we only know about specific athletes and their victories because Pindar wrote about them. The Homeric principle is at work here in the realm of poetics. What Homer was to the heroes of the Trojan War, Pindar became the same type of glory-maker for the athletes of his age.

Everyone has heard, of course, of the Olympics. Yet the Olympics, celebrated at Olympia in honor of Zeus every four years since 776 BC, were just one of four great panhellenic athletic festivals—contests that included participants from all over the Greek-speaking world and, therefore, guaranteed unparalleled prestige and fame for their victors. In addition to the Olympics, there were the Pythian Games, held at Delphi in honor of Apollo every four years after 586 BC; the Isthmian Games, celebrated in honor of the sea god Poseidon at Corinth every two years after 582 BC; and the Nemean Games in honor of Zeus, held every two years beginning in 573 BC. Nemea, incidentally, was also the location of the mythical hero Heracles's first labor—the capture of the Nemean lion. It was consequently a fitting place for yet more heroic glory and fame to be made.

The panhellenic nature of the festivals made them prestigious. Here was a chance to compete against the best of the best, not only in one's own city but with athletes from all over the Greek-speaking world. Many of these places were certainly not known to most participants, and their residents spoke Greek with a different accent. Thus, competitors were not just representing themselves but their cities. Their honor or dishonor would not be their own alone but would reflect back on their city—this was yet another parallel between them and the Homeric heroes, who also were aware of the connection between their own glory and that of their homeland.

Also, just like some athletes today may give credit for their victory to God, the athletes of Pindar's age could not avoid the pagan religious setting of the competitions in which they engaged. All four of the great panhellenic games were held at religious sites and in honor of specific patron divinities. Two of the four celebrated Zeus, the king of the gods. One of the remaining two festivals honored Poseidon, Zeus's brother and god of the sea, and the other was dedicated to Apollo, Zeus's son and one of the twelve Olympian gods.

Athletic contests at these festivals included footraces of different distances, horse and chariot races, wrestling and boxing, and more. Technically, only men were eligible to participate, although the chariot races made it possible for wealthy women to compete by entering their horses and jockeys.[2] The requirements of the contests also ensured that the participants were among the wealthiest and most noble-born people in the Greek world. After all, participants had to pay for their own training. Participants also had to travel to the events in advance to be examined by special panels and accepted into the competition—expensive undertakings in their own right. Horse and chariot races, in particular, were the purview of the wealthiest nobility and royalty. After all, maintaining a team of four horses in peak shape was understandably costly and difficult—not to mention the danger factor involved in racing four-horse chariots at breakneck speed around a narrow track.

It is not surprising, therefore, that the families and patrons of victors wanted to commemorate their achievements in various ways, including through specially commissioned poetry. Pindar's odes in celebrating these athletes are strikingly relatable in some of their content. They often describe the youth and beauty of the victorious athletes, and they note just how difficult it was to achieve victory in a competitive field. Less modern, at first glance, is Pindar's use of mythological stories and parallels to glorify the accomplishments of the athletes. Still, the takeaways are timeless: The immortality of the greatest athletes' achievements reminds us of the same truth that we saw in the Homeric epics and in Hesiod's writings. The gods never die, but mortals—even the most glorious of athletes—do. We are

2. Mary R. Lefkowitz and Maureen B. Fant provide a lengthy list of the resulting women winners in *Women's Life in Greece and Rome: A Source Book in Translation*, 4th ed. (Bloomsbury, 2016), 194–202.

finite and limited, even when we are at the pinnacle of our achievements. So, what does this mean for how we think about the glory we seek and, sometimes, achieve in every realm of life, including athletics? To answer this question, we first need to consider the longings that have always driven athletes to seek victory at the stadium.

Athletics and the Quest for Immortality

In 476 BC, King Hieron of Syracuse, a powerful Greek city-state in Sicily, won the horse race at the Olympic Games and hired Pindar to commemorate the occasion. A single horse race required a jockey on a horse, and we can readily assume that the king himself did not risk his life and limb around the tough corners. Indeed, when we think of the horse races or the chariot races, it is apt to consider their modern successor: the car races. There, cars also slip, collide, crash, and flame up. Sometimes the riders emerge the worse for wear.

But in this race, all went smoothly—perfectly!—for Hieron's horse. And as the one who paid for the training of the horse and its rider, Hieron received the crown and the accolades for this victory. In many ways, such a victory was a celebration of the king's orderly rule and ability to control the elements, human and equine. Indeed, Pindar opens the celebratory hymn for this victory, Olympian 1, by listing the best things of all: Water is the best of elements, gold is the best of metals, and the Olympics are the best of all competitions. By winning the Olympics, Hieron demonstrated his control over all these elements. He is, in other words, a great king, one whose achievements are on par even with the gods', especially in this moment of glory.

Pindar, however, is not one to present facile celebrations. Instead, after the opening compliments and grandiose statements about Hieron, the ode shifts into the mythical segment, so typical for Pindar's celebration odes. Usually, he selected myths that had some connection either to the victor's city of origin or, as in this case, had a subtle moral lesson to offer. Indeed, the myth Pindar tells in this ode initially seems rather unflattering and unfitting for the occasion. It is the tale of Tantalus, a king once beloved by the gods but who lost favor when he tried to test them in the most horrible way imaginable. He cooked his own son, Pelops, in a stew and served the dish at a feast to the gods, just to see if anyone would notice. Spoiler alert: they did, although not before a distracted Demeter nibbled on a piece. In response, Zeus promptly resurrected Pelops and punished Tantalus by eternally surrounding him with delicious fruit and plentiful water that he was unable to enjoy.

Dysfunctional families in Greek mythology are aplenty, and the family of Tantalus is particularly so. Why did Tantalus, a king who had the gods' favor, decide to test their knowledge in such a horrific manner by killing and cooking his own son? And why would Pindar include this myth in his celebration ode for the athletic victory of a great king? Perhaps Tantalus's success was the most fitting way to describe the temptation that the greatest victories of our lives hold over us—they can become a massive boulder hanging over our heads, threatening to crush us.

Success, whether in athletics or in any other area of life, is a dangerously intoxicating drug. It is, on the other hand, something we all crave. What athlete, ancient or modern, doesn't dream of winning at the Olympics? And yet success can be seductive in all the wrong ways, since it tempts us to test the gods (as Pindar saw it) or to test God, as we might admit if we are honest. In our human strivings after power and glory and accomplishments—the things we conflate with immortality and eternity—we can easily make ourselves into our own gods. When victorious in any area of life, we should give glory to the gods, as Pindar said, lest they grow jealous of our success.

Pindar was on to something significant that we know: All our strivings, for victory and success and glory, cease in Christ. In Christ alone, we can rest. Our victories and successes belong to God, but in the greatest moments of victories it is easy to claim these achievements as our own. Of course, Pindar was no fool. He knew which side his bread was buttered on, and he was not going to forthrightly tell one of the most powerful kings in the entire Greek-speaking world that he needed to resist the seductive allure of power. But he could hint at this truth in poetry and through the telling of a well-known myth. You too, O great king, are mortal—a creature of dust and fog.

Youth Athletics

Of course, not all athletes, whether in antiquity or today, are full-grown adults. Youth sports have become in modern America a full-fledged industry in their own right; for example, Friday night high school football draws a larger crowd than any other event in my small Midwestern town of Ashland, Ohio. Annual Halloween trick-or-treating in Ashland is held on the Thursday before Halloween, rather than on the night proper, all to ensure (as the locals tell me) that no trick-or-treating events would ever interfere with Friday night football. We take this event that seriously!

The star athletes of these high school sports command a commensurately high degree of glory. Indeed, the path to a coveted NFL career generally lies through a very clearly marked trajectory: from high school football to college football at a Division I school (on a full scholarship, needless to say) to the draft into the NFL. Very few ever make it into professional football, but this doesn't stop thousands upon thousands of school-aged players each year from trying.

We do not know a lot about children's sports in antiquity, but Pindar's odes celebrating athletic victories offer a tantalizing glimpse.[3] A number of surviving odes celebrate the victories of young athletes, who are probably somewhere between the ages of twelve and eighteen. One of these, Pythian 10, commemorates the victory in a footrace at the Pythian Games of a boy about whom we otherwise know nothing—one Hippokleas of Pelinna. There is a certain irony here: The victor's name means "glory of horses," and his hometown is located in Thessaly, a region in northern Greece that was most famous for its horses. But this boy's victory was not in an equestrian sport—he won by running a middle distance, two laps around the track, on his own two feet.

It is fitting in celebrating a young athlete to consider how his victory reflects on both his city and, especially, his family. Pindar is happy to let us know that Hippokleas's father was also a prize-winning runner—at the Olympics, no less. As the poet notes, the father's seeing his son victorious in this very same type of race is about as high a blessing from the gods that one can reap in this life. Ultimately, this victory ode celebrates its youthful victor by reflecting on what we all desire and glorify in youth sports: health and popularity, which we associate with the good life beyond youth. A successful athlete in youth sports, we assume, will also be a popular and successful grown-up.

Pindar proclaims that assumption as he includes a blessing: May this

3. That said, several of the women athletes mentioned in Lefkowitz and Fant's *Women's Life in Greece and Rome*, 194–202, appear to be girls.

victory bring to Hippokleas the respect of the older men in his community and the admiration of the young girls his age. He is, after all, just a youth and not yet married. This victory is likely to increase both his prestige as an adult and his chances of a great marriage with a girl of his choosing. We may pretend that we no longer think this way today, but think of how many movies set in high school pair the star football player and the best-looking cheerleader. There is, additionally, an implied echo here to another runner from Hippokleas's home region. Thessaly, after all, was the homeland of the Homeric hero Achilles. In addition to being "the best of the Achaeans," Achilles is also labeled "swift-footed" by Homer because he wasn't just the best Greek warrior—he was also the fastest. And, so, could this fastest of Greek boys, Hippokleas from Thessaly, hope to become one day also a great warrior?

Pindar excels at these tantalizing hints: the dreams of greatness yet to come in these celebrations of present greatness. Indeed, that is how we act as humans. Even as we achieve what we had previously thought would be the pinnacle of our lives, even at that moment, even while receiving that victor's wreath, we dream up a new pinnacle: something better that we hadn't thought of before but desire now.

Finally, Pindar has some fun in likening his own work as a poet to athletic events, referring to his poem as the four-horse chariot of the Muses. This is a poignant image. Poetry, at its best, is orderly and organized, following the rules of its genre and art yet trying to do something within these bounds that has never been done before.[4] This doesn't happen easily, just as it is never easy to drive a four-horse chariot around a track faster and better than anyone else—governing the will of four different creatures in the chaotic environment of a race. So why do it? For the glory—why else?

The Homeric epics referred to the glory that the tellers of epics could win, not by doing epic deeds of their own but simply through immortalizing them. Eternity can be won this way by proxy. And so, Pindar also—a mortal poet with no special skills other than the important gift of poetry—is running his own race, guiding the Muses around the track to victory. Perhaps he was right. As we read his poetry now, 2,500 years later, and only

4. For a discussion of how genres work within poetry, see Andrew Judd, *Modern Genre Theory* (Zondervan Academic, 2024), 117–39.

know of most athletes he celebrates through his words alone, we realize that poets really do get the last—and the most lasting—word. And yet reading this poetry, beautiful as it is, also reminds us of the emptiness of such victories. Hippokleas has been dead and gathered to his ancestors for a long time. What was the point of his achievements? We can only hope that they brought him some joy during his fleeting life.

Athletics and the Quest for Honor and Redemption

Pindar's position in celebrating victors of different panhellenic athletic games placed him in a unique position in the Greek world: He celebrated victories of individuals from all over the Greek-speaking world, including from city-states who had at various occasions, including in his own lifetime, been each other's bitterest enemies. So what did he do on these occasions? An immaculate professional, he celebrated the victor and honored the quest for honor and redemption that present-day countries also seek through athletics. Athletes, after all, represent not only themselves.

One particularly striking example of Pindar's diplomatic good sense in mediating such potential drama comes through in Isthmian 7. In this poem he celebrates the victory of one Strepsiadas in the pankration at the 454 BC Isthmian Games. The pankration was known as a particularly vicious sport: It combined no-holds-barred wrestling with boxing. Not surprisingly, it was a special favorite of the Spartans, the most martial state of the age. Victory in this sport was especially prestigious. But in this ode, something else overshadowed the victor's impressive achievement: his city of origin. Strepsiadas was from Thebes.

In the early fifth century BC, the growing Persian Empire invaded Greece twice. In the first invasion, the Athenians dramatically defeated the Persian army at the Battle of Marathon (490 BC). This victory forced King Darius to retreat back home to lick his wounds. But a decade later, following the death of Darius, his son Xerxes was back for another invasion with an even larger army, one that (the historian Herodotus tells us) drank whole rivers dry while on the march. In the course of this second invasion, most of the Greek city-states combined forces against their common enemy, understanding that they could win only if they were united. And win they did—crushing the Persians decisively both on sea at the Battle of Salamis (480 BC) and on land at the Battle of Plataea (479 BC).

But here is the kicker: While most of the Greek city-states indeed worked together to fight the Persians, a few chose instead to "medize," as the Greeks called it—to join the Medes (another term for Persians). The most prominent city-state to medize? Thebes. Strepsiadas himself likely wasn't yet born at that point, a quarter century before his great athletic victory, but this was the generation of his parents. Consequently, knowing his city of origin, everyone watching Strepsiadas's victory would have remembered this recent and painful history.

Pindar is a skilled diplomat, so he goes back to much earlier, mythical history in opening the ode with some nice words about Thebes, the hometown of Dionysus, the god of wine. To be fair, he keeps this story clean, not revealing in detail the uglier aspects of that myth—those were plenty. Next, he turns his attention to the young victor Strepsiadas himself. Sure, he is not in the youth sports category but is quite young—presumably somewhere in his early-to-mid-twenties. And so Pindar expresses admiration for Strepsiadas's youth and beauty, which are on par with the strength he has just proven through his victory in the pankration. His looks, in other words, are not deceptive but demonstrate a matching strength of body and character.

Such a depiction of the victor as someone now proven beautiful in every way is Homeric and deeply culturally ingrained in the Greek world. Just think of the Homeric heroes: All of them were beautiful—as well as strong, skilled on the battlefield, and often adept with words. Beauty and virtue were meant to march hand in hand. By contrast, Homer briefly mentions the "ugliest man who came to Troy" in the *Iliad*. This man, Thersites, is not only ugly but speaks out of turn and dares to criticize the supreme commander-in-chief of the army, Agamemnon.[5] He is the antihero par excellence, deserving nothing but ridicule from Odysseus, who savagely beats him into submission. The Greek army laughs in response to this display of cruelty.

A quarter century before Strepsiadas's magnificent victory, the Thebans had proved the rottenness of their character to the rest of the Greeks when

5. Homer, *Iliad*, 2.250–317.

they sided with the Persians. But now here is a representative of a new generation, one unmarred by a betrayal of the rest of the Greek-speaking world. Wouldn't this be a good moment to let bygones be bygones and celebrate athletic greatness that, in this young man, is fittingly combined with beauty and all the accompanying excellence of character? This is the message that Pindar subtly presents here, as he highlights the city of the victor no less than the victor himself. We thus see a very modern instance of a likeable athletic victor representing his rather disliked homeland well to others abroad.

However, Pindar and his audiences were perhaps somewhat aware of a longing left unfulfilled. This is why there was a huge demand for Pindar's services. The memory of even the greatest victories is fleeting, just like the beauty, youth, and strength of even the greatest of victors. All flowers fade at the end—it is only natural. But we know that God's word stands forever, and this is a comfort that successful athletes today need no less than anyone else.

Pentathlon and *Kalokagathia*

In antiquity, just as today, well-rounded athletes were particularly respected. No Olympic event embodied this idea more clearly than the pentathlon. In this combination of five events, athletes competed over the course of a single intense day in standing long jump, javelin throw, discus throw, foot race, and wrestling. The victors were considered to have demonstrated *kalokagathia*—literally, beauty and goodness, the attributes of the most noble persons.

For the Greeks, internal character and external achievements were connected. Only someone truly good and beautiful, therefore, could win an athletic contest of strength and endurance. Such a victory couldn't be a mere accident of strength—it had to be the result of extraordinary virtue and self-control. However, such an approach yet again adds up to valuing and judging people based on their achievements, determining their worth externally. If only victors are good and beautiful, an uncomfortable Homeric question comes to mind: What does this mean for those who lost?

Each celebration ode that Pindar wrote celebrated someone at the greatest moment of his mortal life—the moment of prestigious victory. But as Pindar well knew, and as we also well know, our bodies were created with limits. This drives our desire to commemorate that great moment, to prove that it really did happen—for in a few decades, it might seem inconceivable that this seventy-year-old man had once been the Olympic champion. No athlete can remain at the peak of his or her game for a lifetime. At some point sooner or later, our bodies grow weak and frail, reminding us, even as we resist this truth, of our finitude.

This reality does not mean that we should not celebrate athletic achievements, but it does mean that we should not make them into idols. These particular idols are especially extremely transitory. Pindar's odes reflect this truth in their very existence—if we do not write down something beautiful and spectacular about the victor and his achievements, both will be forgotten all too quickly. Even the victory itself will lose significance, perhaps. Looking at a dusty trophy decades later, one might struggle to remember what it was all about and why it mattered. Like our very finite bodies, so are our victories.

But another reality of sports is no less important to remember. For every athletic competition that has a victor, there are many more losers. If we define the victors solely by their victories, then we ought to define everyone else by their losses—an uncomfortable conclusion! In other words, most of us are losers in whatever sport we compete, for only one winner can be crowned. The Greeks understood this stark reality even better than we do, since we dole out ubiquitous participation medals and trophies for youth sports and even for adults—cue the completion medals for marathons, for instance.

However, this much-mocked current trend of participation trophies likely gets something important right, albeit without fully realizing it: In

Christ we have not just *a* victory, but *the* victory. This truth is so simple yet so complicated. It should ultimately give us comfort for all athletic endeavors and other competitions by reminding us that whether we win or lose, neither our victories nor our losses define us. That is a comforting thought.

Recommendations for Further Reading

Pindar, *The Complete Odes*. Translated by Anthony Verity. Oxford University Press, 2008.

Questions for Discussion and Reflection

1. Which of the stories of Pindaric victories discussed in this chapter resonated the most with you? Why do you think it did?
2. How should Christians think about athletics or other competitions (if you are not an athlete)? What are some parameters that come to mind for you?
3. If you were Pindar today and were to write a victory ode, whose victory would you celebrate, and how would you approach your poem? If you are feeling inspired, go a step further: Write your own victory ode!

CHAPTER

Herodotus, Thucydides, and Writing Eternity in Prose

> I have written my work, not as an essay which is to win the applause of the moment, but as a possession for all time.[1]

Eternity in Prose

Right around the time of Pindar, another Greek writer was more quietly—and likely for much worse pay—working on his own pet project of writing eternity. But this man, Herodotus of Halicarnassus, decided to attempt something that had not been done at this scope before in Greek literature, even while choosing to do something that was very typical. Yes, he wrote an epic tale of an epic war. And yet the epic war he wanted to explore in detail was historical, not mythological: the Persian Wars. Herodotus's decision was doubtless personal: He was born right at the end of this conflict and his hometown, the city of Halicarnassus in Asia Minor, played a major part in the war. But unlike Homer or Hesiod or even Pindar, he chose to write in prose. In hindsight, we see the significance of his quiet rebellion much more clearly than he had ever imagined. This is why we call Herodotus "The Father of History"—a title that establishes him as the free-spirited experimenter who started something new: the writing of history.

---

1. Thucydides, *The Peloponnesian War*, trans. Richard Crawley (Random House, 1982), 1:22.

When we read translations of ancient literature, including poetry, sometimes we forget that a decision to write about a recent war—the war of his parents, which Herodotus surely grew up hearing about from family, neighbors, and friends—and in prose, to boot, was so revolutionary—but it was. Herodotus's visionary decision attests not only to the Greeks' willingness to experiment with other genres but also confirms the rise of a new creature in Classical Greece: readers. While poetry is easy to memorize and was composed and meant to be presented orally, prose was meant to be read. Such reading would be done not only in public but also by private individuals who had the means to purchase scrolls to read at home.

And so, with his massive work of nine books—nine separate scrolls—that formed his history of the Persian Wars, Herodotus became the model for all future historians. His goal, as he tells us from the get-go, was to preserve the great deeds of men—both Greeks and non-Greeks—from extinction. This aim has been the mission of historians ever since. While historians are also people and often take sides in their own interpretations of events, they are also aware of their duty to preserve an often messy and complicated past.

Herodotus's experiment became a massive success, although some read it more for the esoteric stories of weird things Greeks and non-Greeks have done than for the grand history narrative. He was, it seems, a businesslike personality up front yet a jocular entertainer in the back. But the historian whom we tend to place beside Herodotus, the Athenian Thucydides, who wrote a history of the Peloponnesian War (431–404 BC), was most assuredly all business and no fun. Ever. To be fair, this was perhaps not Thucydides's fault: The life he lived was decidedly complicated.

While Herodotus was just a guy who had wealth and connections sufficient for the ample travel that he undertook while researching his book for decades, Thucydides was an Athenian aristocrat and politician whose career culminated in becoming a general: a prestigious yet stressful office. Furthermore, Thucydides was significantly closer to the war that he documented than Herodotus was to the Persian Wars: He served in the Peloponnesian War until he was exiled for botching an important military operation in 424 BC. He subsequently spent the rest of the war traveling away from Athens à la modern war correspondents.

Each of these two historians documented the most important war of his lifetime for not only the Greek world but the entire Mediterranean world.

Each was convinced that it was necessary to set the history of this conflict in writing to preserve its memory for future generations. In this regard, we find Herodotus and Thucydides also operating with the Homeric mindset: Great deeds, whether good or bad or neutral, must be preserved both to render the glory due to the past and to benefit the future. In other words, both Herodotus and Thucydides saw the writing of history as a timeless, weighty duty—the work of preserving the past for eternity. History was, as Thucydides hopefully and ambitiously described, "a possession for all time." It was the work of glory—past, present, and future.

It was the work of eternity.

The Historian at Work

Hesiod may have encountered some rude Muses on the hillside where he herded sheep, but Herodotus and Thucydides had no such sources for their historical quests. Without divine inspiration, they instead had to pursue research to gather information about the events they were describing. They understood their task well. Both men conducted significant original research: oral interviews with witnesses and participants, consultation of any documents they could find, and so much travel to visit sites of relevance that one modern scholar wrote an article titled "Herodotus the Tourist."[2]

Facts, however, do not stand alone. The historian needs to decide which facts fit best into the story and what order and purpose they should follow. Indeed, the historian must set forth a purpose first of all. Herodotus's methodological prologue to his *Histories* made this initial declaration of purpose an essential and henceforth expected feature of the genre of historical writing that subsequent Greek and Roman historians followed.[3] Historians still generally follow this approach today—which is why your history teachers and professors ask you to have a thesis statement in your history papers.[4] So, how did Herodotus see his work?

2. James Redfield, "Herodotus the Tourist," *Classical Philology* 80, no. 2 (1985): 97–118.
3. See John Marincola, *Authority and Tradition in Ancient Historiography*, 2nd ed. (Cambridge University Press, 2025).
4. For an overview of historical methodology and goals of study from a Christian perspective, see John Fea, *Why Study History? Reflecting on the Importance of the Past*, 2nd ed. (Baker Academic, 2024) and Sarah Irving-Stonebraker, *Priests of History: Stewarding the Past in an Ahistoric Age* (Zondervan Reflective, 2024).

> Here are presented the results of the enquiry carried out by Herodotus of Halicarnassus. The purpose is to prevent the traces of human events from being erased by time, and to preserve the fame of the important and remarkable achievements produced by both Greeks and non-Greeks; among the matters covered is, in particular, the cause of the hostilities between Greeks and non-Greeks.[5]

Human beings are liable to die, and therefore human events are forgotten, erased by time. The only antidote that protects the glory of events from eternal extinguishment is, Herodotus concludes, to write them down. Fair enough!

Herodotus's emphasis on the importance of the achievements of both Greeks and non-Greeks may surprise us at first glance. When we recount the events of wars from our fathers' or grandfathers' generations, we likely prefer to condemn the enemy openly than to commemorate the enemy's achievements. I think, for instance, of my two Russian grandfathers who fought in World War II; both remarkably survived the Battle of Stalingrad. Their generation most assuredly would not have thought of anything their German enemies did as remarkable or worth remembering. But this mission also appears readily Homeric for Herodotus—recall that the *Iliad* also depicts moments of glory on and off the battlefield for both the Greek and Trojan heroes.

We do not need to guess that Herodotus was thinking of Homer while writing his introduction. He makes this clear for us himself as he proceeds to tell his theory about the origins of the Persian Wars. It all started, he says, with a series of kidnappings of women—first, the Phoenicians abducted a Greek princess, taking her to Egypt. Next, Greeks visiting Tyre in Phoenicia kidnapped the king's daughter from there.

A generation later, Herodotus tells us, the Trojan prince Paris decided to kidnap Helen. He assumed from previous historical precedent that this wouldn't cause any trouble—but, alas, he was wrong. This kidnapping sparked the Trojan War. In this way through his prologue, Herodotus manages to connect his new experiment—writing history in prose—to the more respected epic of Homer. Furthermore, we see his reflection on historical

---

5. Herodotus, *The Histories*, trans. Robin Waterfield (Oxford University Press, 1998), 3.

causality: Events like the Trojan War do not exist in isolation. Rather, events have a bearing on other events.

But, wait, you might be asking right now: What does this catalog of abductions of random princesses have to do with the Persian Wars? And doesn't the Trojan War, with its tales of gods and demigods, belong to the realm of mythology rather than history? Herodotus saw an obvious response to the first question: Troy was located in Asia Minor, part of the Persian Empire of his day. The Trojans were, in Herodotus's mind, the ancestors of the Persians. So the Persians took the Trojan War personally and sought a way to avenge the disaster and dishonor they had suffered. This makes sense—or, at least, it did to Herodotus.

As for the second matter, the distinction between myth and history did not exist as clearly for Herodotus as it does for us today. For him and his readers, the Trojan War was certainly a faraway event, but it was unquestionably historical—and its effect on the Persian Wars was, therefore, perfectly logical. Herodotus was not the only person who sought to mix mythology and history. We will see later, when we get to the Roman poet Vergil, that the Romans also had an interest in connecting their history to the Trojan War (and to Trojans specifically).

Thucydides started his own project within a couple of decades from the time when Herodotus had completed his. He seems to have looked down on his predecessor; in a brief jab, he apparently contrasted Herodotus's project unfavorably with his own:

> The absence of romance in my history will, I fear, detract somewhat from its interest; but if it be judged useful by those inquirers who desire an exact knowledge of the past as an aid to the interpretation of the future, which in the course of human things must resemble if it does not reflect it, I shall be content. In fine, I have written my work, not as an essay which is to win the applause of the moment, but as a possession for all time.[6]

Look, Thucydides wants you to know that he is a *serious* historian—not like that Herodotus guy, unnamed but clearly referenced here. He is

6. Thucydides, *The Peloponnesian War*, 1:22.

not one who courts his readers through gratuitous entertainment. And so Thucydides insists that he doesn't care for the "applause of the moment." If his work manages to educate readers to understand how historical events unfold, he will be content. It is perfectly fair for us to note that Thucydides doth protest too much. Surely, he did care about winning glory for his work; after all, every writer who has ever existed has wanted to be read and appreciated. Furthermore, such a concern for glory was in Thucydides's very DNA as a Greek man! And yet we also see in his words a somber variation on that worn-out modern adage that "those who don't know history are doomed to repeat it": If you know history, you will at least understand what is going on when it repeats itself, as it invariably does. Then at least you'll be equipped to say "I told you so" to everyone around you.

While Thucydides takes great effort in his prologue to separate his work from that of Herodotus, ultimately both men have a common goal in mind. As historians, they want to document epic wars in their own times and give their own updates on Homer, as Hesiod and Pindar had each personally done. Hesiod wanted to show that everyday events could also be the stuff of epics, while Pindar glorified athletic victories, setting them on par with the heroic achievements of Achilles and his ilk. But Thucydides and Herodotus go a step further, proclaiming that each age and each warlike generation can have their own epic war that is worthy of historical writing. These epics, furthermore, have a way of educating their readers—forming their very character. Let us consider now two further ways in which they do so.

History as Literature

Thucydides may have taken jabs at Herodotus's excessive use of entertainment in his history to attract the attention of his readers. But nothing Herodotus did (at least as far as he tells us) is likely to garner as much of a shock from the modern reader as Thucydides's explanation of how he approaches speeches in his history:

> With reference to the speeches in this history, some were delivered before the war began, others while it was going on; some I heard myself, others I got from various quarters; it was in all cases difficult to carry them word for word in one's memory, so my habit has been to make the speakers say

what was in my opinion demanded of them by the various occasions, of course adhering as closely as possible to the general sense of what they really said.[7]

Over the years, I've heard students describe this admission as "shocking," "shameless," "mic drop," and "bombshell." I myself have joked to students that they can't abide by this method of citing information in their college papers. Can you imagine a historian today ever borrowing a page from Thucydides's playbook to admit outright: "I included quoted speeches in my book wherever I thought that such a quoted speech was necessary. I did hear some of these speeches. But for some of them I wasn't actually present in person, and I'm not entirely sure that a speech was even delivered on that occasion. But I just wrote what I thought should have been said on that occasion. Oh, and I won't tell you which speeches I heard and which ones I made up."

Obviously, we would consider such a methodological approach from historians and journalists today to be utterly scandalous and outrageous. But before we get overly angry at Thucydides's free hand in wholesale making up some speeches in his history, let us recall that some of his literary predecessors (e.g., Hesiod) were getting their information directly from the Muses. And so, more than anything else, when we read Thucydides's description of how he composed speeches in his history, we should be reminded of the close connection that ancient historical writing bore to more fictional genres of literature, especially the epic. In this regard, historical speeches are similar to historical battle narratives; both try to paint a picture fitting to the occasion, leaning on art to present what looks like reality.

For example, one genre of speeches in Herodotus, Thucydides, and subsequent Greco-Roman historical writers is the pre-battle exhortations that generals give to their troops. Modern historians have wondered if such speeches actually happened.[8] How can we even know? These historians have discussed the logistics of addressing large crowds before the availability of

7. Thucydides, *The Peloponnesian War*, 1:22.

8. See Mogens Herman Hansen, "The Battle Exhortation in Ancient Historiography. Fact or Fiction?" *Historia: Zeitschrift für Alte Geschichte* 42.2 (1993): 161–80, and "The Little Grey Horse—Henry V's Speech at Agincourt and the Battle Exhortation in Ancient Historiography" *Histos* 2 (1998): 46–63.

voice amplifiers. Could a general really speak to several thousand men at once and be heard by all of them? But, to consider a more recent parallel, the eighteenth-century evangelist George Whitefield could address thousands of listeners in urban settings with a clear, sonorous voice—which an initially skeptical Ben Franklin confirms in his autobiography.[9] Just as opera singers have traditionally projected their voices to be heard throughout an entire large hall, so could some talented public speakers. In other words, these pre-battle speeches could certainly have happened more or less as ancient historians describe.

But perhaps such speculations are not the point. Rather, these speeches are another feature of the new prose epics that Herodotus and Thucydides were writing. Speeches heighten the drama: They present participants in the historical narrative as real characters rather than flat one-dimensional figures. In the process, they make historical accounts more interesting. Additionally, both Herodotus and Thucydides use battle narratives not only to describe real events as accurately as they can but to create Homeric epics in prose. Here is one example.

During the thick of the Battle of Marathon (490 BC), one Epizelus, an Athenian soldier, had a vision: "It seemed to him that he was confronted by a huge man in heavy armour, whose beard overshadowed his whole shield; but this phantom passed him by and killed the man next to him. That is Epizelus' story, according to my informants."[10] Following this encounter, Epizelus immediately went blind—despite having no visible wound nor even the merest scratch on his body—and remained blind for the rest of his life.

Modern historians have mentioned Epizelus as a classic example of PTSD on the battlefield, and that is certainly true. But we also see remarkably Homeric features in this episode. Here again, in a chaotic battle narrative a single warrior is singled out by name, and we see the presence of the supernatural—an encounter with an entity similar to Homeric descriptions of the gods fighting on the battlefield right alongside the mortals. Seeing a god

---

9. Benjamin Franklin, *The Autobiography*, in *Benjamin Franklin: Autobiography, Poor Richard, and Later Writings*, ed. J. A. Leo Lemay (Library of America, 1997), 669. Franklin further remarks, "[Whitefield's preaching] reconcil'd me . . . to the antient Histories of Generals haranguing whole Armies, of which I had sometimes doubted."
10. Herodotus, *The Histories*, 6:117.

generally carried consequences, and so Epizelus's blindness makes sense in this regard. But more than anything else, Epizelus's close call with death in battle reminds us that war leaves scars, visible or invisible, upon all its participants. Is the glory that the greatest warriors obtain in battle worth such sacrifices? We already saw in Homer's epics that some warriors felt conflicted over this very question. And so, Thucydides realized, sometimes war as literature becomes more closely connected not to the genre of epic but tragedy. Perhaps a more famous example of this genre shift involves a small island that wanted to remain neutral during the Peloponnesian War.

In 416 BC, the Athenians set their eyes on the tiny island of Melos, which had up until that point remained neutral during the Peloponnesian War—refusing to back either Athens or Sparta in the conflict, unlike what practically all other Greek city-states had done. At this point, Thucydides himself has been an exile from Athens for almost a decade. Where he got his information about these proceedings is unclear, but we find a short tragedy in his narrative: an episode we refer to today as "the Melian Dialogue."[11] Thucydides allows us to eavesdrop on a conversation between the Athenians and the Melians, casting it as a tragic dialogue—a conversation he himself certainly did not witness and which may never have happened. But the spirit of the event is clear. Through the Athenians' brutal ultimatum to the Melians—join Athens or die—Thucydides shows the corruption of human character that war perpetrates. The Athenians, noble proponents of democracy at the beginning of the war, are now savagely insisting to the Melians that natural order has created the weak to submit to the strong, because there is no other alternative.

The Melians, whether overly noble or foolish or both, refuse. Athens then besieges the island, captures it, and slaughters all male inhabitants, selling the women and children into slavery—the unfortunate classic outcome of ancient wars for the defeated. The overconfident Athenians, convinced of their strength, next embark upon the Sicilian Expedition, seeking to conquer the entire island of Sicily as a side project even while the domestic war with Sparta is still ongoing. Predictably, the Athenians suffer a horrific disaster that wipes out their entire fleet and eliminates most of their generals.

11. For a translation of the Melian Dialogue, see academics.wellesley.edu/ClassicalStudies/CLCV102/Thucydides--MelianDialogue.html. This excerpt is from the Richard Crawley translation, also used in *The Landmark Thucydides*, ed. Robert Strassler (Free Press, 1998).

Thucydides could have narrated the events at Melos in a matter-of-fact style, chronicling what happened as the nationless observer that he now was. But by recounting the events at Melos as a tragic dialogue, Thucydides did something much more powerful: He called all readers, present and future, to confront the moral questions that war always brings up. In the process, he reminds us that history, like all of life, is never neutral. Living in light of eternity requires us to confront right and wrong all around us. Additionally, the consequences of moral failure will also at some point reverberate on the offenders, as the Athenians found out too late in their Sicilian catastrophe.

Herodotus and the Battle of Thermopylae (480 BC)

Perhaps the most famous episode from Herodotus's *Histories* is the iconic Battle of Thermopylae. It is a Homeric contest par excellence: Three hundred Spartan warriors (and some other Greeks, who are overshadowed by the glorious Spartans) take on the entirety of the Persian army—these hordes that drank rivers dry. And while the Spartans die to a man (except for the two guys who missed the battle because of pink eye, really), they win immortal glory. Indeed, one could argue, their glory continues to live on in such modern media portrayals as the film *300*.

Stories like this one from the Persian Wars gave the Greeks real Homeric heroes: real people they could look up to. These stories also created, for the first time, a sense of panhellenic identity—all of the Greeks could now work together because their autonomous small city-states had to unify against a common enemy. In other words, the Homeric epics had given a common culture, but it took the Persian Wars and battles like Thermopylae to create a sense of a common cause.

Eternity and the Quest for the Good Life

Perhaps we can't achieve eternity in the here and now, after all. All of the authors we have considered so far gently whisper this truth to us under their breath, even while humoring us with their tales of failed quests of individuals and states for eternal glory through earthly acts. Gilgamesh was right, after all. The most prominent thing that defines us as people is, most assuredly, our mortality. Nevertheless, something else that defines us is our desire to dream big. Even in the days between the early knowledge of the one true God and the arrival of the gospel with Christ's birth, we find pagan thinkers and writers dreaming of the good life and wondering what it is all about. If the good life is not eternity, what else is there? This is a question that Herodotus also confronts through a remarkable side story early in his history about the encounter of King Croesus of Lydia with the Athenian lawmaker and sage Solon.

Solon, who supposedly ruled Athens as a lawmaker in 594 BC, is a figure more legend and smoke than flesh and blood. But, then, the entire conversation Herodotus documents between him and Croesus is likely to be more legend than reality, anyway: How could Herodotus have been privy to the private discussions of a king and a sage? At any rate, the story Herodotus tells is significant in illustrating the Greeks' quest for the good life.

During his travels, Herodotus tells us, Solon pays a visit to King Croesus of Lydia, then at the height of his power and wealth—it is no coincidence that "wealthy as Croesus" became a byword. Croesus takes Solon on a tour of his treasuries, and afterward casually asks if Solon has ever seen anyone more blessed than himself.[12] Solon responds by telling a story about an Athenian family man, Tellus, who lived a happy family life and then died in battle during a small war. He fought well and was buried on the battlefield as a hero with honors.

Taken aback, Croesus asks Solon to name a runner-up for "the most blessed man ever" award. He is sure that even if he has lost the first prize, he at least has the second place in the bag. Solon, spoilsport that he is, happily obliges by telling the tale of two brothers, Cleobis and Biton. When their mother, a priestess of Hera in Argos, was running late for a festival, the

12. For this conversation, see Herodotus, *The Histories*, 1:30–32.

two brothers yoked themselves to her chariot in place of oxen and brought her to the ceremonies on time. She then prayed to Hera to give her sons the best reward of honor they could receive. Accordingly, following the festival, the brothers went into Hera's temple, fell asleep, and never woke up. An outraged Croesus then asks Solon if he considers Croesus's obvious wealth, power, and success to be worthless. Solon next presents a key truth that is still important to us today: The story is not yet over. How can he name anyone who is still in the middle of life as the most blessed of all? He must see, first and foremost, how Croesus's story will turn out. Subsequent events, which involve the dramatic fall of Croesus's kingdom, will vindicate Solon's judgment.

Herodotus's tale has more significant theological implications for us than he could ever have fully realized. We are all, in our heart of hearts, like Croesus. Created with eternity stamped deep within us through the *imago Dei*, we yet want to boast in the visible, in the obvious, and in the here and now—at least when things are going well for us. But we are too small to see any sort of big picture, as the fate of so many earthly kings from Croesus to the Bible and beyond reminds us time and time again.[13] God alone knows eternity, feels it, and is master over it. The longing for eternity, knit into every human being, is but a longing for God. Nevertheless, since we live in the earthly mortal realm, we have to come to terms with our nature as citizens and participants in the politics of our state. We turn to this theme in the next part of this book.

Recommendations for Further Reading

Herodotus, *The Landmark Herodotus*. Edited by Robert B. Strassler. Translated by Andrea L. Purvis. Anchor Books, 2009.

Thucydides, *The Landmark Thucydides*. Edited by Robert B. Strassler. Translated by Richard Crawley. The Free Press, 1998.

13. Lucy S. R. Austen makes this point in her essay on writing biography as a Christian: "What Hath Faith to Do with Biography?" *Current*, October 19, 2023, https://currentpub.com/2023/10/19/what-has-faith-to-do-with-biography/.

Questions for Discussion and Reflection

1. Which of the two historians in this chapter do you find more relatable—Herodotus or Thucydides? Why?
2. Have you ever thought about writing a history of an event? Which event is it, and how would you approach telling its story?
3. How does the idea of the *imago Dei*, the awareness that every human being who has ever existed is made in God's image, change our view of history?

PART

The Formation of Virtuous Citizens

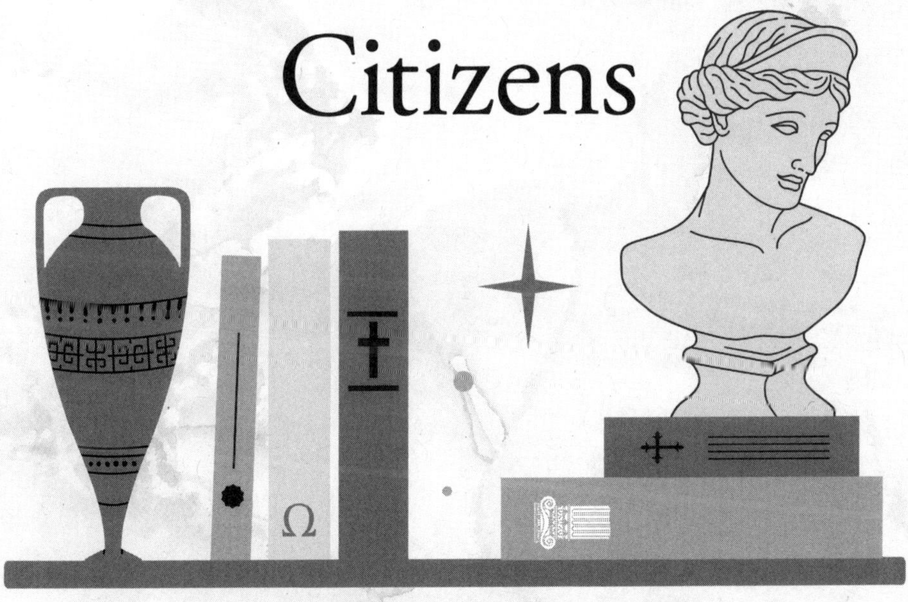

CHAPTER

Aeschylus and the Formation of Virtuous Citizens

> I shall fight as long as I live, and I shall not consider it more important to be alive than to be free . . . and I shall do whatever the generals command. Those who die, of the allied fighting-men, I shall bury on the spot and I shall leave no one unburied. After beating the barbarians in battle I shall tithe the city of the Thebans . . . If I remain faithful to the oath's terms, may my city be free from sickness; if not, may it become sick.[1]

Forming Virtuous Citizens: The School of Hellas

When a determined army of Athenian hoplites furiously charged the Persians at the Battle of Marathon in 490 BC, among the many citizens who fought with distinction that day was a young man named Aeschylus. The battle made an impression on him. Decades later, as an old man writing an epitaph for his tomb, he would request that his status as a Marathon veteran be listed there rather than the achievement for which he is still well-known two and a half millennia later—his tragedies, which effectively created the genre of Greek tragedy as we know it. But there was, of course, a connection

1. This is the Athenian oath taken before the battle of Plataea (479 BC). See Charles W. Fornara, ed. and trans., *Archaic Times to the End of the Peloponnesian War*, 2nd ed., Translated Documents of Greece & Rome 1 (Cambridge University Press, 1983), 57.

between his distinguished military service and his art: He wished to use both to serve and preserve the Athenian democracy.

On a cold winter day in Athens in 430 BC, a good quarter century after Aeschylus was laid to rest in his tomb, streaming crowds filled every narrow street in the small ancient city, shivering against the bitter winds and longing for the warm fires of their homes. Except for an important political assembly, a public festival, or—very recently in this case—a foreign invasion, it was rare for so many people to visit the city all at once from the countryside, abandoning their responsibilities to the farms where most of the region's residents dwelt and labored. But the occasion that brought them within the city walls on this particular day wasn't a festival; rather, it was a day of public mourning.

The winter of 430 BC marked the end of the first year of the Peloponnesian War, the brutal conflict between Athens and Sparta in which all Greek city-states were ultimately forced to join one side or the other. They had no idea that this war would continue for twenty-seven long years.[2] On this frigid day, the Athenians were commemorating the soldiers of the city killed during the first year of the war in a magnificent state funeral. In a city that was, in effect, a public fishbowl, where everyone was connected to everyone else, every citizen was guaranteed to know someone who had been killed. For some, of course, the losses were devastatingly intimate—the death of sons, fathers, husbands, friends, neighbors, or members of civic or social organizations.

In what was widely seen as the culmination of the day's events, Pericles, Athens's leading statesman, delivered to the intent crowds what would become his best-known speech: "The Funeral Oration." We have what may be a close transcript of this speech because none other than the historian Thucydides was present in that crowd and straining to hear over the coughing, shuffling, and mournful sobs of thousands of attenders.[3] It is entirely possible that this speech fits Thucydides's own admitted practice of sometimes reporting simply what he thought someone should have said

2. For an overview of the first part of the Peloponnesian War, see J. E. Lendon, *Song of Wrath: The Peloponnesian War Begins* (Basic Books, 2010).

3. For a translation of Pericles's speech (Thucydides, *The Peloponnesian War*, 2:34–46), see https://sourcebooks.fordham.edu/ancient/pericles-funeralspeech.asp. This excerpt is from the Richard Crawley translation, also used in *The Landmark Thucydides*, ed. Robert Strassler (Free Press, 1998).

on that occasion—but the speech we have is what we have. And this speech expresses Pericles's concern over a topic of timeless significance: the responsibility of the state for the formation of virtuous citizens.

Just how are virtuous citizens formed, in Pericles's view? In a nutshell, the response is: location, location, location. That location, of course, is Athens. Pericles proudly refers to the city as "the school of Hellas"—the example to all others across the Greek-speaking world of excellence in government, literature and the arts, and law. This environment cannot but call citizens—both those of Athens and those of other city-states who come into contact with the Athenians—to virtue. The locale of Athens inspires goodness in people through surrounding them by all aspects of the virtuous life, including a willingness to serve the city even by laying down one's life. Pericles's speech was, in some ways, one of a kind, like Pericles himself. Still, his audiences were used to hearing regular reflections about the virtues of Athenian citizenship and the calls to be virtuous citizens, even as they regularly struggled to embrace the rigorous requirements that citizenship in the Athenian democracy imposed.

As historian Matthew Christ has convincingly argued, bad citizens were commonplace in Athens. He particularly notes the predilection of citizens to shirk military service, skip jury duty, and avoid voting and other types of public service as much as possible.[4] Greed was a particularly common Athenian vice.[5] In some ways, we could say, this is a tendency we also saw in Homer's epic heroes: the prioritizing of one's own glory and desires above those of others, including one's own army. Or, more precisely, we could observe that this desire to proclaim "my own will be done" has been human nature since the fall. So, how did the Athenian state try to reel in these human tendencies of citizens to be selfish and greedy? How did the state try to form citizens so they could love the city-state and fellow citizens more than themselves? This is a question no less relevant for us today—as parents, as citizens, and as political participants with a stake in the well-being of our own state. The response is: Moral formation of citizens is key. But how can we achieve this?

Starting with at least the days of Aeschylus, the institution that arguably

4. Matthew Christ, *The Bad Citizen in Classical Athens* (Cambridge University Press, 2006).
5. Ryan Balot, *Greed and Injustice in Classical Athens* (Princeton University Press, 2001).

did more than any other to contribute to the moral formation of Athenian citizens was state-sponsored entertainment: Athenian drama. You likely thought that attempts at moral formation through entertainment, such as films or television programming, were a modern phenomenon. Of course, these types of entertainment are, alas, a reminder that moral formation for ill is just as possible as for good. The story of Athenian dramatic festivals, with their performances of tragedies and comedies for the public at state expense, is inseparable from the story of the Athenian democracy. Developing around the same time in the late sixth and early fifth centuries BC, they rose and declined together over the course of the following two centuries. The concerns the events in the tragedies and comedies reflect were real concerns of life in a democratic state—indeed, they also look very familiar for citizens of a democratic state today.

We all want to be the masters of our own affairs and, preferably, also those of the state. We resent anyone telling us what to do and how to do it. But the life of citizenship calls us to regular compromise and even self-sacrifice. We like this call about as much as the Athenians did. And, so, through what was effectively a regular state-sponsored refresher course in good citizenship, Athenian dramatic performances tried to inculcate shared virtues in the citizens through giving them a unified body of shared literature over which to think, weep, agree, and (quite often) disagree. In the second half of this chapter and in the two chapters that follow, we will examine the virtues (and vices) on which the different dramatic writers focused. First, however, this idea of tragedy and comedy as shared literature that contributed to the flourishing of a democratic state and the education of its citizens merits just a little bit more of our attention. Just how did this work in practice?

Shared Literature for the Education of Citizens

It was citizen assembly morning, and important matters of state were up for discussion.[6] Therefore, one citizen dutifully made the early morning trek to the assembly. On arriving at the designated meeting space, he saw . . . no one else. Annoyed with his fellow citizens' disdain for the democratic

6. This section is adapted from my essay, "Democracies Need Shared Literature," *Front Porch Republic*, October 26, 2023, https://www.frontporchrepublic.com/2023/10/democracies-need-shared-literature/.

process, he caustically remarked that if this were a free public comedy performance, everyone would have been present on time—even early, so they could get the best seats.

This citizen is the fictional creation of the late fifth-century BC Athenian comic playwright Aristophanes (we will meet him again in chapter 7). Even then, jokes make the best sense when rooted in reality. This joke was itself part of Aristophanes's free public performance of his comedy *Acharnians* (425 BC), and it mocked how the most democratic space of the Athenian democracy was the free dramatic performances: the tragedies and comedies that the city put on for the benefit of all citizens at public expense. Voting or assembly meetings did not even come close to garnering similar attendance.

Before we condemn the Athenians as selfish, entertainment-addicted bad citizens—which, to be fair, they sometimes (or often?) were, just like us—it is worth considering what such shared democratic spaces of entertainment facilitated. I contend that the enormously popular Athenian tragic and comic performances, held at multiple festivals throughout the year, provided the Athenians with shared occasions to weep and to laugh—achieving that catharsis of emotions which Aristotle later wrote about in his *Poetics*. This was cheaper than therapy.

Comedic plays often used mythological or other fictional storylines to comment on current events. For instance, in *Acharnians*, the protagonist, Dicaeopolis, fed up with politicians' ineptitude during the Peloponnesian War, secedes from Athens. He then declares his little farm a kind of Switzerland and signs an individual peace treaty with the Spartans, who are at war with Athens. In another of Aristophanes's comedies, *Knights*, a humble sausage seller who would like peace and prosperity for the Demos (the people) faces off against a war hawk villain who is obsessed with acquiring more power for himself. The villain, as original audiences would have recognized, was clearly based on an actual politician—Cleon, whose hawkish policies made it impossible to pursue a peace treaty until he was killed in battle.

On the other hand, playwrights also used tragedies to provide commentary on everything that could go wrong in a man's life—expressing shared fears and giving opportunities for shared mourning. In the next chapter, when we look at the work of the tragedian Sophocles, we will consider the famous mythical king Oedipus. What if the gods are angry at a man and even his city, all because of a curse that he knew nothing about?

Even though Athenian tragedies are heartbreaking, they are also fiercely patriotic, since they show most of the worst disasters that could befall someone happening in other city-states. By contrast, resolutions to the worst tragedies imaginable are found in Athens, the proud giver of justice for all the Greeks. Consider, for instance, the mythical protagonist of Aeschylus's trilogy *Oresteia*. Orestes is persecuted by the Furies, the goddesses of revenge, for killing his mother—which the gods had ordered him to do to avenge his mother's murder of his father (and you thought your family was dysfunctional?). He finally finds justice in Athens. Also, consider Euripides's Medea, the wronged common-law wife of the Greek hero Jason and the protagonist of the tragedy *Medea*. When Jason abandons her to secure a better marriage, Medea orchestrates the deaths of his new bride and that bride's father, then kills the children she had with Jason. At the end of the play, she acts as her own *dea ex machina*, dramatically escaping in a dragon-drawn chariot bound for Athens, where she too, like Orestes, will find a safe haven and a place to mourn all she has lost.

For the citizens of the Classical Athenian democracy, such plot lines offered an occasion to feel a range of emotions, but ultimately (and most importantly) they allowed citizens a chance to be proud of their city. At the same time, they provided an escape from many citizens' mundane lives of farming or trading and gave them shared stories to consider together. Citizens certainly not only attended plays together but also continued to talk about them for weeks and months afterward. Jokes from comedies likely entered popular language, whereas tragic storylines inspired reflection, mourning, and even fear: Could my own wife turn into a Medea? Furthermore, the poetic format of these plays made it possible to memorize long chunks wholesale—just as we can recall many songs from memory, regardless of whether we tried to learn them or not (here's looking at you, "Baby Shark"), but must work much harder to memorize a famous speech in prose.

In other words, the stories that the Athenian citizens saw on stage provided a common literary canon for their democracy—a shared body of treasured texts and stories for people who otherwise could agree on virtually nothing else. It is difficult to overestimate the significance of such a shared ongoing and growing canon for a city-state whose citizens held incredibly diverse political views—ranging from the most progressive "power to the people" demagogues to the most conservative oligarchs who opposed the very existence of a democratic form of government. But this canon obviously required poets who shared this vision to use drama and their creative genius for the moral formation of fellow citizens. This brings us back full circle to Aeschylus. It is perhaps fitting that after defending Athens during the first Persian invasion of Greece in 490 BC, Aeschylus used a famous battle from the second Persian invasion as the subject of his first surviving tragedy. *The Persians*, performed to great acclaim in 472 BC, portrays the events of the Battle of Salamis (480 BC).[7] In the process, it explores the quintessential Persian vices and the corresponding Athenian virtues.

Persian Vices and Athenian Virtues

Ten years after the Greeks, including Aeschylus, had defeated his father at the Battle of Marathon, Persia's new king, Xerxes, made his own trek westward with an army so massive that it supposedly drank entire rivers dry. His goal: to punish the upstart Athenians (along with the rest of the Greeks) and blot out his father's shame.[8] But, first, in practical terms, he had to master another enemy: geography.[9] He had to cross from his own region of Asia Minor, completely under Persian control, over to the Greek territories. The strait of Hellespont, about three quarters of a mile wide at its narrowest point, seemed a logical place for this purpose. And, so, Xerxes ordered a bridge of pontoon boats to be constructed to allow his army to march across the Hellespont, as though on dry land. Easy peasy.

However, a storm destroyed the first bridge. Outraged at the sea's disobedience and not accustomed to encountering this kind of resistance, the great self-titled King of Kings decided to teach it a lesson. Xerxes ordered the sea to be given a thorough whipping—three hundred lashes—and also threw chains into it and branded it so it could be reminded that it was his slave. He then built a second bridge, promptly crossed over to Greece, and managed to surprise the Greeks at Thermopylae (the famous story of the three hundred Spartans!). However, Xerxes ultimately was defeated by the

---

7. Having taught this battle multiple times to undergraduate students, I must include the obligatory explanation that the stress in "Salamis" goes on the first syllable, thus distinguishing its pronunciation from everyone's favorite Italian lunch meat.
8. For a biography of Xerxes, see Richard Stoneman, *Xerxes: A Persian Life* (Yale University Press, 2015).
9. Herodotus describes these events in *The Histories*, 7.21–35.

Greeks both on sea (the Battle of Salamis, 480 BC) and on land (the Battle of Plataea, 479 BC).

But, wait, we should ask, just as the Greeks did, how did this powerful king, with his drinking-rivers-dry army, lose to the scrappy Greeks? With the exception of Sparta—and those guys had just lost a lot of their forces at Thermopylae!—they didn't even have a properly trained standing army, being used to throwing together a semiorganized ragtag militia on an as-needed basis. These men had to bring their own armor, snacks, and all else that was needed for every campaign. This is a legitimate question to ask. Indeed, the Greeks appear to have been shocked by their victory over the Persians, but they had a clear explanation in hindsight: It all had to do with the moral character of both individuals and their leaders. More specifically, it had to do with how the gods also think about character.

By every action and decision of his—sea-whipping and all—Xerxes displayed hubris: an over-haughty pride that exposed his thinking of himself as not merely a great earthly king but as a master of the universe and a rival of the gods. Therefore, his defeat, miraculously achieved by puny Greeks, was concrete proof that the gods were paying attention and had punished him for disrespecting them. We have here a clear *memento mori*, Greek style: Mortal, remember who you are. For dust you are, and to dust you will return. Xerxes's hubris, we could say, is the real tragic hero of Aeschylus's *The Persians*, set in the wake of the devastating loss at the Battle of Salamis.[10] Taking place during the day of the battle in Susa, the Persian capital, the tragedy examines the Persians' emotions surrounding this battle and the invasion: Initially assured of the rightness of their cause, they are devastated by the news of the loss. The great king Xerxes himself arrives home (and on stage) later in the play. As the Athenian audiences knew, he had only recently whipped the Hellespont but now is a broken man.

Greek tragedies operated by a number of clear rules, which we also see at work here. The plot took place within a single day—from sunup to sundown. Only two actors in Aeschylus's day performed all the parts in a play. Thus, only two characters are on stage at any moment, lending added poignancy to dialogue. In addition, there is a chorus—of Persian elders,

10. The Reading Greek Tragedy Online project partnered with Out of Chaos Theatre to perform *The Persians*: "The Persians, Aeschylus—Reading Greek Tragedy Online," The Center for Hellenic Studies, streamed live on May 13, 2020, YouTube video, https://youtu.be/-k1xdQ1FYKY.

in this case—providing additional reflection, commentary, and questions about the events unfolding on stage. The tragedy of *The Persians* shows one man, Xerxes, as he belatedly realizes that his hubris is the vice that destroyed not only him but his army. We see that the character of leaders matters—perhaps even more than the character of their followers.

But if Xerxes's vice of hubris, of desiring to be a king above human rules and limitations, destroys him, the Athenians' love of freedom is their corresponding virtue, since their freedom is the thing for which they had fought. Aeschylus emphasizes these contrasting dynamics, placing this report strikingly in the words of the Persian messenger who tells the events of the battle to Xerxes's mother, the Persian queen Atossa:

> A song that echoed all about us from every rock and crag on the island. A song of terror that engulfed us all. Fear shook everyone of the barbarians. Their hopes of victory was [*sic*] proven false.
>
> This was no solemn song the Greeks were singing. This was no song of grief and of defeat. This was a song sprung from deep [in] their war-clogged hearts. They were charging into the battle with fearless zeal and, right through their whole line, the trumpet's voice fired them up into brave action.
>
> And suddenly, their flat oars obeyed some command and they sliced the salty waters of the deep. Almost immediately after that, they were there, in front of us!
>
> First came their right wing: orderly, calmly and then, close behind it, came the rest of their fleet. They rushed hard at us with a great shout: "Charge! Greek men, set your country free! Save your children, your wives, the holy temples of your fathers' gods, the sacred tombs of your ancestors! Now is the time to fight for all these things!"[11]

Greek tragedy most commonly presents commentary on current events through selecting a mythological tale that clearly echoes those events. But in this case, Aeschylus brilliantly selects a recent historical event, less than

11. For a translation, see Aeschylus, *Persians and Three Other Plays*, trans. George Theodoridis (self-pub., 2020), vv. 390ff. The online version is at George Theodoridis, "Aeschylus' '*Persians*,'" Bacchicstage, accessed March 6, 2025, https://bacchicstage.wordpress.com/aeschylus-2/persians/, vv. 390ff.

twenty years removed at the time of the performance, and presents it specifically through the eyes of the (fictionalized) Persians. In putting the Persians on stage and telling the tale of their loss in their own imagined words, having them admit their acknowledged vices to the virtuous Athenians, Aeschylus gave the Athenians of the post-Persian Wars generation something of which to be proud—a healthy type of proud, of course, not the hubristic kind. Over fifty years later, Pericles would call Athens "the school of Hellas," but Aeschylus's play showed Athens also schooling the Persians.

Aeschylus won the first-place award for the trilogy of which *The Persians* was part. Clearly his words resonated with his audience. But selling the virtues of good citizenship to citizens was not a one-and-done kind of effort; regular refreshers were clearly necessary. Besides, some Athenian virtues required more work than others.

Phrynichus, *The Sack of Miletus*

In 494 BC, the Persians viciously sacked the Greek city of Miletus. Located in Asia Minor, it wasn't in mainland Greece. And yet the suffering of fellow Greeks who lived there hit the Athenians hard. When the Athenian tragedian Phrynichus wrote a tragedy about the event two years later, *The Sack of Miletus*, the performance did not go as he expected.

The Athenians found themselves reliving the tragic suffering of the people of Miletus all over again and required Phrynichus to pay a massive fine for upsetting the sensibilities of the *polis* so gravely. What is going on? This event gives us a glimpse of just how involved the audiences were in watching tragedies. This was no passive entertainment; the citizens were invested in what they saw. Seeing the suffering of fellow Greeks on display here proved to be more than what they could handle. Overcome with grief, they punished the playwright. So much for mere entertainment!

Selling Citizens on the Virtues of Jury Duty

A few years ago, when my middle son was just a few months old, I received my first-ever jury duty summons. An existential dread filled me once I opened and read the letter. To be fair, I was still nursing a baby every few hours—he had never agreed to take a bottle—and I was juggling homeschooling with my job as a full-time tenured professor. So, the thought of disrupting or adding anything to my usual daily schedule seemed unfathomable. To put it simply, it was inconvenient for me to serve the democracy when I had no time or regular opportunity for sleep. I can anecdotally attest that my reaction to this summons is fairly common. My husband is the only person I have ever met who has wistfully mentioned his desire to get summoned for jury duty, just so he could experience this noble democratic process in action. If you work for the court and could make this happen, take note! To my great relief, however, I found out that primary caretakers of infants as well as primary homeschooling parents are eligible for a deferment of jury duty service, so it all worked out just fine for me.

Still, it appears that the Athenians shared my lack of enthusiasm for this particular democratic duty, even though they were paid for their jury service. Thus, we have a dilemma. The flourishing of a democratic court system requires the existence of a jury of peers. At the same time, such service—lasting a full day or longer, taking one away from regular obligations—is highly inconvenient. It is a small illustration of the kinds of self-sacrifice that a democracy regularly requires of its citizens. The state cannot run unless there is clear buy-in from the citizens in all democratic institutions. The courts are just one example.[12]

Civic duty is a central theme in Aeschylus's play *The Eumenides* (or *The Furies*), the concluding installment of *The Oresteia* (458 BC), the only complete trilogy of tragedies to survive from antiquity. Like most Greek tragedies, this one is based on a mythological tale. Agamemnon, the commander-in-chief of the Greek armies, arrives home after the Trojan War in the first play of the trilogy, *Agamemnon*.[13] His wife Clytemnestra,

12. For an overview of Athenian law and the courts, see Adriaan Lanni, *Law and Order in Ancient Athens* (Cambridge University Press, 2016).

13. For a performance of this play by Out of Chaos Theatre, see "Oresteia: Agamemnon, Aeschylus,"

however, promptly assassinates him in his bathtub—for many complicated reasons, he apparently really had it coming. Years ago, as a graduate student traveling around Greece, I saw a local hotel named "Clytemnestra" advertising "rooms with bath." I did not choose to stay there for the night.

Things get complicated after this first murder. The god Apollo promptly orders Orestes, the exiled son of Agamemnon and Clytemnestra, to kill his mother to avenge his father's murder. Orestes carries out these orders in the second play of the trilogy, *The Libation Bearers*.[14] But this seriously messed-up family drama runs into a conflict that even the gods can't fully disentangle. On the one hand, murder of kin must be avenged. This means that Orestes, as far as Apollo is concerned, had to kill his father's killer. On the other hand, the murder of kin by a blood relative must also be avenged. And so the Furies, primordial goddesses in charge of avenging such murders, persecute Orestes in *The Eumenides*.[15] The goddess Athena offers to resolve the conflict by holding a fair trial for Orestes in (where else?) Athens.

In putting on this first-ever murder trial, Athena gives a rousing speech about the virtues of her citizens, lauding them *en masse* as virtuous, selfless, and eager to pursue justice not only for Athenians but for all of Greece. This is a "name it, claim it" kind of philosophy, flattering the citizens in the audience. Athena claims that every Athenian, simply by virtue of being an Athenian, is perfectly suited for this work of administrating justice. Location, location, location, yet again. The citizens responded with applause, awarding Aeschylus yet another first-place victory in the dramatic contest that year. Seeing a horrific family tragedy resolved by the virtuous work of an Athenian citizen jury, featured as the secondary hero in this play, perhaps temporarily made jury duty seem great again to the Athenians.

The Center for Hellenic Studies, streamed live on October 21, 2020, YouTube video, https://youtu.be/X2KihPrvPog.

14. For a performance of this play by Out of Chaos Theatre, see "Oresteia: Choephoroi (Libation Bearers or Women at the Graveside), Aeschylus," The Center for Hellenic Studies, streamed live on October 28, 2020, YouTube video, https://youtu.be/nFhfG3l8yjA.

15. For a performance of this play by Out of Chaos Theatre, see "Oresteia: Eumenides, Aeschylus," The Center for Hellenic Studies, streamed live on November 4, 2020, YouTube video, https://youtu.be/zCkWZCx1x-g.

Confronting Our Hubris

The reminder to confront our hubris is latent even in such ordinary exhortations to citizens as the call to jury duty. For whipping the disobedient seas is not the only way we can act as tyrants ruling our own small worlds. Rather, as Aeschylus realized, such urges are part of human nature. Therefore, virtuous citizenship in a democracy is always going to be a difficult call because we will always feel unpleasant when we admit that we ourselves are not "King of Kings." Abuses of power always come naturally to leaders and citizens, whereas self-sacrifice always feels like a loss of something to which we are entitled. This is a truth that Christians can see powerfully in the story of the fall and expulsion from the garden of Eden. Abusing power is the story of all earthly kings and rulers ever since, it seems. It is also the story of too many ordinary citizens—at least in their desires, if not in reality. Indeed, the history of the Athenian democracy includes plenty of such mournful tales that show the abuse of power by the citizens themselves. Athena's perception of her citizens' virtues, it appears, was overinflated.

It is no mere coincidence, then, that tragedians after Aeschylus continued to explore the virtues of good citizenship and the abuses of power of both leaders and citizens in their works. In the process, they continued to call Athenian citizens to love their state more, abhor the negative examples of tyrants, and vow to protect the Athenian democracy. As Aeschylus's younger contemporary, Sophocles, realized, one of the best ways to teach these lessons to Athenians was to show the horrors of life in a city without democratic virtues. Consequently, he proceeded to show that something was rotten in the land of Thebes.

Recommendations for Further Reading

Aeschylus, *Oresteia*. Translated by Peter Meineck. Hackett Publishing, 1998.

Aeschylus, *The Persians and Other Plays*. Translated by Alan H. Sommerstein. Penguin Classics, 2010.

Aristophanes, *Acharnians, Knights*. Edited and translated by Jeffrey Henderson. Harvard University Press, 1998.

Questions for Discussion and Reflection

1. In what ways did Athenian dramatic performances work to strengthen Athens' democracy?
2. We are certainly not kings, but we are still prone to some of their sins—like hubris. What is hubris, and why is it a problem? Can you point out some concrete examples of hubris that you have observed—whether in real life, other books, or movies?
3. What are the duties of citizenship you find the most appealing, and what are the duties of citizenship you find the most challenging? Why?

6

CHAPTER

Sophocles Plays *Clue*

Thebes is dying. A blight on the fresh crops
and the rich pastures, cattle sicken and die,
and the women die in labor, children stillborn,
and the plague, the fiery god of fever hurls down
on the city, his lightning slashing through us—
raging plague in all its vengeance, devastating
the house of Cadmus! And black Death luxuriates
in the raw, wailing miseries of Thebes.[1]

Clue: Something Is Rotten in the Kingdom of Thebes

If you have ever played the game *Clue*, you may recall the challenge and the thrill of untangling a glamorous murder mystery set in a sprawling mansion with extravagant rooms such as the conservatory and the billiard room. Never has the scene of a violent crime looked better.

The players know at the game's outset that there is a body—Mr. Boddy. But which one of the players killed him? Where? And by what means? Was it Miss Scarlet in the parlor with a candlestick or rope? Or Mr. Green in the library with a pistol or a wrench? The players gradually unveil this mystery, clue by clue, as the game unfolds, until in a dramatic denouement one player lays out his theory, solving the mystery in one fell swoop. In my

1. Sophocles, *Oedipus the King*, in Sophocles, *The Three Theban Plays*, trans. Robert Fagles (Penguin Classics, 1984), vv. 31–38.

house, this person is somehow almost always my husband—whose character in the game is always Professor Plum. Yes, each member of our family has designated roles in *Clue*!

When Athenian audiences turned out at the theater in 429 BC to see the latest tragedy of Sophocles, *Oedipus the King*, they may not have known at first that they were attending a *Clue*-style whodunit—but they were. First, they would have found art imitating life.[2] As the play opens, the bodies are literally piling up in Thebes—a devastating plague is ravaging the city. While the play ostensibly tells a mythological tale, the audiences would have been intimately familiar with a very similar, still ongoing plague of their own day. Modern medical researchers who have compared the description of symptoms of the Athenian plague that the historian Thucydides describes with the plague Sophocles outlines concluded that the two are one and the same. So much for mythology![3]

Disturbingly, a plague in Greek mythology is usually a punishment, a sign of religious pollution or a divine curse—a sign of something deeply wrong.[4] Just think of the plague at the beginning of Homer's *Iliad*, which turned out to be the god Apollo's punishment upon the Greek army at Troy. Likewise, the plague in Sophocles's play is a sign that something is rotten deep within the land of Thebes. But, then, when is it not? While in the previous chapter we saw how Aeschylus openly talked about the virtues of the Athenian citizens in his plays, encouraging them to live up to such lofty praise, we see here Sophocles often taking a different approach toward this same audience. He instead emphasized what life looked like in the ultimate anti-Athens—Thebes.

A historical grudge was afoot, to be sure. Thebes had sided with the Spartans against Athens at the outbreak of the Peloponnesian War, two years ongoing at the time of this play's performance. Historical memory went much farther back, however. As I mentioned in chapter 3, the Thebans had

---

2. For a performance of this play by Out of Chaos Theatre, see "Oedipus Tyrannus, Sophocles," The Center for Hellenic Studies, streamed live on June 10, 2020, YouTube video, https://youtu.be/VCvHfVK50ck.
3. Antonis A. Kousoulis et al., "The Plague of Thebes, a Historical Epidemic in Sophocles' Oedipus Rex," *Emerging Infectious Diseases* 18, no. 1 (2012): 153–57. https://pmc.ncbi.nlm.nih.gov/articles/PMC3310127/.
4. For an overview of pollution in Greek religion, the most comprehensive source remains Robert Parker, *Miasma: Pollution and Purification in Early Greek Religion* (Oxford University Press, 1983).

medized by joining the side of the Persians during the Persian Wars, hoping for a reprieve by betting on the surer party to win. Against all expectations, the Greeks had prevailed, and all the Thebans got out of their deal was decades of disdain from their fellow Greeks. In the context of this heavy historical baggage, it makes perfect sense that when Athenian dramatic poets needed a foil to Athens, a place as corrupt and rotten to the core as one could possibly imagine, and a place that showed a cautionary tale of what happened if rulers and their people did not adopt the virtues of democratic citizens—well, that place in Athenian drama was more or less always Thebes.

If, as we saw in the last chapter, the key for flourishing citizen virtues is location, location, location, so it is for the promotion of the anti-virtues. And yet, as Sophocles gently but persistently hints, there is something unifying, both encouraging and terrifying, about our anthropology—the very nature of all human beings, whether Athenians or Thebans. For we are all mortals—finite creatures, certainly, but oh-so-impressive still.

The story of our Mr. Boddy and the hunt for his killer reveals a world rife with anxiety. Anthropology is inseparable from theology. Sophocles is investigating human nature and the place of the gods in the world, but he doesn't tell us so up front. Instead, he makes us work to understand the clues to this larger investigation through his plays about the Theban royal house. Thus, he configures the tragedy in *Oedipus the King* as a murder mystery. Let us follow along on the same path that the original audiences traveled and see if we can make sense of the clues, solving a murder and addressing our fears.

Mr. Boddy at a Crossroads

The Greek mythological version of *Clue* has a built-in possibility for attaining clues outside of reliance on the powers of deduction alone—oracles and prophets. And so, early in *Oedipus the King* we learn that Oedipus has done the responsible thing to uncover the reason for the plague: He sent his brother-in-law Creon to Delphi to consult the oracle of Apollo. Since Apollo was the god of plagues—you may once more recall that he had also unleashed the plague in the *Iliad*—this makes obvious sense.

Creon arrives back with an important clue. In this case, the oracle, generally known for being remarkably unclear, was surprisingly direct in laying out the reason for the plague: Laius, the king before Oedipus, had been murdered, bringing about pollution. Apollo demands that the killer be punished. He also gives one more clue: The killer is in Thebes. The whodunit is set in motion. We now have the identity of this Grecian Mr. Boddy: He is none other than Laius, the previous king of Thebes. And so Oedipus begins the investigation, assisted by the rest of the cast of characters: the blind seer Tiresias; his wife Jocasta, who is also the widow of Laius; Jocasta's brother Creon; the chorus of the city elders; and a slave who happens to be the lone witness of the murder of Laius.

As I mentioned in the last chapter, the plot of a Greek tragedy takes place from sunup to sundown within the space of one day. In this span we see the investigation unfold, even though we are aware that this particular game is rigged. Just like with the original audiences, many of us have heard this myth before watching or reading this tragedy, and so we know how this story turns out: Oedipus is the culprit. Those who had first seen the play performed received their thrills from seeing the clues and how the characters, including Oedipus, interpret them.

Although Tiresias from the beginning tries to tell Oedipus the truth, Oedipus has to follow the clues for himself. Jocasta ends up providing the first devastating clue that will shake Oedipus: the precise location of the murder of Laius, at a crossroads of two major roads, one of them leading from Delphi. In a striking reversal, she will also describe Laius's physical characteristics to Oedipus. Normally the suspect's physical characteristics are described in the process of an investigation, but here the focus is on Mr. Boddy, who is never present on stage yet whose murder drives the action of the play.

But perhaps the important query to ask in this play is: Is there one body or two? Jocasta muses over this question early in the play as she remembers the original Delphic prophecy that had, decades before, predicted that her baby with Laius would kill his father. Instead, her baby is presumably dead, exposed at birth, and Laius had also died later on.[5] There is a possibility that both of these bodies exist, negating the original prophecy. But the clues eventually lead to a key discovery: There is only one body, that of Laius. The exposed baby—Oedipus—is alive. But this truth takes time to emerge in the play. In the meantime, Jocasta's question

5. Sophocles, *Oedipus the King*, vv. 794–800.

about the possibility of two bodies, rather than one, causes some characters to undergo an existential crisis.

What does this tell us about the gods? Could they be just plain wrong? The chorus of Theban elders has a grimmer reaction to this possibility than does the queen:

> Never again will I go reverent to Delphi,
> the inviolate heart of Earth
> or Apollo's ancient oracle at Abae
> or Olympia of the fires—
> unless these prophecies all come true
> for all mankind to point toward in wonder.
> King of kings, if you deserve your titles
> Zeus, remember, never forget!
> You and your deathless, everlasting reign.
>
> They are dying, the old oracles sent to Laius,
> now our masters strike them off the rolls.
> Nowhere Apollo's golden glory now—
> the gods, the gods go down.[6]

The question of the chorus has much to tell us about pagan theology, in which the gods are powerful but not all-powerful. The gods have to prove to their followers that they are still worth worshiping. The chorus verges on blasphemy here, addressing Zeus, king of the gods, in a gut-wrenching plea: "King of kings, if you deserve your titles." There is deep desperation here in the voices of people who crave truth and feel that it is just out of their grasp.

Why worship the gods if they cannot even fulfill their own oracles, their own promises? This question makes sense in the pagan quid-pro-quo view of the relationship between the gods and mortals. But there is a greater fear at hand to provoke anxiety. The story of Oedipus ultimately is a story of a family curse that Oedipus had known nothing about. Once Oedipus and Jocasta know at the end of the play that the original prophecy—and the curse—has come true after all, they do not have faith in the gods. Instead

6. Sophocles, *Oedipus the King*, vv. 985–97.

they fall into despair, leading Jocasta to commit suicide while Oedipus gouges out his own eyes.

Consequently, the search for Mr. Boddy and then the search for his killer—all under the shadow of a divine curse—brings to life a horrible fear for us all. It is a pagan fear, but Christians can also hold it. What if I (or my community) are cursed but don't know about it? What if we don't even know the cause of this curse? What if we're guilty of something we don't even realize we did? These questions have important implications for our view of not only our relationship with God but also for our relationships with fellow citizens. The Greeks realized instinctively something that we are conditioned by modernity to deny—the collective nature of society. True, each of us is an individual with responsibilities and gifts and callings. And yet none of us are an island unto ourselves. As citizens we are always a part of the whole, and what any one citizen does reverberates for the rest. As Paul reminds us in the description of the body of Christ in 1 Corinthians 12, this is no less true for the church than for the broader society.

One Nation Under Curse?

Let us go back one important step and consider how our search for Mr. Boddy and his killers began. It all started with a plague, which clearly suggested to the Thebans that they were under a curse. Oedipus had first sent Creon to Delphi to consult the oracle so the nature of the curse could be known. After all, the second step in eliminating a curse (after the first step—admitting you're under a curse) is finding out the reason for this curse.

But we find out that while the curse in question results from the actions of one man, its ramifications extend to the entire community. All citizens suffer for it. Thebes, put simply, is one nation under curse. This dire fact shocks no one in the play, nor would it have shocked anyone in the original audience. In the process of telling the story of Oedipus, Sophocles reminds his readers that part and parcel of citizenship in any state—just as much in Athens as in Thebes—is participating in the curses that are bestowed upon one's nation.

Indeed, the Greek myths that form the foundational plots of Greek tragedies are rife with curses. Usually these are family curses affecting a single royal house. Lasting for three generations (just long enough to kill everyone off), a robust family curse combines at least two of the trifecta of the greatest evils imaginable: incest, murder of kin, and cannibalism. Furthermore, although each curse is the lot of one particular royal family, it always affects the well-being of the entire state.

Let's take the example of the family of Orestes, son of Agamemnon. Agamemnon had sacrificed his own daughter, Iphigenia, to the goddess Artemis so that his army could safely sail to Troy. But in the generation before this, Agamemnon's father Atreus had killed the children of his brother Thyestes and served them to him for dinner. If you think this is bad, this isn't even the first time we get cannibalism in this particular family. (It's a wonder any of them still dared gather together for dinner!) The father of Atreus and Thyestes was none other than Pelops, the son of Tantalus. As I described in chapter 3, Tantalus was forever cursed in the underworld because he had tested the gods by cooking Pelops and serving him in a stew to them to see if they would notice. Zeus had resurrected Pelops, who eventually married and had children, enabling this gruesome culinary cycle to continue.

However, the Theban royal house certainly gives the house of Atreus a run for its money. Laius, Oedipus's father, brought down a curse from the gods on his line by raping the young son of a friend. His victim committed suicide. This curse leads to the murder of kin—Oedipus murders a stranger, who turns out to be his father. In addition, we have incest—Oedipus marries his mother. Finally, in the next generation, the two sons of Oedipus die by each other's hand. In this whole process, the citizens of Thebes also bear the cost of this curse.

What should we make of Sophocles's accounts of the sufferings of the Theban people? Oedipus endures unimaginable pain, so many of his unnamed subjects die of the plague, and his two sons later perish in a devastating civil war because they could not agree to share the throne. As Christians, there is much we can agree on in the worldview that Sophocles presents in this whodunit: All citizens really are in it together, whatever the "it" happens to be in any given moment for their community. And we can agree, just as the Greeks did, that one's love for their city is important. Last but not least, even though we don't like to agree on this final detail, we really are a people under curse—and by "we" I mean the human race, not Americans or any nation specifically. But what do I mean here?

Perhaps the best illustration of the theological concept involved here is one that C. S. Lewis provides in *The Lion, the Witch and the Wardrobe.* Remember that interminable winter—but never Christmas—in which Narnia and all of its inhabitants labor when the Pevensie children first stumble into it? It is a land under a curse—the curse of the White Witch. The return of Aslan, the glorious king, breaks the curse and brings spring and joy and hope back to the land. Lewis wasn't just making up a pretty story here—at least, not entirely. The tale is theological in nature, harkening back to the state of the world since Adam's fall and expulsion from Eden. We have all labored under a curse ever since then.

Thankfully, our story doesn't stop here. Unlike Sophocles's audience, who felt the unfairness and cruelty of the world around it and blamed it on curses from the gods, we know that God comes to restore creation. "Far as the curse is found," we sing every Christmas, often without dwelling sufficiently on the glory of this promise. But God's promise to remove the curse makes the Christian message different from anything Sophocles could have imagined. Yes, sometimes this world feels like a land under a curse, but we have God's promises of blessings—indeed, the greatest of them: eternity with Christ. This idea of future blessings that will overcome the curse was unfathomable to the Greeks of Sophocles's time, whose view of the divine had no space for such blessings. This striking theological message—that God cares for us so much that he wants to bless us rather than leave us to keep living under Adam's curse—brings us back full circle to the connection between theology (how we think about God or gods) and anthropology (our view of people—including ourselves).

How Oedipus Found Salvation at Athens

Many people have heard the basics of the myth of Oedipus. But did you know that in some versions, his story concludes with a redemption in Athens? In Sophocles's tragedy *Oedipus in Colonus,* whose action takes place between *Oedipus the King* and *Antigone,* the self-blinded

Oedipus travels to Athens, led by his daughters as guides, and petitions for asylum. Cursed by all others, he finds refuge in the village of Colonus just outside of Athens proper—Sophocles's own home.

This story fits into the larger pattern in Greek myths as presented on the Athenian stage. The wronged, the tragic heroes, the bereaved, and the long-suffering all find welcome in Athens after being driven away from everywhere else. The Athenians were not, in practice, so tolerant of immigrants and foreigners. Without the theological conviction that every human being is priceless in God's eyes because he or she is made in God's image, there was no reason for them to care for the plight of foreigners and tragic heroes. And yet we see a desire come through at times in Greek tragedy to show compassion in a world where compassion was sorely lacking. After all, the story of Oedipus reminds us that such a curse could befall any of us.

"What Is Mankind That You Are Mindful of Them?"

In Psalm 8, as David worships God, he reflects on the connection of having a proper theology (understanding of God) to formulate a healthy anthropology (understanding of the nature of humanity). Understanding God's greatness, in David's eyes, makes it all the more incredible and beautiful that God cares about us, mere people:

> Lord, our Lord,
> how majestic is your name in all the earth!
>
> You have set your glory
> in the heavens.
> Through the praise of children and infants
> you have established a stronghold against your enemies,
> to silence the foe and the avenger.
> When I consider your heavens,

the work of your fingers,
the moon and the stars,
which you have set in place,
what is mankind that you are mindful of them,
human beings that you care for them?

You have made them a little lower than the angels
and crowned them with glory and honor.[7]

Just as the Hebrews—and then the early Christians—worshiped God, so did the pagan inhabitants of the Greco-Roman Mediterranean world write hymns to worship their gods. The Homeric hymns—worship songs in Homeric language and style though clearly not composed by the authors of the epics—go back to the seventh century BC, and praise both major and minor gods. But Sophocles alone dared compose a hymn to people.

While *Oedipus the King* provides the first chapter of the tragic story of the Theban royal house, Sophocles did not write his tragedies on these myths in order. His first foray into these stories came over twenty years earlier, in the tragedy *Antigone* (ca. 441 BC), which is really a sequel to *Oedipus the King*. In that play, a young girl, Antigone, is the only one in all of Thebes who stands up to evil, insisting on burying her brother even at the cost of her own life. But before any of these events happen, the chorus of Theban elders, men well acquainted with the sorrowful history of the city and its divinely cursed royal house, takes a brief breather from talking doom and gloom. It delivers what is probably the most famous choral ode in *Antigone*, and one of the best known in all of Greek tragedy. The "Ode to Man" is a poetic list of all the accomplishments and inventions of humanity from time immemorial. It celebrates the height of the *technê* of mankind:[8]

Numberless wonders
terrible wonders walk the world but none the match for man—
that great wonder crossing the heaving gray sea,
driven on by the blasts of winter

7. Psalm 8:1–5.
8. Adrienne Mayor, *Gods and Robots: Myths, Machines, and Ancient Dreams of Technology* (Princeton University Press, 2018), 62.

on through breakers crashing left and right,
holds his steady course
and the oldest of the gods he wears away—
the Earth, the immortal, the inexhaustible—
as his plows go back and forth, year in, year out
with the breed of stallions turning up the furrows. . . .

And speech and thought, quick as the wind
and the mood and mind for law that rules the city—
all these he has taught himself
and shelter from the arrows of the frost
when there's rough lodging under the cold clear sky
and the shafts of lashing rain
ready, resourceful man!
Never without resources
never an impasse as he marches on the future—
only Death, from Death alone he will find no rescue
but from desperate plagues he has plotted his escapes.[9]

Reading the "Ode to Man" alongside Psalm 8 brings the anxiety of the pagan world into greater focus. We saw the theological nature of this anxiety in *Oedipus the King*. In *Antigone*, Sophocles focuses more on this anxiety's anthropological nature. People of both the past and the present are amazing in so many ways—great and awful and surprising (and sometimes all of these at once). People keep aiming—and achieving—so much, both good and evil. Always resourceful, people are only bounded by death, as Sophocles states matter-of-factly. Two and a half millennia later, even as science continues to make incredible advances, Sophocles's observation remains true. Humanity's tragic flaw, as this choral ode reminds us, is that one desires to fashion oneself as one's own god. This was as true for the pre-Christian pagans as it continues to be the driving desire for many of us, the children of (post)modernity. But unlike the pre-Christian world, Christians have a hope that defeats death. This hope defines the stories of

9. Sophocles, *Antigone*, in Sophocles, *The Three Theban Plays*, trans. Robert Fagles (Penguin Classics, 1984), vv. 377–85 and vv. 395–405.

those who find it, and it also affects how we perceive tragedies—whether they be literary, historical, or even personal. As someone who had come to discover that hope in Christ at the age of thirty, I find myself needing it no less in my historical writing than in my own daily life.

As I think about fictional and historical people from the ancient world, I am repeatedly reminded that no one's story is truly insignificant. After all, God made each and every one of us, including the many people of the past who had spiritual longings but never knew Christ. In studying the literature and history of the ancient world, we get to know their stories of struggles, failures, and successes—some ordinary and others extraordinary. These stories fit into larger patterns, for not even the most isolated recluse ever lives in a vacuum. These larger patterns, I believe, extend from antiquity to the present.[10]

The ancient world was comfortable with violence and suffering, and this unpleasant reality comes across in the hopeless stories people told and lived. Mythical tragedies taking place in Thebes mirrored the calamity of the real-life plague in Athens, which carried away relatives of so many in the audience that saw the first performance of *Oedipus the King*. The world Sophocles describes is dark and hopeless. There is no escape from the bitter curses that are dealt to some people, fictional or real, for no fault of their own. But the gospel continues to offer a revolutionary and countercultural hope. The beauty of that hope continues to enthrall me as a believer, historian, and, yes, citizen of my community.

The world of Sophocles and that of Psalm 8 powerfully contrast each other. While curses in the pagan world came from the petty and vengeful gods, for reasons that someone like Oedipus might not even know, Christianity offers a different story. Yes, curses do fall upon this world and into our lives—they come from both ourselves and our sinful nature since the fall—but this sober reality is not the end of the story. Rather, our story is filled with blessings—promises of blessings past and many more to come from God. This anthropology gives us individual hope to triumph over despair. But, even more so, it gives hope to us as citizens of our communities, for it reminds us that our citizenship here is but training for the citizenship of heaven.

---

10. Daisy Dunn's *The Missing Thread: A Women's History of the Ancient World* (Viking, 2024) particularly drives this point home in describing how we think about the historical significance of women and anyone who wasn't a famous leader.

Recommendations for Further Reading

Sophocles, *The Three Theban Plays: Antigone, Oedipus the King, Oedipus at Colonus*. Translated by Robert Fagles. Penguin Classics, 2000.

Questions for Discussion and Reflection

1. Sophocles intended his tragedies to evoke powerful emotions in the audience. What emotions did you experience in reading the story of Oedipus?
2. What is biblical anthropology, and how does it contrast with the anthropology that dominates in Sophocles's tragedies?
3. What do we learn from the contrast between the "Ode to Man" and Psalm 8?

CHAPTER

Aristophanes and Euripides Remember the Ladies

He seems like the gods' equal, that man, who
ever he is, who takes his seat so close
across from you, and listens raptly to
your lilting voice . . .[1]

Gas Clouds over the Acropolis

About a decade after Sophocles's *Oedipus the King* moved the Athenian audiences to tears of mourning, another dramatic poet used his craft to move them to tears for a different reason. Audiences who turned out to the performance of Aristophanes's *Peace* in 421 BC witnessed a curious opening scene: a farmer fattening a dung beetle, all so that he could fly on this poor man's "Pegasus" to visit Zeus, king of the gods, and beg him for peace. This was still the era of the Peloponnesian War, as you may recall, although the Peace of Nicias, a fragile treaty, had just been implemented, and the comedy's focus on seeking peace reflects this state of affairs. Ending the war and obtaining peace was certainly a great desire of the Athenian farmers, including those in attendance at the play.

After the farmer Trygaeus finally saddles his humble transport, he turns

1. Sappho, fragment 31, trans. Chris Childers, *Literary Matters* 9:1 (Fall 2016), https://www.literarymatters.org/1-1-sappho-31/.

to the audience and asks, "As for all of you, for whose sake I'm performing these labors, stop farting and [pooping] for a period of three days; because if this thing picks up the scent while airborne, he'll toss me off head first, and go off to pasture."[2] Shocked? You're not alone. When I taught a seminar on Athenian democracy a few years ago, a graduate student confessed that he did not expect to encounter this much toilet humor in Athenian literature. "I thought the Athenians were serious people," he mused, "but there are so many fart jokes."

Indeed, the comedies of Aristophanes universally display humor related to all kinds of bodily functions. At least fart jokes transcend both time and cultures—but not all jokes do. The political humor that is likewise present throughout these comedies is more challenging to understand; even Greek historians today are not entirely sure about some of the references. This makes sense. If you watch political satire from just a decade or two ago, some of the jokes might pass you by unless you remember the particular people and events in question. And then there are the various sexual jokes, innuendos, and rape humor—these are not so funny to us anymore as we reflect on the dignity of all image-bearers.

For jokes to be funny, they have to be relatable—and they were to their original audiences. These were all citizens—Athenian men (and never women) of eighteen years or more. As mentioned in chapter 5, attending plays together was a political act for Athenian citizens, but this was certainly more fun than jury duty or voting, as Aristophanes himself notes on occasion. The performance of a tragedy or comedy was a school of democracy and a school of virtues for all citizens to experience together. But it was a school in the original meaning of *scholê* (leisure) rather than in the stricter sense that the English derivative "school" implies.

A well-known example of this Athenian "schooling" occurred in 425 BC, when Aristophanes put on a play about Socrates. Named *The Clouds*, it portrayed the famous philosopher and teacher floating above the stage in, well, clouds. Socrates was suspended above the city and his adoring students, pontificating on some fairly outrageous nonsense. This comedy

---

2. Aristophanes, *Peace*, trans. Jeffrey Henderson (Harvard University Press, 1998), vv. 149–53. I substituted "pooping" in place of a much cruder term, altering this one word in Henderson's translation—and his translation is faithful to the Greek original in its crudeness.

is our first glimpse of how ordinary Athenians (as opposed to, naturally, Socrates's own adoring students) truly saw Socrates. In this play, we get hints that Socrates's teachings may have been seen as dangerous to public morality, muddling the Athenians' discernment of what is good or bad. Socrates in the play, as in real life, aimed to teach his students critical thinking skills, requiring them to question everything. But taking this approach to an extreme, as Aristophanes suggests, is all rather funny, especially once you add in the requisite number of fart jokes.

The humor of scenarios like the performance of *The Clouds* ultimately challenged Athenian citizens to consider important and rather serious political and social developments in their city. Even though these plays offered irreverent and funny commentary, they nevertheless forced one to think. Perhaps even Socrates, that much more serious public intellectual, saw the value in this practice. Comedy reminds us that disagreement between citizens is a guaranteed part of life in a democracy. In fact, this conflict begins right in your own home and raises uncomfortable questions. For example, did any Athenian wives ever bring up the concern that Abigail Adams once famously raised to her husband, the future president John Adams? "Remember the Ladies," she noted in a letter in 1776.[3] Her world was millennia removed from the Athenian democracy, and yet still one that held women in a similarly powerless position. Her reminder went unheeded in some ways, but it doesn't mean that John Adams and his contemporaries did not have questions about women's role in the state.

This analogy can be extended to the Athenian democracy. While only men attended Athenian dramatic performances, both tragedies and comedies display a significant degree of interest in understanding women, these strange beings with whom the men in the audiences lived and shared the city-state. Some comedies wondered quite openly: What is the nature of women as human beings? How are they different from men? And how might they govern the state, should this very hypothetical possibility ever materialize? For starters, perhaps they would bring about peace and no dung beetles would be necessary.

---

3. Abigail Adams to John Adams, March 31–April 5, 1776, Massachusetts Historical Society, accessed January 31, 2025, https://www.masshist.org/digitaladams/archive/doc?id=L17760331aa.

The Good: Aristophanes's Peace-Making Wives

Ten years after the dung-beetle-facilitated peace, the Peloponnesian War was still raging in earnest. Aristophanes consequently wrote another play in his long series of comedies that envisioned outrageous schemes for obtaining peace. This play, *Lysistrata* (411 BC), would have seemed a howler unlike any other its audience had previously seen. For one thing, the male-only audience would have been surprised to find out that most of the characters were women—although, as always in Athenian drama, all actors were still men.

In this comedy, Lysistrata, a regular Athenian wife, summons a meeting and calls the other Greek women together. In this group, the Spartan representative attracts the most attention with her incredible fitness level. "Just look at the muscles on this gal!" the other women gush. You could bounce quarters off her abs or derrière! But everyone eventually calms down and hears out the plan Lysistrata has cooked up: Since the men have repeatedly failed to agree to a peace and end the war, the wives will withhold connubial privileges from them until peace is concluded. This scheme seems so simple, yet brilliant. We see here a comic version of Pericles's vision of Athens as "the School of Hellas" in action—here is an Athenian wife who demonstrates brilliant thinking. In other words, the Athenian men are not the only intellectual leaders.

Once this premise is set into play, hilarity ensues. Husbands are trying to seduce their wives, while their wives, who would really like to be seduced, are having a hard time resisting all advances to stay on task. In the end, the wives win: The husbands want to restore domestic peace and intimacy so much that they speedily sign a peace treaty, and everyone lives happily ever after. The play concludes with singing and dancing from the Spartans and the Athenians, as each man takes his wife and happily goes home. A victory for marriage and families!

The dialogue is crude and vulgar, and yet the basic premise of this comedy is something significant: War is the enemy of domestic life. Furthermore, the point is comically made that perhaps peace is simpler than the men on both sides think. For in this play, unlike in the earlier comedy *Peace*, the peace treaty is not the result of divine intervention—no Zeus or the goddess Peace comes to help here. Rather, it is all the work of women.

If, as Aristophanes suggests to his audiences, women ran the Greek world, perhaps Athens would already have peace rather than this war that keeps dragging on for decades.

Admittedly, seeing women's thoughts and voices projected entirely through the writing and acting of men, which was normal in Athenian comedy, raises questions for us. To our modern sensibilities, this phenomenon only emphasizes that we have no idea what real Athenian wives thought, felt, and imagined. Women's voices are an acutely felt absence in Greek literature, highlighting that we are missing the experiences of the weak in a way that denies their full personhood. However, as classicist Daisy Dunn reminds us, some of these absences are problems of survival. There were a lot more women writers in antiquity than we think; unfortunately, their works didn't survive. For example, Dunn cites "Pamphila, a seminal first-century AD female historian from Epidaurus in Greece (her thirty-three-book work of *Historical Commentaries* is sadly lost but was quoted from by male writers in antiquity)."[4]

Literacy rates in antiquity are notoriously difficult to measure, but it appears that most men could read well enough to comprehend public decrees and other similar documents that were set up to provide essential information for citizens—laws, announcements of military drafts, or sales agreements for land. And, indeed, by the fifth century BC we have enough of a hint that literature for men existed—we might mention such authors as Herodotus and Thucydides. By contrast, most women did not have such high levels of literacy, as they were not expected to read public documents. We would be wrong, however, to assume that there was no women's literature at all. Besides, some women writers, like Pamphila, whom we just mentioned, did not write for women—Pamphila was a historian, writing for diverse audiences.

All this said, in Aristophanes's comedy we see women's desires pointing to one key thing: happy marriage. This is the goal that drives Lysistrata's plot to end the war. It is no coincidence that Sappho, the best-known woman poet from the Archaic Greece era, wrote poems that express this same desire. She was an aristocrat who lived on the island of Lesbos in the late seventh and early sixth centuries BC, and her songs celebrate marriage

4. Daisy Dunn, *The Missing Thread: A Women's History of the Ancient World* (Viking, 2024), 81.

and love within the confines of marriage as the highest goal and expectation for women of her time. These poems and (likely) those of other poets in this same genre were, furthermore, the quintessential women's literature of Archaic and Classical Greece. But most women likely never read these poems; rather, they learned to sing them as choral songs.

Surviving merely as fragments quoted by later authors—yet again, in other words, surviving through the voices of men—Sappho's poems vividly express a highly charged language of desire. Just consider Fragment 31, the epigraph for this chapter, in which we see a couple in love:

> He seems like the gods' equal, that man, who
> ever he is, who takes his seat so close
> across from you, and listens raptly to
> your lilting voice . . .[5]

Who performed these songs, and where? Scholars like André Lardinois have suggested that many of Sappho's poems were *epithalamia*—wedding songs. Furthermore, although Sappho or other soloists may have performed some of these songs, they were also often performed by choruses of unmarried young women who were around the same age as the bride.[6] Such songs were both expressions of celebration for the bride and reminders for the singers that their day would yet come. Catchy in their poetic rhythm and, likely, also in their tunes, these "hits" were cherished by the teenagers who learned them. We can imagine these teenage girls continuing to sing or hum such songs to themselves as they went about their days, dreaming just like their modern counterparts of that perfect love that will someday arrive to sweep them off their feet.

Scholars' view of women's lives in Greek society is rightly grim. Since women lacked the full rights of citizenship in a society that favored arranged marriages of younger women to somewhat older men, they were in danger of being abused. And yet both Sappho's marriage songs and Aristophanes's *Lysistrata* give us some glimpses of happy pairings and the ideal of marriages

---

5. Sappho, fragment 31.
6. André Lardinois, "Who Sang Sappho's Songs?" in *Reading Sappho: Contemporary Approaches*, ed. Ellen Greene (University of California Press, 1996), 150–73.

so happy that husbands might likely make the right choice if pressed to choose war or the restoration of harmony in the home.

The Bad: Assemblywomen Take Over

Lysistrata portrays a hypothetical scenario in which the women do not use openly political tactics to effect their desired outcome in the Greek world, rather brokering a peace entirely through their domestic powers. Aristophanes had taken an ingeniously original approach to the question of women in society, and he would have another chance to tackle this issue.

The Peloponnesian War ultimately ended with an ignominious defeat for Athens and the overthrow of its democratic government. But the bloodthirsty "Tyranny of the Thirty," a Spartan-supported oligarchy, lasted less than a year and democracy was restored in 403 BC. However, all was not well. Heading into the early fourth century BC, we see a power vacuum in the Greek-speaking world. Both Athens and Sparta had been significantly weakened by the Peloponnesian War, and against this backdrop of domestic economic and political instability—in short, just general unhappiness—a much older and grittier Aristophanes yet again decided to portray a scenario of women taking over the state. In this case, however, the women take an openly political approach.

In *Assemblywomen* (391 BC), the women form a plot: They dress up as men, come to the citizen assembly very early in the morning before the men can get there, and pass a new legislation disenfranchising the men and giving exclusive citizen rights to women alone. So far, so good. But what do women want? In *Lysistrata*, the women wanted peace—and their own husbands safely home with them. In *Assemblywomen*, however, the humorous investigation into women's innermost desires and how they might rule the state takes a darker turn. The women, it turns out, just want to party all day and all night and sleep with any men they wish. That's basically it. And so the affairs of the city, as the play tracks them, disintegrate into utter chaos, since the selfishness of the women's very physical appetites allows no room for anything else. Far from the humorous yet pro-family stance of *Lysistrata*, the humor of *Assemblywomen* is downright misogynist, showing women as not fully human in their intelligence and certainly more animal than human in their desires.

But then, such humor had a long-standing tradition in Greek poetry. In the seventh century BC, the Greek poet Semonides of Amorgos wrote a poem documenting the ten different types of wives.[7] It is a sort of scientific guide for men to distinguish the different sorts of women that one might happen across—or, worst of all, marry. The list of animals to which Semonides likens different women shows that misogyny across human traditions is remarkably uncreative. Some insults used toward women even today still borrow the same animal language that Semonides includes. There is the sow—the filthy and fat pig of a wife, whose home is a total pigsty. There is the "bitch"—she is cunning and all bark. There is the stubborn she-donkey, who requires much beating (says the poet). Worse yet, she's promiscuous, happy to sleep around with anyone. Same goes for the weasel. And then there's the horse woman—so pretty (look at that flowing mane!), but very high-maintenance. She won't do any housework and also won't let her husband touch her, lest he mess up her hair or outfit. And so the list continues.

Only the tenth and final type of wife—the bee—is good. She is hardworking, kind, loving, and a treasure to her husband and entire family. But she's quite rare. So, the poet asks the logical question after this depressing analysis: Why did Zeus create women, anyway? The answer: He wished to curse and punish men. So, here are all the men now, each praising his own wife but suffering in secret.

However, such descriptions of wives and marriage as a curse exist in tension with the tender description of love that we see in the marriage songs of Sappho, Semonides's rough contemporary. How might we explain the existence of both? We could attribute it to gendered language and settings—the contrast of women's gentle songs about love and men's "locker room" talk about women's flaws with its generally rough-and-tumble humor. But even more so, we see the difference of genre expectations. The job of invective poetry was to make the listener laugh, albeit through attacking the subject under discussion. Invective poetry was never going to be nice in its insults; rather, the more shocking, the better. Semonides certainly was a master of this genre just as Aristophanes was the master of comedy, a related genre.

But there is one more genre that considers women's place in society and

---

7. Semonides of Amorgos, *Women*, poem 7, trans. Diane Arnson Svarlien, Diotíma, accessed March 6, 2025, https://diotima-doctafemina.org/translations/greek/women-by-semonides-of-amorgos-poem-7/.

the state seriously and displays a remarkable degree of tenderness and sympathy toward their plight. This is the genre of tragedy, with which we are already a little familiar from the previous two chapters. In tragedy, we see suffering that shows hints of something redemptive, even though the pagan writers could never name it in those terms.

The Redemptive: Suffering Heroines in Greek Tragedy

Greek boy meets barbarian girl. They fall in love. Sure, her father disapproves, but such is love. And so they elope together, as he also steals her father's most treasured possession (aside from his daughter, of course). Oh, and to delay her father's pursuit as they elope over sea, she kills her brother and throws bits of his body off the ship. As her father stops to pick up each part, she and her beloved are able to escape to safety.

Is this what "happily ever after" is built on? This woman was so sure it would be. The couple had two children in quick succession, and life seemed to slow down a bit. And then the man delivers a bombshell: He has decided to marry a princess, someone more suitable to his stature as a Greek man of royal lineage. Since this other woman, the mother of his children, was not a Greek nor a legally wedded wife, he could leave her just like that. Her desires didn't matter: She was to be discarded, free to go anywhere she wanted—which is, really, nowhere where she could survive alone. At least, in a gesture of what he thought to be kindness, this man asked to keep their two children and raise them in the royal palace with his new wife.

This is the story of the famous hero Jason (of Jason and the Argonauts fame) and Medea. Children's mythology books generally focus on the first part of the story—how Jason built the first ever ship, the *Argo*; how he assembled the heroic Argonauts; and how they bravely sailed across the known world to capture the Golden Fleece. But the less heroic and more tragic section is that second part of the story—the tale of Medea, Jason's common-law wife, who had helped him obtain the Fleece and get back home safely. In his tragedy *Medea*, Euripides, the youngest of the three great Athenian tragedians, tries to give a voice to this woman scorned and abandoned. Athenian audiences, perhaps along with modern readers, would have wondered: Is she to be pitied or feared?

Both pity and fear seem to apply to Medea in equal measure. She mulls over the difficulties that men and women face in their respective spheres of life, only to conclude, "I would rather stand three times with a shield in battle than give birth once."[8] Why did Euripides, an Athenian man, put this haunting comment in his play? And how did his audiences—his fellow Athenian men—react to it? They had known plenty of women who had carried children and given birth, sometimes dying in the process. Commemorative funeral sculptures remind us of this sober fact even today, just as they did for those who had originally commissioned them and walked by them day in and day out in the great city of Athena.

I first encountered *Medea* in intermediate Greek class in college. I memorized in Greek the speech of Creon, the father of Jason's new princess bride, which he delivered to Medea in a tense conversation. He began with the admission, "I am afraid of you—there's no need to hide behind a cloak of words—afraid you will do my child some irreparable injury. There's plenty logic in that fear. You are a wizard possessed of evil knowledge. You are stung by the loss of your husband's love. And I have heard of your threats—they told me of them—to injure bridegroom and bride and father of the bride."[9]

Creon's fear for his daughter's safety here turns out to be justified—later in the play they both will die a horrible death, courtesy of Medea's poison. She will send her children to deliver a wedding present to the princess: A beautiful robe soaked in a powerful poison—or, as folklorist Adrienne Mayor has suggested, napalm.[10] Once she puts it on, the princess will burn to death, along with her father who tries to extinguish the flames with his own body. Deaths pile upon deaths at this point in the tragedy: Medea will then slaughter her children and escape out of town driving a dragon-drawn chariot, bound for Athens, where she has been promised asylum. Thus, Jason the opportunist will, in a single day, lose his old lover and children

---

8. Euripides, *Medea*, ed. and trans. David Kovacs (Harvard University Press, 1994), v. 250. The text is also online at the Perseus Digital Library, accessed February 3, 2025, https://www.perseus.tufts.edu/hopper/text?doc=Perseus:abo:tlg,0006,003:249.
9. Euripides, *Medea*, in *Ten Plays by Euripides*, trans. Moses Hadas and John McLean (Bantam Classics, 1969), vv. 282–88.
10. Adrienne Mayor, *Greek Fire, Poison Arrows & Scorpion Bombs: Biological and Chemical Warfare in the Ancient World* (Princeton University Press, 2022), 251–52.

and his new intended wife. If it weren't for all the other horrifically mournful deaths, one might say that this tragedy couldn't have happened to a nicer guy.

Other characters in a tragedy may need a *deus* or *dea ex machina* to save them or somehow resolve the plot that is otherwise bent on universal destruction. However, Medea alone is her own savior. In the Greek world, where she was a non-person and a non-entity, she really did not have anyone else to save her.

New Discoveries in Greek Tragedy

Two classics scholars in 2024 spent months poring over a 10.5-square-inch papyrus fragment before concluding that the excerpts on the fragment were from two previously lost tragedies of Euripides, *Polyidus* and *Ino*.[1] It is an understatement to say that this discovery is exciting. Euripides wrote about ninety plays, but only eighteen survive. Getting to know a bit more about two other works is, therefore, a welcome gift.

One of these plays, *Polyidus*, introduces a lesser-known myth. After Glaucus, a young prince, drowns in a vat of honey (yes, really!), his distraught parents, the Cretan king and queen Minos and Pasiphaë, ask the seer Polyidus to raise him back from the dead. The newly discovered excerpt is a debate between Minos and Polyidus: Is this resurrection ethical? It appears that they ultimately agree; thus, this tragedy (unlike most) concludes with a resurrection rather than a pile of bodies.[2]

1. Bill Allan, "Greek Tragedies from an Egyptian Tomb: Discovering a New Euripides Papyrus," *TLS*, September 6, 2024, https://www.the-tls.co.uk/classics/greek/new-euripides-papyrus-essay-bill-allan.
2. Clay Bonnyman Evans, "Uncovered Euripides Fragments Are 'Kind of a Big Deal,'" *Colorado Arts and Sciences Magazine*, University of Colorado Boulder, August 1, 2024, https://www.colorado.edu/asmagazine/2024/08/01/uncovered-euripides-fragments-are-kind-big-deal.

Mary's Magnificat: Tragedy Redeemed

A little over half a millennium after Euripides, a teenage girl in Galilee faced an unexpected and unplanned miracle pregnancy. Notified of this miracle by an angel, no less, she bravely claimed the blessing and sang of it:

> My soul glorifies the Lord
> and my spirit rejoices in God my Savior,
> for he has been mindful
> of the humble state of his servant.
> From now on all generations will call me blessed,
> for the Mighty One has done great things for me—
> holy is his name.
> His mercy extends to those who fear him,
> from generation to generation.
> He has performed mighty deeds with his arm;
> he has scattered those who are proud in their inmost thoughts.
> He has brought down rulers from their thrones
> but has lifted up the humble.
> He has filled the hungry with good things
> but has sent the rich away empty.
> He has helped his servant Israel,
> remembering to be merciful
> to Abraham and his descendants forever,
> just as he promised our ancestors.[11]

The song of this woman, Mary, is a powerful response to not only pagan female poets like Sappho but also to tragic heroines like Medea and comic figures like Lysistrata. Like the words of these other women, Mary's words are also preserved because a male writer—Luke, in this case—took care to write them down. But the similarities stop here. Sappho puts words of longing for a good marriage in her singers' mouths, and Medea bemoans the loss of her marriage and decries the physical and emotional pain and

11. Luke 1:46–55.

suffering that have defined her life. But Mary, politically powerless in her own society just as these other women were in theirs, has something—someone—greater to look to. God's tenderness and care for her, so unlike the treatment she could expect from her society, move her to this song of joy and gratitude.

Earthly kings do not have the final word, Mary insists. In fact, even in this world, God can and does remove rulers from power while blessing the powerless and the humble. In other words, Mary's response to the pagan women of Greek tragedy and comedy is a more holistic picture of what it means to be a citizen. Thus, our citizenship is not just earthly. In God's kingdom, we will be citizens and—even more—we will be beloved sons and daughters.

Recommendations for Further Reading

Aristophanes, *The Complete Plays*. Translated by Paul Roche. Berkley, 2005.

Euripides, *Ten Plays*. Translated by Moses Hadas. Bantam Classics, 1984.

Questions for Discussion and Reflection

1. What different images of marriage do we get from the different writers in this chapter (Aristophanes, Sappho, Semonides, Euripides)?
2. What are the stereotypes about women that Aristophanes presents in his comedies? Why do such stereotypes matter? Why are they problematic?
3. What is Mary's response to Sappho and Euripides?

8

CHAPTER

Plato and Aristotle Teach Civics

> Now, in discussing the Athenian constitution, I cannot commend their present method of running the state, because in choosing it they preferred that the masses should do better than the respectable citizens; this, then, is my reason for not commending it. Since, however, they have made this choice, I will demonstrate how well they preserve their constitution and handle the other affairs for which the rest of the Greeks criticise them.[1]

On the Streets of Athens

The tourist was not happy. There he was, walking down the street in Athens after a good night's rest at the home of his guest-friend, having eaten a nice breakfast of freshly baked bread and local olives (not bad, really). Now, out for a stroll in the morning air, he was observing the busy life of the city and growing more and more alarmed. Unlike in the modern world, if you were a respectable man, as he most assuredly was, you wouldn't just stay at some hotel when traveling. No: If you traveled to another city-state, you would only stay at the home of your guest-friend (*xenos*) in that city. Hereditary friendship (*xenia*) was passed down for generations, connecting well-born men to each other.

1. *The Constitution of the Athenians*, in *Aristotle and Xenophon on Democracy and Oligarchy*, trans. J. M. Moore (University of California Press, 1975), 37.

Perhaps my favorite example of *xenia* in practice is in Homer's *Iliad*. A hero, Glaucus, fighting for Troy, and Diomedes, fighting for the Greeks, meet on the battlefield and (as one does on the battlefield) challenge each other to a duel.[2] Of course, each hero recites his genealogy before they fight to the death. But they swiftly discover that they are hereditary guest-friends—their grandfathers were friends! Obviously, this means they can't fight each other. They hug it out, exchange armor (just like modern BFFs might trade T-shirts), and depart the battlefield to go get dinner or drinks together.

But let us go back to our tourist who, again, wasn't happy at this moment. Athens had profoundly shocked his civilized sensibilities. The greatest source of his discomfort? It was impossible to tell who was slave or free from a simple glance while walking down the street. As this man explained later in his treatise *The Constitution of the Athenians*, he saw this as a serious problem:

> Slaves and metics [i.e., resident non-citizens] at Athens lead a singularly undisciplined life; one may not strike them there, nor will a slave step aside for you. Let me explain the reason for this situation: if it were legal for a free man to strike a slave, a metic or a freedman, an Athenian would often have been struck under the mistaken impression that he was a slave, for the clothing of the common people there is in no way superior to that of the slaves and metics, nor is their appearance.[3]

In other words, our tourist was appalled that he couldn't just hit any slaves or resident aliens on the street if he felt like it; he was presumably used to performing this kind of behavior at home.

Alas, we do not know this stranger's name. Modern historians have nicknamed him "the Old Oligarch," because his grumpy tone makes him sound like someone's crotchety grandpa. As for the "oligarch" part, well, his critique of the Athenian democracy makes that clear. We do not know if our "oligarch" friend was from Sparta (probably not), but he clearly admired its approach to government more than Athens. In his view, social hierarchy should be readily visible.

---

2. Homer, *Iliad*, 6.120–232.
3. *The Constitution of the Athenians*, 39.

Two particular terms that the Athenians and the Spartans respectively used to describe their constitutions serve to illuminate the differences between a democracy, which recognizes the collective rule of the people (*demos*), and an oligarchy, where a select group of aristocrats rule. While the Athenians prided themselves on their state of *isonomia* (equality of the laws for all citizens), Spartans and other oligarchic states prided themselves on their *eunomia* (having good laws). This difference seems subtle at first glance, but is not minor in reality. Would you prefer to live in a state where the same laws apply in the same way to all citizens, noble or not? Or would you rather live in a state where laws may apply differently at different points to different groups of people—perhaps giving aristocrats much more leeway to get away with offenses?

Most ancient states, including the Roman Empire, could be described as operating under the principle of *eunomia*: They had laws, which worked for these states in keeping order and stability—most of the time. But were these laws equally just for all citizens? No—but then, of course, that is the point. Choosing *eunomia* over *isonomia* means acknowledging that maybe some people are more important than others. And so, our stranger's frank remarks about the Athenian constitution show just how unusual Athenian *isonomia* seemed to contemporaries from other city-states. Of course, the Athenians themselves delighted in being weird, and believed that their strangeness made them superior to other Greeks. After all, Pericles had called them "the school of Hellas." They were teaching others the right way, and their city's incredible economic, legal, and civic success and stability were the proof that their approach worked. Although the Athenian democracy was overthrown twice in the last decade of the Peloponnesian War (first in 411 BC and then in 404 BC), each time the coup was short-lived and democracy was swiftly restored by the citizens themselves.

Socrates Holds Class Outside

As the Old Oligarch was meandering through town, trying to understand this strange city, he had high odds of running into the man who was, in the eyes of the Athenians themselves, one of the strangest fixtures of their community—Socrates. Alas, this encounter may have never happened—or, at least, our tourist friend doesn't mention it. And so, we're going to bid him adieu now. He has served his purpose well and is ready to leave Athens to travel back home. But we're now ready to meet Socrates in earnest.

You may recall that I mentioned Socrates in relation to Aristophanes's comedy *The Clouds* (425 BC) in the previous chapter. This play ridiculed him as a dreamer floating in the clouds above the stage, making nonsensical statements and teaching questionable ethics to impressionable youth. Aristophanes seeks to show how sophists—in this case, private teachers who teach (for a fee) how to win any argument, no matter how corrupt—are bad for democracy. If this were the only thing we knew of Socrates, perhaps we would have less regard for him. None of Socrates's own writings survive, after all. And yet we know quite a lot about Socrates—or, at least, we think we do. Most of our information comes from highly stylized philosophical dialogues written decades later by his adoring student and successor, Plato. Plato gives us a much more positive view of Socrates and his role in the formation of Athenian citizens. But even through Plato's rose-colored glasses, the picture we get of the legendary teacher and his famed Socratic method is still rather complicated.

When you hear the term "Socratic method," what comes to mind? You are likely thinking of an idyllic classroom setting where someone poses questions, spurring a productive conversation. To learn via the Socratic method is to actively participate in the educational process by asking and answering questions about a topic, in respectful dialogue with one's teacher, fellow students, or friends. It is the opposite of the passive lecture approach, whereby a sage on the stage is just dispensing knowledge. While Socrates's approach was not quite a typical lecture, it was a far cry from what we imagine when we think of the Socratic method today.

Imagine street preachers of the sort that many today dread seeing or running into. Even for sincere and earnest believers, these guys with megaphones at the corner of a busy intersection just seem a bit extra, you know? That is precisely the vibe I imagine Socrates had. A street preacher—but for philosophy. Sure, he sounds grand in theory, but would you want to be ambushed by a guy you barely know in broad daylight, on the street, who will then keep following you around and bombarding you with probing questions until nightfall finally forces him to knock it off?

Comical or extreme as this sounds, such is the premise behind practically every Socratic dialogue that Plato wrote. Each dialogue proceeds generally along a certain formula. First, while out and about in Athens, Socrates meets one or more conversationalists. He asks his conversationalist(s) to define an important concept or answer a question. (What is courage? What is justice? What is rhetoric? What is the ideal state constitution? What is virtue? What is temperance?) The conversationalists always seem to think that they may have a decent answer at first, but Socrates repeatedly stumps them by follow-up questions. Finally, after a few hours of intense back-and-forth, it gets dark outside and the other side begs for mercy, admitting to Socrates that they don't really know anything and pleading to go home. This is all in a day's work, as far as Socrates is concerned!

To be honest, if I had to be stuck in this sort of conversation for five or more hours, I would say anything just to get out of there! And it does seem that while some Athenians appreciated Socrates, many others considered him a general pest—*The Clouds* shows us hints of that. Perhaps Socrates realized this himself and rather relished in his reputation—in Plato's *Apology*, he described himself as a gadfly stinging Athenians into discomfort with his questions.[4] Or, more precisely, this is the portrayal of Socrates's opinion on the matter that *Plato* presents—again, we must remember that we only get to know Socrates filtered through Plato.

From the plethora of surviving dialogues, we get the impression that Socrates just kept following his philosophical formula for decades—meandering the streets of Athens, asking difficult questions from anyone who might be willing to engage with him, and annoying people. The Athenians eventually got so fed up with Socrates that they put him on trial in 399 BC, charging him with corrupting the youth and disrespecting the gods. The verdict: death by hemlock poison, which the seventy-year-old Socrates accordingly drank. Socrates did advocate for a strange version of monotheism, it appears. At the very least, he rejected the irrationality of the pagan gods. And yet, while Socrates perhaps did see some hints of transcendent truths, he seems to have been blinded more by his love of his own wisdom. Indeed, when we read Plato's Socratic dialogues, we should focus not only on the wisdom that we can gain from them—which is considerable!—but also on the limits of wisdom apart from God.

The limitations of the Socratic method speak for themselves—none

4. Plato, *Apology* 30e.

of Socrates's dialogues ends with a clear answer. What is courage? What is virtue? What is the ideal state constitution? The conclusion in every case is that we cannot know for sure—because apart from God we really cannot know for sure. This is an ironic truth, even though Plato (and presumably Socrates) did not realize it. As over half a millennium later Paul will write to the Christian believers in Rome, "There is no one righteous, not even one; there is no one who understands; there is no one who seeks God."[5] Left to our own devices, we easily slip into a Socratic mode of the worst kind, questioning everything and becoming wise in our own eyes. And yet, even in the midst of questioning, Plato's Socrates repeatedly returns in dialogue after dialogue to one transcendental desire—to seek the good, the true, and the beautiful. This desire is perhaps most obvious in humanity's search for love.

Evening Seminar: Let's Talk About Love

Socratic discussions were not limited just to the streets of Athens. Sometimes they took place in the context of aristocratic dinner parties—perhaps with a more refined audience in attendance. The *symposium*, literally meaning "drinking together," means to us today a sophisticated intellectual event—perhaps a more intimate alternative to "conference," which implies something larger. Perhaps our conception of a symposium, rather than the semi-rowdy drinking party that such events usually were in reality, is similar to the one that Plato describes in his dialogue *Symposium*. This work is meant to be a transcription of sorts of a real dinner party conversation, which, if it happened, took place in 416 BC.

At this dinner, a small and intimate gathering of aristocrats, plus Socrates, decides that since they are still hung over from overindulging the previous evening, perhaps a more intellectual form of entertainment would be best. And so they go around the room, as we sometimes do in seminar class discussions, and each person in his turn gives a speech on the selected topic of the seminar—love. While Socrates is, of course, one of the guests at this event and offers his own speech for this occasion, the symposium setting moderates his usual intensity. The choice of love as the focus of conversation is striking, as is the variety in the speeches that result—some

5. Romans 3:10–11.

earnest and some more cheeky, yet all hinting at the glimpses of the eternal and the transcendent realities that loving someone presents to all men. However, by "men," we really do mean just those of the male species, as they are the focus of this dialogue apart from Socrates's reference to a wise woman, Diotima, in his speech.

A century ago, in the introduction to his edition and translation of *Symposium* for the Loeb Classical Library, scholar W. R. M. Lamb wrote, "Love is here treated with a sense of its universal importance and with a reach and certainty of insight which do not appear in any other of the great religious or moral teachers. This confident mastery was one of the extraordinary powers of Socrates which Plato at this stage of his writing was intent on portraying."[6] While Lamb singles out Socrates's speech on love in this dialogue, the speech that has always stood out the most to me is that of Aristophanes—yes, this is the comic poet who put Socrates in *The Clouds*. Here he is, eight years after *The Clouds*, sharing the evening with Socrates as a fellow dinner party guest!

In his speech, Aristophanes is as tongue-in-cheek as we know him from his comedies, and he tells the story of how originally, in addition to men and women, there was a third and perfect sex—both man and woman combined together. Envious of their unity, which seemed to rival the gods, Zeus sliced each of them in half. Ever since, Aristophanes claims, we've all been chasing for that missing half that will make us whole. Admittedly, he does note casually that for some men, it means chasing other men. So, how do we read this dialogue as Christians? For one thing, Lamb's explanation is obviously inadequate. Does Plato's dialogue, and especially this speech of Socrates, really offer the kind of insight into our understanding of love that no other "great religious or moral teachers" have articulated? After all, Jesus has frequently been described even by non-Christians, like Gandhi, as a great religious and moral teacher—although, as the only-begotten Son of God, he was certainly also much more than that.

When Christians talk about love, such a conversation should begin with recognizing the unfathomable love of God for us—something unthinkable in any other religion. And so, as we read the *Symposium* we see all the more clearly the importance of Socrates's general practice of asking questions

6. W. R. M. Lamb, *Plato: Lysis, Symposium, Gorgias* (Harvard University Press, 2001), 74–75.

while simultaneously also seeing the shortcomings of such a practice if it is separated from belief in God. What is love? How can we talk about love without acknowledging that "God so loved the world that he gave his one and only Son, that whoever believes in him shall not perish but have eternal life."[7] Such a love offers a foundation for who we are as citizens and political beings. No less significant is the search for the missing half—we all do feel that we're missing something. We feel that yearning that we cannot articulate and which so often ends up being described as romantic love. But as Augustine will write eight centuries after Plato, our souls are restless when apart from God. It is God alone who completes us, not other people.

Xenophon on the Education of Cyrus

In the mid-sixth century BC, Cyrus the Great brought together several smaller kingdoms to create the Achaemenid Persian Empire. This was the same empire that invaded Greece twice in the early fifth century—we considered Herodotus's writing of that history in chapter 4.

But Xenophon, writing around 370 BC nearly two hundred years after Cyrus's rise to power and a century after Herodotus's work, was interested in a different question than Herodotus: How did Cyrus achieve this kind of success? He proposed an answer: It's all about a virtuous education that forms one's character for success.

The Education of Cyrus is not a historical treatise, although it pretends to be one—and perhaps even Xenophon thought it was. Still, the figure of Cyrus offers Xenophon, himself a historian and a student of Socrates, the opportunity to consider the ideal education of a ruler. The key to building, conquering, and ruling an empire is, ultimately, all about the virtuous character of both the ruler and his subjects.

7. John 3:16.

Aristotle's General Education Curriculum for the Formation of Virtuous Citizens

Although other people do not complete us, we do have to know how to live with them well; God calls us not only into relationship with himself but also into relationships with other people. In any state, ancient or modern, this has meant recognizing that the flourishing of the state is inextricably connected to the flourishing of its citizens. The formation of virtuous citizens is consequently important. Indeed, this instruction of citizens was Socrates's goal in his decades of wandering through Athens like a street corner preacher. He meant well, but—as some Athenians thought—he failed at the end.

When the bloodthirsty thirty oligarchs came briefly to power in Athens in 404 BC, after the city's defeat by Sparta in the Peloponnesian War, several of these tyrants, including the worst of them all, Critias, had been former students of Socrates. Sure, they used their excellent rhetorical education to rise to positions of authority, but they showed no virtues of temperance or mercy or love for fellow citizens while in power. Instead, they unleashed a merciless bloodbath, motivated at least partly by greed.

Should we judge teachers and schools by the fruit of their students? Should we judge parents by their children? This is a difficult question, but at least we must partly admit that, yes, God holds us responsible for those whose stewardship he has entrusted to us. The Athenians agreed too: As the fourth-century orator Aeschines notes, the Athenians had voted to condemn Socrates to death because Socrates had taught Critias.[8] But it is no less important to admit that in education, just like in parenting, just talking about ethical topics, as Socrates did with his students, is not enough in and of itself. Perhaps the famed fourth-century philosopher Aristotle felt likewise. Unlike Socrates, he left us plenty of his own writings, but he displayed a different approach than Socrates for training up virtuous citizens.

While Socrates seems to have believed in the importance of extensive dialogue on virtues and difficult life questions as the key educational method, we could see Aristotle as the first and greatest proponent of a solid general education for everyone. That is, you know, those classes that (as

8. Aeschines, *Against Timarchus*, 1.173.

the stereotype goes) students have to take in high school and in the first couple of years of college before they're allowed to get on with the study of the topics they really like. To be fair, I get it. I went to a university whose honors program allowed students to skip the general education requirements entirely. Nothing made my heart skip more beats in joy than bypassing all math and science classes after high school. Aristotle would not have approved of this mentality, and, with the distance of a quarter century, I can reluctantly admit that maybe he was right.

Aristotle was a polymath unlike any other until, quite possibly, the European Renaissance. Indeed, there is a reason we use the term "Renaissance man" to describe someone proficient in a broad array of academic subjects. But Aristotle was a "Renaissance man" long before the Renaissance. Among the many treatises he wrote—and, therefore, among the many subjects he taught his students—are topics as varied as politics and history, grammar and rhetoric, ethics, music, physics, biology and zoology, human and animal sexuality, geography, astronomy, literature, economics, spiritual matters, and psychology. This is not a comprehensive list—but you get the idea.

Aristotle's ability to write about so many varied topics is unquestionably impressive. At the same time, we can now also acknowledge that his level of competence varied. Unlike the Word of God, Aristotle's writings are not infallible or divinely inspired, although some thinkers, pagan and Christian alike, have treated them as if they were. He was wrong about a number of matters. To note just a couple of examples: His description of women as incomplete or mutilated men continued (and buttressed) the long tradition of ancient scientific misogyny, while his incorrect understanding of how the heart works and how blood circulates in the human body misled doctors for the entirety of the Middle Ages.[9] So, we should approach Aristotle with this tension in mind: He gives a model of an ambitious curriculum. Related and similarly crucial is his repurposing of the Homeric military term *aretê*, originally referring to martial excellence, to mean virtues in the intellectual realm and in citizenship. But we should also remember that we cannot master everything and humility is a virtue. It is appropriate for us to recognize our limits—indeed, this is a key theological truth.[10]

---

9. Dhun Sethna, *The Wine-Dark Sea Within: A Turbulent History of Blood* (Basic Books, 2022).
10. Kelly Kapic, *You're Only Human: How Your Limits Reflect God's Design and Why That's Good News* (Brazos Press, 2022).

Still, Aristotle's defense of general education for the formation of virtuous citizens gives us a model for education today. It develops, we could say, Plato's exhortation to seek the good, the true, and the beautiful by recognizing that this search is not limited to just one area of life or art or science but is built into the world around us. It is a reminder, Christians could say, that a world filled with such truth, goodness, and beauty was made—and, therefore, clearly has a Maker. Let us now consider in brief one example of this education at work—Aristotle's treatise *Poetics*.

What is poetry, why do we need it, and what makes poetry a public good? These are the questions that Aristotle sets out to answer in this short treatise, which reads very much as an introductory class lecture—perhaps because that's what it originally was. This means, by the way, that while Aristotle did not write anything expressly about pedagogy, we can gain useful lessons here. Aristotle begins with definitions: Just what does he mean when he speaks of the art of poetry? Poetry, he goes on to explain, is not defined solely by its poetic meter. It is, in many ways, the most instinctively imitative art for people. Poetry allows us to imitate the sounds of the world around us in a more creative and whimsical way than prose typically does. And so the art of poetry appeals to all of us from childhood onward—just consider the popularity of such masters of the craft as Dr. Seuss or Shel Silverstein. The sound of their poetry could make each of my children laugh long before they fully understood every word!

But plot also matters in the art of poetry. Aristotle explains the similarities and differences between the work of historians and poets as follows:

> The function of the poet is not to say what *has* happened, but to say the kind of thing that *would* happen, i.e., what is possible in accordance with probability or necessity. The historian and the poet are not distinguished by their use of verse or prose; it would be possible to turn the works of Herodotus into verse, and it would be a history in verse just as much as in prose. The distinction is this: the one says what has happened, the other the kind of thing that would happen.
>
> For this reason poetry is more philosophical and more serious than history. Poetry tends to express universals, and history particulars.[11]

11. Aristotle, *Poetics*, trans. Malcolm Heath (Penguin Books, 1996), 16.

To our modern sensibilities and an imagined rigid line between fiction (stuff that's made up) and nonfiction (stuff that really happened), this explanation that poetry is "more serious than history" might seem shocking at first glance. But Aristotle's point is that by presenting universal scenarios, poetry, just like philosophy, prepares one to understand anything that comes in life. Isn't this what education in a fast-changing world should be about? The best education prepares people to understand universals—those facts of the human condition that will not change, even as the technology all around us does, minute to minute.

These universals, ultimately, involve understanding other people, because being a good citizen requires living with other people (who may be difficult) in both good and bad times. This leads Aristotle to declare tragedy the pinnacle of poetic art. And the most perfect of all tragedies, he contends, is none other than Sophocles's *Oedipus the King*. We have now come full circle, in a sense. In chapter 5 I mentioned the importance of shared literature, of the sort that tragic and comic performances afforded, for fostering community among citizens in a democracy. It is this shared literature—more specifically, shared poetry with its transcendent beauty and emotional appeal—that Aristotle emphasizes in his *Poetics*.

General education, in Aristotle's eyes, was important for the formation of citizens. But had he been forced to choose just one subject as supreme for creating good citizens, I guarantee he would have chosen poetry.

Is the Kingdom of God *Isonomia* or *Eunomia*?

If there is one basic takeaway from the Greek writers interested in citizenship, it is that being a good citizen of one's city is not easy. This isn't earth-shattering news, but it reminds us that the struggles we observe in our own society are nothing new. At the same time, we saw that the different writers over the course of the four chapters in this section expressed interest in shaping the character of citizens in one's state for the better through education. Virtuous neighbors, after all, are the best kind of neighbors. Anyone living in any state in any period of history would agree with this principle. Reflecting on our identity in Christ, however, pushes us to think further than the Greeks did.

As Christians, we live in this world, but we long for the kingdom of God still to come. This means that although we are citizens of our communities, states, and nations, we are also citizens of another kingdom—one that is not visible. This does not stop us from asking questions. Might God's kingdom be more of a democracy, with equal laws equally applied to all? Or is it an oligarchy, in which a privileged few have all the power? Perhaps it is neither of these. Rather, the kingdom of God reminds us that words have power—after all, in the beginning was the Word. That is a power that people have recognized from well before there was writing or what we would call rhetoric.

Recommendations for Further Reading

Aristotle, *Introductory Readings*. Translated by Terence Irwin and Gail Fine. Hackett Publishing, 1996.

Aristotle, *Poetics*. Translated by Anthony Kenny. Oxford University Press, 2013.

Moore, J. M. *Aristotle and Xenophon on Democracy and Oligarchy*. University of California Press, 1986.

Plato, *Five Dialogues: Euthyphro, Apology, Crito, Meno, Phaedo*. Translated by John M. Cooper and G. M. A. Grube. 2nd ed. Hackett Publishing, 2002.

Plato, *Republic*. Translated by G. M. A. Grube. Hackett Publishing, 1992.

Plato, *Symposium*. Translated by Alexander Nehamas and Paul Woodruff. Hackett Publishing, 1989.

Questions for Discussion and Reflection

1. What do we learn about Socrates and the Socratic method from Plato and Aristophanes?
2. What is the difference between *eunomia* and *isonomia*? Why does it matter?
3. Why did Aristotle consider poetry so important for the education of citizens? Do you agree? Why or why not?

PART

Words of Power and the Power of Words

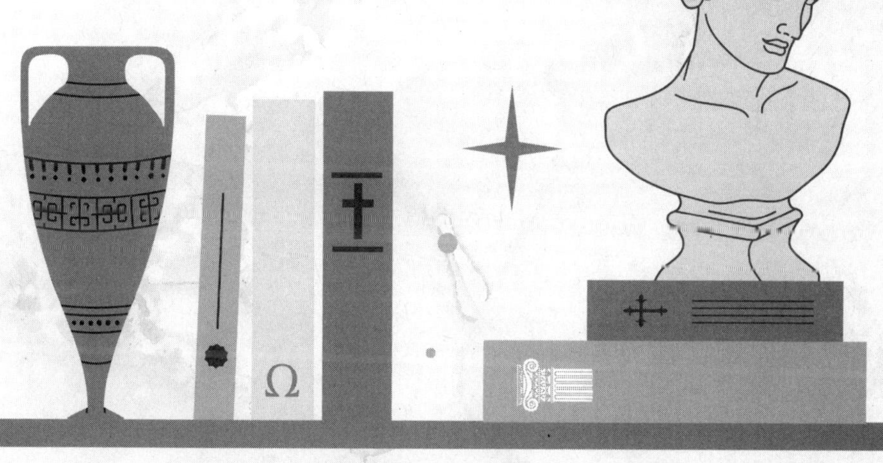

CHAPTER

The Athenian Forensic Speechwriters

> Well then, men of Athens, when you executed Sokrates the sophist, because it was shown that he had taught Kritias, one of the Thirty who overthrew the democracy, is Demosthenes to plead his associates off in your court? This man who has exacted such monstrous revenge from ordinary people loyal to the democracy for their free speech?[1]

Leocrates Goes on Vacation

Almost a century after Aristophanes's fictional farmer Dicaeopolis stood on the Athenian comic stage and guilt-tripped his fellow citizens for skipping such essential civic duties as assemblies and voting, a real flesh-and-blood citizen, one Leocrates, stood trial for not performing his civic duties. The precise charge? Treason. But if treason to you readily elicits images of caught spies, mutinous officers, or maybe an elaborate assassination plot, Leocrates's story will disappoint you. It is far less juicy. Or, rather, it is juicy in a different way.

Hard times were still ongoing for Athens. After the Athenians and the Spartans had lost much of their military and political strength in the wake of the Peloponnesian War, different players jostled for control over the

1. "Case XV: Aischines 1—Against Timarchos," in Christopher Carey, *Trials from Classical Athens*, 2nd ed. (Routledge, 2012), 197.

power vacuum during the course of the fourth century BC. Then in 338 BC, Philip of Macedon—a backwater region in northern Greece to which no one had previously paid significant attention—defeated the combined Greek armies at the Battle of Chaeronea. This decisive victory ultimately consolidated the hitherto independent Greek city-states into a large kingdom under Philip's hegemony.[2]

The news of Philip's victory caused mass panic in Athens. During the chaos, Leocrates, a regular Athenian citizen, decided to skip town—just as Athens was issuing an emergency decree enlisting all citizens to military service. He loaded his ships with essentials (including his mistress) and quietly absconded overnight for a leisurely multi-year tour of the Greek isles. Our unlikable antihero was by all accounts a nobody—albeit a reasonably wealthy nobody. And so, he clearly thought that no one had been paying attention to him when he returned to Athens in 331 BC, hoping to live on in a now stable city under new management as if nothing had happened. However, Leocrates had miscalculated.

The following year, the prominent statesman and orator Lycurgus brought a lawsuit against Leocrates, charging him with treason for abandoning the Athenian democracy at its time of direst need. In his powerful speech, one of the greatest Classical Greek arguments for patriotism in a democracy, Lycurgus describes Leocrates's decision to run away:

> And so he disappeared, a deserter, untouched by pity for the city's harbors from which he was putting out to sea, and unashamed in face of the walls which, for his own part, he left undefended. Looking back at the Acropolis and the temple of Zeus the Savior and Athena the Protectress, which he had betrayed, he had no fear . . .[3]

Lycurgus spares no argument in building his case against Leocrates. If the accusation of kicking puppies or cute kittens was as emotionally serious to wield against someone in Athens as it is today, Lycurgus would

2. Part of this section is adapted from Nadya Williams, "Bad Citizens in a Democracy," *Current*, August 8, 2022, https://currentpub.com/2022/08/08/bad-citizens-in-a-democracy/.
3. Lycurgus, *Against Leocrates*, trans. J. O. Burtt (Harvard University Press, 1962), 1.17. The text is also online at the Perseus Digital Library, accessed February 4, 2025, https://www.perseus.tufts.edu/hopper/text?doc=Perseus%3Atext%3A1999.01.0152%3Aspeech%3D1%3Asection%3D17.

have also thrown it in. In the middle of his speech, he gives a particularly dramatic recitation of the ephebic oath, the citizenship oath that ephebes (eighteen-year-olds) in Athens undertook at the beginning of their two-year military garrison service. Going through this military oath of loyalty clause by clause, Lycurgus shows how Leocrates had violated it. Failing his promise to stand fast next to his fellow soldiers in the hoplite phalanx? Check. Not defending the ancestral fruit trees? Yeah. Not thinking about the gods of the city? That, too.

In Lycurgus's masterful speech, Leocrates emerges as the ultimate anti-epic hero, the foil to Homer's Odysseus. Instead of setting out from home to fight for glory, he quietly shirked all responsibility. He didn't think of his family, much less the city-state. When he finally returned from his self-imposed odyssey of leisure, this also wasn't an act of love for his state but an act of self-love and convenience. Lycurgus's rage at Leocrates's extraordinary selfishness translates well across time and culture. By the time I finished reading this speech for the first time, two and a half millennia removed from his betrayal, I was ready to also convict Leocrates.

In the end, however, Leocrates narrowly escaped conviction—the jury of several hundred citizens deadlocked in a tie vote, acquitting him.[4] It appears that while some Athenians were outraged at Leocrates's betrayal of his duties as a citizen, just as many could awkwardly identify with his decision to put his own interests first in a time of crisis. This tension can certainly feel familiar—and we explored aspects of it in previous chapters. To be a citizen requires each of us to put the state's interests ahead of our own, at least part of the time. The Athenians liked this idea about as much as we do (meaning, not very much).

Additionally, another important detail of Lycurgus's brilliant speech is easy to overlook. From a legal perspective, the charge of treason is a serious stretch in Leocrates's case. The only reason the charge sounds convincing as we are reading the speech—indeed, it is the reason that Leocrates only barely made it out of the courtroom a free man—is because Lycurgus's

4. For an overview of the Athenian legal system, I recommend Adriaan Lanni, *Law and Justice in the Courts of Classical Athens* (Cambridge University Press, 2006), and Michael Gagarin and David Cohen, eds., *The Cambridge Companion to Ancient Greek Law* (Cambridge University Press, 2005).

words are so powerful and ingeniously composed. Indeed, we could say that rhetoric artfully employed is the real hero of this case.

The Art and Science of Rhetoric

Over the next four chapters, we will explore ways that words of power—and the power of words—shaped the Athenian democracy and the Roman Republic. Rhetoric and public speaking were a key component of education in antiquity and modernity up until very recently—and for good reason. I hope that considering the power of rhetoric in different settings will encourage you to enhance your own skills in this area. Can you speak convincingly to present your perspective on a matter and persuade someone?

Rhetoric is still an essential skill for us—not only at home and in conversations with friends, but also at work, at school, and more—even though we don't always think about the intricacies of the art of persuasive speaking today. And yet we spend a lot of our daily time engaged in seeking to persuade someone else—such as when my son is trying to convince me to make pizza for dinner, my daughter is trying to cajole someone in the house to play a game with her, or (on a more serious note) when we are trying to persuade someone to hire us for a job during an interview. We begin in a place where the power of words in a democracy was particularly obvious on a daily basis, ever since the mythical days of Orestes's murder trial: the Athenian law courts.

In the days before forensic evidence and professional lawyers, orators—those who had a way with words—could make or break a case in Athens. Both plaintiffs and defendants had to speak for themselves in court, but they didn't always compose their own speeches. Those whose own rhetorical skills were subpar could hire a good orator (assuming they could afford one) to write a speech for them to recite in court. About a hundred of the speeches that different professional orators wrote for such cases survive from fourth-century BC Athens. The cases addressed range from murder to assault and battery, inheritance fraud, property disputes, citizenship cases, and more. The speeches, assembled and published under their writers' names, give us an idea of the talents and the names of the men who plied this trade—such as Lycurgus, Demosthenes, and Lysias.

Because these orators later collected and published their speeches, many courtroom speeches survive without context—they are the only piece of evidence that we have from a particular case and trial. Even the outcome of the case is unknown for many of these speeches. And yet the themes that recur in these speeches can tell us much about what words wielded the most power in the democratic courtroom. Why else would professional speechwriters have turned repeatedly to the same themes and topics? Because they knew what worked. And what worked was character testimony—a consideration of virtues and vices.

No less important than recognizing *what* worked is also acknowledging *why* it worked. Aristotle explains early in his guide to rhetoric:

> Rhetoric then may be defined as the faculty of discovering the possible means of persuasion in reference to any subject whatever. This is the function of no other of the arts, each of which is able to instruct and persuade in its own special subject; thus, medicine deals with health and sickness, geometry with the properties of magnitudes, arithmetic with number, and similarly with all the other arts and sciences. But Rhetoric, so to say, appears to be able to discover the means of persuasion in reference to any given subject. That is why we say that as an art its rules are not applied to any particular definite class of things.[5]

Aristotle goes on to describe the three particular means of persuasion that generally work together. There is, at the most obvious level, *logos* (the argument itself). There is also *pathos* (the emotion that the speaker brings into the argument and brings forth from the audiences). Finally, there is *ethos* (the character of the speaker).

In other words, rhetoric works because the speaker knows both his subject matter and, crucially, his audience and how that audience will react to his (or her) words. Words of power are not powerful simply in and of themselves.[6] They are only powerful if employed correctly to persuade people to whom these arguments are particularly suited. Reading the room is a key

5. Aristotle, *Rhetoric*, trans. J. H. Freese (Harvard University Press, 1926), 1.2.1. The text is also online at the Perseus Digital Library, accessed February 4, 2025, https://www.perseus.tufts.edu/hopper/text?doc=Perseus%3Atext%3A1999.01.0060%3Abook%3D1%3Achapter%3D2.
6. See Andrew Judd, *Modern Genre Theory* (Zondervan Academic, 2024), 43–44, for an example of how this works with such a document as a parking ticket: A prank ticket can terrify, but only a real ticket written by a real parking official will have a legal effect.

ingredient for speaking persuasively. And in the Athenian democracy, this meant recognizing the shared values of all the citizens in the proverbial room—in this case, the courtroom.

Life in a Fishbowl

For most Athenian lawcourts, all we have is either the speech from the prosecution or the defense, and we often do not know how the case turned out. But based on common themes and tactics used in surviving speeches, we can see trends of what was effective. One of the most common types of evidence used is character testimony, which was often based on the person's past military record. A good citizen honorably served with distinction, while a bad citizen was clearly a coward. Why did character testimony—the recitations of virtues or vices of citizens—work so well when presented in court?

I've described the Athenian democracy as a fishbowl to all my students. Everyone knew everyone else's business, seeing it as relevant for the city-state. Virtues and vices were public knowledge for the simple reason that good citizens are good for the city, whereas bad citizens are not. Consequently, people had a long collective memory of different individuals' virtues and vices. Even decades after someone's despicable offense that was never prosecuted—e.g., shirking military duty or getting into a drunken brawl in an alleyway—that old offense might be used against that individual in court. We commonly believe today that people can change (a concept rooted in the Christian reliance on the Holy Spirit regenerating believers), but the Greeks did not agree with this idea.[1] A good person is a good person—always. However, someone wicked will always show his true colors in the end—puppy-kicking included.

---

1. Ephesians 4:30; 1 Thessalonians 5:19–24; Titus 3:5–7. See also Matthew Barrett, *Salvation by Grace: The Case for Effectual Calling and Regeneration* (P&R, 2013).

One Evening in Athens: Lies, Adultery, and Murder

One evening in Athens, a previously quiet and law-abiding citizen came home—and found his wife in bed with another man. He promptly killed the man on the spot. But Euphiletos, the surprise killer, was no cold-blooded murderer. To understand this case, we must back up a bit and learn about the events leading to that fateful evening—just as the original jury would have done. It all began with that "curse" that Hesiod and Semonides had so wisely advised against—marriage.

When Euphiletos got married, he tells the jury—or, rather, the professional speechwriter Lysias tells in the speech Euphiletos commissioned from him for his defense—that he first kept a close eye on his new wife. Sure, he wasn't mean about it, but he was cautious. However, once their first son was born, he gave her much more leeway. The downstairs section of their two-story home in the city was her own private wing, where she could sometimes sleep as she nursed the baby at night. So, their wedded bliss was indeed initially quiet and comfortable. As a proper Athenian man, Euphiletos left the house every morning to go do manly things. His wife, as a proper well-to-do Athenian woman, stayed home in seclusion, taking care of the baby and the home. By the way, due to these standards of propriety, we never even get the name of Euphiletos's wife in this speech. She wasn't present in court to hear this speech, either.

Alas, one day Euphiletos's mother died. At her funeral, Eratosthenes, a known Athenian serial adulterer, saw Euphiletos's young wife and set his eye on her. At this time, Eratosthenes was already carrying on with another woman (a detail important to this case), but he started sending messages to Euphiletos's wife through a slave girl who went to the market daily. And so, the affair began. For a long time Euphiletos suspected nothing, although he saw warning signs in retrospect. For instance, why was his wife wearing makeup, even though she was in mourning for her brother who had also recently died? Indeed, Euphiletos only found out about the affair because this other woman became jealous when Eratosthenes began dividing his attention. She then sent her own slave to inform Euphiletos.

Those who say that knowledge is power have never been in this kind of situation. Euphiletos apparently did not find this particular knowledge empowering. Rather, in this speech we get the impression of a heartbroken husband and father. He is shocked to find out that his happy family life has been a lie. But another kind of knowledge does prove to be empowering to him: knowledge of Athenian law. And in Athenian law, which Euphiletos makes sure to read in full in court—a common practice—homicide was justified in a few select circumstances. One of these was, of course, self-defense. But another was adultery—and this case shows us just how serious the Athenians considered it.

Specifically, the law stated that if a man caught an adulterer in his own home with his wife, he was allowed to kill the man on the spot or demand a monetary compensation from him for this offense. Such murder cases, incidentally, were tried in a separate court—the Delphinion, reserved exclusively for cases of alleged justified homicide. In those cases, everyone on the jury knew from the onset that the person on trial really did kill the victim. The trial's goal was, therefore, to establish if the homicide was legally justified. In other words, when Euphiletos, the husband, stood trial for the murder of Eratosthenes, no one had any doubt as to who killed whom or why. Rather, the matter under dispute was whether the murder was legally justified. This meant that Euphiletos had to establish clearly that he had no other grudge against Eratosthenes, and that he fulfilled all of the requirements of the law. Did he? Let's go back to the night of the murder.

Once Euphiletos knew about Eratosthenes and had done his research on the law, he arranged for his slave girl to inform him the next time the adulterer was in the house while he was out. Euphiletos also arranged for friends to be on standby and act as his witnesses. All preparations made, all he had to do was wait. Once he finally received the message that Eratosthenes was in his house, Euphiletos brought his friends with him, barged into the room, and found the adulterer with his wife.

We should imagine a crowded and chaotic scene in Euphiletos's small bedroom. The wife, perhaps, is quiet, embarrassed, and utterly in shock. However, Eratosthenes seems to have known the Athenian adultery law himself quite well, as he immediately offers to pay off Euphiletos for his trouble. No matter—Euphiletos kills him on the spot, in front of the witnesses. And in front of his wife—whom he never physically harms. Rather, as he describes throughout his speech, she is a victim, a weak one who was deceived. She was never in control of her actions, and he doesn't seem to blame her. We do know, however, that this affair left the family in a vulnerable legal position.

While Euphiletos does not mention it in this speech, Athenian law required husbands to divorce wives caught in adultery. His wife's public life was now over, and she was unlikely to ever remarry. But there is another concern and potential future legal nightmare as well—the status of the kids. Athenian law only recognized the children of legally wed Athenian citizens as citizens themselves. While Euphiletos is certain that his sons are his own, this public trial cast a shadow over their paternity. Surviving cases of inheritance disputes show that someone years down the road might dispute these children's status as legitimately born, thus challenging both their citizenship status and their right to inherit their father's estate. Therefore, we would not be exaggerating to say that Eratosthenes ruined this family's life for generations.

With this unpleasant potential future in mind, Euphiletos appeals to public sympathy in the conclusion to his speech, arguing that he was an honorable and law-abiding citizen of Athens whereas Eratosthenes was a lawbreaker and a corrupter not just of individuals but of public morals. After all, he had established earlier that Eratosthenes was not a one-time offender but a serial one. Whose wife would have been in danger of being seduced next by Eratosthenes, if Euphiletos hadn't stopped him? Thus, Euphiletos's act of killing is a public punishment on behalf of the entire city:

> In my opinion, gentlemen, this was not a private punishment for my own sake but for the whole city. For people who act in this way, once they see the prizes set up for such offences, will be less likely to commit them against others, if they see that you are of the same mind. Otherwise, it is far better to expunge the established laws and make others which will impose the punishments on men who protect their own wives and grant full immunity to men who wish to offend against them . . . For I now find my person, my property, everything else, in danger, because I obeyed the city's laws.[7]

Unfortunately, the disappointing, spotty nature of source survival means that we do not know how this case turned out. We only have this speech. Therefore, we have no idea what Eratosthenes's relatives, who must

7. Lysias 1.47–50, in Carey, *Trials from Classical Athens*, 33.

have acted as the prosecution here, said in his defense. I do suspect that Euphiletos won his case. If he did, I think his concluding appeal that the punishment which he meted out to Eratosthenes was on behalf of the entire city would have been particularly convincing for his fellow citizens on the jury. Euphiletos named here every citizen's worst fear—that his trusted wife and the mother of his children had been corrupted by someone else, destroying not only his marriage but potentially putting the status of his very children and heirs into question. Putting this common fear into words was perhaps the most powerful statement Euphiletos could have made.

All for One and One for All

Sometimes one gets the possibly accurate impression from the Athenian forensic speeches that Athens had a crime problem. Sometime in the mid-fourth century BC, a young man, Ariston, was walking home one evening from the shrine of Persephone in Athens. Suddenly, a middle-aged man named Konon along with his son and a couple of other associates jumped him. They shoved him in the mud, stripped him of his clothes, and beat him up to within an inch of his life:

> They left me in such a poor condition that I could neither stand up nor speak. And as I lay there I heard them saying many dreadful things. Much of it is abusive and I should hesitate to repeat some things in your court; but one thing, which is evidence of his arrogance and an indication that he was the leader in the whole business, I shall tell you. He crowed in imitation of victorious cocks, and the rest urged him to flap his elbows against his sides by way of wings.[8]

Ariston admits that he had a dispute with Konon's sons during their service in garrison duty together a couple of years earlier, but the present attack had no other provocation. And so, when he finally recovered, Ariston brought a charge of assault. However, he notes in the speech that he could have pursued the even more serious charge of hubris.

We last encountered hubris in the tale of the Persian king Xerxes lashing

---

8. Demosthenes 54.8–9, in Carey, *Trials from Classical Athens*, 80.

the Hellespont after the sea had destroyed his pontoon bridge. When the Greeks subsequently defeated him, they saw their victory in part as divine punishment on Xerxes for his hubris—a pride that rivaled the gods. We also see Konon exercising such a pride here in his unprovoked attack upon a law-abiding private citizen. His hubris is demonstrated by his crowing like a rooster in triumph over the respectable young man whom he had just bloodily beaten. This instance of hubris is not only an offense against the gods but also a violation of the city's laws. Konon's nose-thumbing reveals his conviction that he can do whatever he wants without any consequences. Consequently, this offense is not just against Ariston and his dignity but against the entire city of Athens.

As we look at the words that had the most power in Athenian forensic oratory, the clearest way to sum them all up is the slogan made famous by *The Three Musketeers*: "All for one, and one for all." The emphasis that the offense in question is not just against one individual but against the entire city appears frequently in Athenian courtroom speeches, and we see it in all of this chapter's examples. Each speaker reminds his listeners that his pursuit of justice is not just for himself but for the rest of his fellow citizens. Citizens whose actions are defined by their vices rather than virtues deserve to face repercussions—especially when they abuse good citizens. If these villains are left unchecked, who knows whom they will attack next—this person could be you!

Therefore, words of power in the democratic law courts emphasized the citizens' desire to see justice as a collective shared endeavor. Sure, selfish citizens just wanted to win their case—who doesn't? But in trying to achieve a legal victory, they ironically used a more collective and enthusiastic language of citizenship than perhaps anywhere else. Nevertheless, although the speechwriters used impressive and powerful words, we ultimately see the limitations of human language in pursuing justice. The uncertainty of our knowledge in reading these speeches only highlights this further. Such speeches contain eloquent words, and surely many of them achieved their aim, winning the day at court for the speaker. But did each person rightly win each trial? We just don't know. But we can safely assume, knowing the sinful nature of human beings, that at least sometimes the winning rhetoric in antiquity—just as in today—is not the words of justice. One can speak powerfully and win a case without being on the side of justice.

By contrast, we know that God's justice is perfect and he knows the hearts of men, as Solomon notes during his prayer of dedication when the ark of the Lord was first brought into the newly built temple. In this prayer, Solomon particularly emphasizes God's role as the only true judge, the one who can administer justice perfectly in a way that we never can (1 Kings 8:31–53). It does makes sense: This is who God is—the only one whose speech is so powerful that it created the world and everything in it.

Recommendations for Further Reading

Aristotle, *The Art of Rhetoric*. Translated by Robin Waterfield. Oxford University Press, 2018.

Carey, Christopher. *Trials from Classical Athens*. Routledge, 2012.

Questions for Discussion and Reflection

1. Think of an instance recently when you were successful or unsuccessful in persuading someone. Why do you think your speech succeeded (or didn't) in that situation?
2. What is character testimony, and why does it matter? Can you think of an example in your life when you have used character testimony to make a decision?
3. Aristotle considered *logos*, *pathos*, and *ethos* as essential components of rhetorical persuasion. What is each of these components? Think of an example of each in a real-life situation.

How to Do Anything in the Ancient World

> You yourself can alarm an enemy at night by giving your herds of heifers—and other draught-animals—wine to drink and then driving them with bells on into the enemy camp.[1]

The Practical Power of Manuals and Handbooks

Sometime in the second century AD, a wealthy Roman man hosted a banquet in his home. It was a typical fancy affair, complete with everyone overindulging in food and wine. Voices only grew louder from joy and fine drink as the evening went on. The floor grew correspondingly slippery from spilled crumbs, drink, and maybe even some rogue fish and pheasant bones casually discarded by less well-mannered guests. Of course, the enslaved servants would have tried to surreptitiously sweep everything away without disrupting the festivities.

Maybe, as we read in the tale of one fictional banquet, the menu included a roasted boar whose cut-open belly dramatically released some flying thrushes.[2] Hopefully these birds then didn't poop on anyone's dinner

1. David Whitehead, *Aineias the Tactician: How to Survive Under Siege* (Bristol Classical Press, 2003), 81.
2. See Petronius, "Dinner at Trimalchio's," an episode from his larger novel *Satyricon*, which did not survive in full: Petronius, *The Satyricon*, trans. P. G. Walsh (Oxford University Press, 2009).

plate! Pastries shaped skillfully into swans, piglets, and sheep, served on green salad leaves as though they were actual animals grazing on a meadow, may have completed the repast. Finally, late in the night, the host sent his guests home bundled in their litters, safely accompanied by their torchbearers. Then—at last!—he slept.

Most importantly for our purposes, this host dreamed. It was an uneasy dream—a fox was chasing a wolf as a sword hung over them both. Upon waking, he went to his home library, pulled a scroll off his shelf, and looked up the meaning of this dream by finding its individual components in the reference manual to dream interpretation, the *Oneirocritica* (*The Interpretation of Dreams*) of Artemidorus. Or maybe he used another, earlier manual. No matter—but our sleeper had a question and knew where to find the answer. He found out that the fox meant a sly enemy was scheming to attack him in secret. Could this enemy have been present at the dinner party the night before?

This is a hypothetical scenario; I am not telling the story of any particular man. However, we can be sure that such occasions occurred. We tend to think of manuals and handbooks as a modern phenomenon because they are ubiquitous—just look around any bookstore. The popular (and unfortunately named) *For Dummies* series has installments on every topic imaginable—from philosophy and a wide range of academic subjects to the appreciation of music, art, and food, along with such practical matters as childrearing and skincare. Higher-brow manuals also exist on all of these topics and more. Cookbooks, in particular, are a staple of most homes, even for those that do not have many other books.

We know of manuals and handbooks dating as far back as at least the fifth century BC. They cover such diverse topics as medicine, all aspects of war and military affairs, rhetoric, dating, pagan theology, the Roman religious calendar, and—yes—even cooking. Admittedly, not all of them were directed for an immediate practical purpose. For instance, many of the military manuals that survive from antiquity were likely an armchair warrior genre—works written for the fascination of those who might never serve in war but who still enjoyed learning about it. However, most manuals likely were practical. We will focus on these particular manuals in this chapter as we consider the power of such written words to educate people in different situations, shaping behavior as well as character.

First, Do No Harm

Once upon a time, there lived a doctor named Hippocrates. Just as his older contemporary, Herodotus, later acquired the moniker "The Father of History," so Hippocrates became "The Father of Medicine."[3] There were similar reasons for granting these two men such venerable titles. Because of Herodotus, history became a true science containing its own methods and questions that the historian should pursue based on genuine inquiries, research, and investigation. Likewise, Hippocrates is credited with making medicine a genuine science based on research and examination of evidence—for instance, creating case notebooks documenting the course of a disease for individuals who were sick.

Honestly, the case notebooks, *Epidemics*, are depressing. On day such-and-such the patient is throwing up. The very next day, the patient is getting worse. Finally, the patient dies. The doctor is seemingly powerless to do much else other than observe in the shadows, painstakingly taking notes. Yet there is much power in observation. Today's scientific method relies on it: A scientist must sometimes simply observe, often for a long while before acting. Such observation reflects a trust in the beneficial continuity of knowledge: Accumulating it over generations will benefit others, even though initially it may not help the observer and his own patients.

Additionally, the observer himself might also present theories in progress. We see attempts to formulate theories based on observations in some Hippocratic treatises, even though they may often seem strange to us today. For example, in his treatise *Airs, Waters, Places* Hippocrates formulates a theory of the different ailments to which people are prone, based on the geography of the locations where they live. He concludes that northern climes generally tend to be healthier than warm southernly ones. This take is perhaps simplistic and, as some have noted, smacking of scientific racism. *Airs, Waters, Places* nevertheless recognizes the importance of being in the right location for both our physical and spiritual wellbeing. Our very health is also local—as is our medical care. In other words, the best physician is no

3. For an overview of the history of ancient medicine up to Hippocrates, see Robin Lane Fox, *The Invention of Medicine: From Homer to Hippocrates* (Basic Books, 2020).

modern telehealth specialist—this person is present, well acquainted with the places where patients receive care.

Hippocrates is a much murkier figure than Herodotus. Many treatises are attributed to him that he certainly did not write. Still, as we read the Hippocratics (as some refer to the texts in the Hippocratic corpus), we learn much about Classical Greek views of the body and disease, the role of the doctor in society, and the rise of medical ethics. We will briefly focus on this ethics aspect as we consider the best-known and most influential of all Hippocratic texts: the Hippocratic Oath. This oath is a foundational text for what we would today term bioethics—the study of the ethics of what doctors should do, especially when multiple courses of action are available.

Doctors around the world today still take a version of the Hippocratic Oath while they are students first embarking on medical training. The oath is no longer standardized; rather, many medical students create their own version. This is akin to modern-day marriage vows, which are increasingly individualized by couples.[4] And yet a key aspect remains that we should not forget: Oaths are deeply religious. They are, in their original intent in the ancient polytheistic world, agreements between people and gods. In other words, even pagans recognized that the responsibility of healthcare did not seem to be a typical earthly profession. Those who cared for bodies had a suspicion that they were also caring for souls, even though they lacked a theological framework for it.

The Hippocratic oath is likewise religiously explicit. It opens by listing the divinities who enforced it: "I swear by Apollo the healer, by Aesculapius, by Health and all the powers of healing, and call to witness all the gods and goddesses that I may keep this Oath and Promise to the best of my ability and judgment."[5] The clause "to the best of my ability and judgment" is important: It keeps the doctor accountable while also acknowledging that even with the best intentions the doctor still lacks absolute power over the outcome. However, intent still deeply matters throughout this oath, getting even more specific in particular instances:

---

4. Lydia S. Dugdale, "Bring Back Hippocrates," *Plough*, October 7, 2022, https://www.plough.com/en/topics/community/education/bring-back-hippocrates.
5. *Hippocratic Writings*, ed. G. E. R. Lloyd, trans. J. Chadwick and W. N. Mann (Penguin Books, 1983), 67.

> I will use my power to help the sick to the best of my ability and judgement; I will abstain from harming or wronging any man by it.
>
> I will not give a fatal draught to anyone if I am asked, nor will I suggest any such thing. Neither will I give a woman means to procure an abortion.
>
> I will be chaste and religious in my life and in my practice.[6]

Here it is, in the fifth century BC: A physician's oath swearing by the gods that he will not assist a patient in suicide, will not kill a patient whether asked or unasked, and will not assist in an abortion. The strikingly simple statements here are in sharp contrast to the debates in the secular modern medical profession: Some of the earliest allowances for abortion, even before abortion on demand was legalized in *Roe v. Wade* (1973), included the mental health of a mother. As for physician-assisted suicide, as of this writing euthanasia is the sixth leading cause of death in Canada.[7] Modern disdain for human life would apparently have appalled even pagan doctors.

But we might ask why this oath was already necessary in the fifth century BC. Oaths, being contracts between human and divine agents, are words of special power because their enforcement by powers outside our own is implied. While not a medical manual per se, the Hippocratic Oath undergirds all other medical texts and manuals from antiquity, reminding doctors who used them: First do no harm.

How to Survive Under Siege

On a spring morning sometime in the mid-fourth century BC, a young mother woke up in a besieged city. Her husband had just returned home from nighttime guard duty. She kissed the toddler and the baby, hugged her husband, and left her home in the charge of her aged parents while she herself donned some pots and pans to pass for armor. Thus strangely attired, from afar she seemed to be a real soldier, and this was better than trying to wear her husband's own heavier armor. She then went to stand guard on the

6. *Hippocratic Writings*, 67.
7. Benjamin Crosby, "Where Are the Churches in Canada's Euthanasia Experiment?" *Plough*, February 27, 2023, https://www.plough.com/en/topics/justice/culture-of-life/where-are-the-churches-in-canadas-euthanasia-experiment.

city walls for the next few hours. Her job, while an artifice, was important: She and the other mothers, dressed in their kitchen's finest pots, were standing guard during the day while most of their husbands rested. Thus, from the enemy's distant perspective the city's garrison strength was twice what it actually was. Never expecting to fight, the women consequently served an important purpose in this siege. By the way, they learned this trick from a handbook.

We do not have any testimonials assuring us that this event really happened, but it likely did. We do have the handbook recounting this trick, at any rate. Nevertheless, it is helpful to briefly remember the historical context of sieges in that era. The year 399 BC saw the invention of one of the most important technological advancements of antiquity: the catapult. Up until then, siege warfare was a protracted affair, seeking to slowly starve out those besieged until their surrender. For instance, the Trojan War lasted ten years—which was no surprise to those involved. While the siege of Troy is mythical, its extreme length demonstrates challenges involved in real sieges. If a city's walls were good, it could withstand any attacks. The inhabitants within were safe—until the catapults arrived.[8]

The earliest catapults, to be sure, were not battering rams and could not inflict damage upon city walls. Rather, they were able to shoot projectiles of various sorts at a much greater distance than before—for instance, hurling scorpion bombs into besieged cities. What were those? The name is quite apt: A hollow jar-like object would be filled with live scorpions and shot into the city.[9] Catapults ensured that no one inside a city under siege was now safe; overnight, all noncombatants also became targets. In other words, catapults challenge our otherwise neat picture of premodern warfare. Until very recently, historians describing ancient warfare too easily focused on men upon the battlefield, ranged in orderly ranks and facing off honorably. That is, of course, the general flavor of war in the *Iliad*. However, we did see that things were a bit more complicated even in the *Iliad*. Civilians, after all, could and did get regularly brutalized in all kinds of awful ways. Their supplies and animals were requisitioned by enemy troops, and, as we saw,

---

8. For a history of the catapult, see Tracey Rihll, *The Catapult: A History* (Westholme, 2007).
9. For a full overview of such projectiles and similar unexpected techniques, see Adrienne Mayor, *Greek Fire, Poison Arrows, and Scorpion Bombs: Unconventional Warfare in the Ancient World* (Princeton University Press, 2022).

even they themselves could be kidnapped and enslaved long before the war was officially over.

Still, civilians could ostensibly feel a sense of safety, however fragile and imperiled, within the city walls during a siege—at least so long as the food and water supplies held out. But once the catapult arrived, any remaining security vanished. Scorpion bombs or other terrifying projectiles shot into a city did not discriminate between military personnel and innocent women and children. What could people do now? In the wake of this frightening innovation, one retired military general, Aeneas Tacticus, decided to put the tricks of his trade into handbook form—but with a twist. Having spent his career as a successful general besieging cities into submission, in the mid-fourth century BC Aeneas wrote a manual for nonmilitary personnel who might find themselves besieged in an undefended city.

Aeneas's advice is practical and simple, walking nonexperts through procedures step by step. Had you never put together a force for defending the city, patrolling the streets, and keeping everyone to a shift schedule? No need to fear—just follow this checklist. A meticulous researcher, Aeneas also cites examples of sieges where various advice was implemented well—or where things went terribly awry. In particular, there are disturbingly so many ways to compromise the integrity of the bolts that keep the city gates shut! Aeneas accordingly reminds us of a key historical truth about siege warfare: Treachery always looms. The vast majority of sieges in world history have ended through someone opening the gate from the inside.

At the end, Aeneas's manual is so powerful because his words almost literally stand between life and death for some of his readers. In other words, the circumstances of reading this text imbue his words with power. By contrast, as I read Aeneas's manual from the safety of my modern home, at the kitchen counter with some coffee, I'm merely entertained. We can also likewise consider the entertainment angle of another set of ancient manuals—those related to cooking. In this process, we will seamlessly transition from the Greek world into the literary traditions of the Romans. Those upstart Mediterranean neighbors had (according to tradition) been around since the founding of Rome in 753 BC, but did not begin writing literature in earnest until the second century BC. One of them, the late first-century BC poet Horace, later noted on this matter:

"Captive Greece captured, in turn, her uncivilised conquerors."[10] That is, the Romans may have militarily triumphed, but Greek culture in turn conquered them.

Meal-Planning, the Roman Way[11]

I am writing this chapter as spring settles in for good, heralding the end of this school year. I have seen several seasonally updated family meal plans and recommendations for the fastest and easiest yet also most nutritious ways to feed one's ever-hungry brood. Sure, my pantry is well-stocked with granola bars and who knows how many types of crackers in the shape of many (but not all) creatures great and small, denizens of land and sea.

Still, endless streams of yogurt tubes, crackers, and granola bars are just not enough to fuel the day for my energetic crew. Are you, like me, looking for new inspiration to diversify your spring family meal plan and get you out of your wintertime meals rut? Thankfully, courtesy of Apicius, a first-century AD Roman gourmet whose cookbook survives, we have plenty of Roman recipe ideas to meet every nutritional need and level of culinary adventure. The key to success here is to think local. Let us creatively envision the following scenarios you might undertake if you seek to enjoy the cuisine that the Romans relished.

Chicken is boring and is so 2020, when Americans stress-bought out all the baby chicks.[12] By this time, if you have followed in the Romans' footsteps, you long ago (*Deo volente*, "God willing") successfully raised those baby chicks, protected most of them from your backyard dog and other domesticated and wild predators, and finally ate them. At any rate, if you are tired of chicken recipes but are looking to continue your experiments in domestic meat-raising, why not start your own backyard *glirarium* (dormouse-raising farm), à la Romans in the first century AD? Home-raised

10. Horace, *Epistles* II.1.156–67, trans. A. S. Kline, Poetry in Translation, accessed April 3, 2025, https://www.poetryintranslation.com/PITBR/Latin/HoraceEpistlesBkIIEpI.php.
11. This section was previously published as "Springtime Meal Planning with the Romans," *The Arena* (blog), *Current*, May 5, 2023, https://currentpub.com/2023/05/05/springtime-meal-planning-with-the-romans/. It has been edited for smooth integration into the surrounding content.
12. Yes, really. See Tove Danovich, "America Stress-Bought All the Baby Chickens," *New York Times*, March 28, 2020, https://www.nytimes.com/2020/03/28/style/chicken-eggs-coronavirus.html.

dormice were all the rage for a while. Rumored to have superior taste and fat content to its wild brethren, a well-seasoned home-raised dormouse tastes just like squirrel, which tastes just like chicken. Or so I hear.

Cramped on space? You can still raise your own dormice at home even without a backyard. Archaeologists have found small individual dormouse-sized jars with grooves. These allowed the dinner-destined rodents to stay contained and get sufficient exercise while awaiting their fate. And if your family is larger (thus ruling out single servings), bigger dormouse jars have also been discovered, allowing you to use more dormice for dinner prep. It's like the Roman equivalent of those live lobster tanks at the grocery store!

Speaking of other meat options, Book 8 of Apicius's work is dedicated to recipes involving quadrupeds. Our motto here should be: Think beyond beef![13] (No, not *that* Beyond Meat.[14]) Recipes are readily adaptable for the slow cooker. How about wild boar slow-cooked all day in some sea water and sprigs of laurel? And if you like chicken and dumplings, you would surely enjoy a goat kid or lamb cooked in a peppery broth with some green beans, white beans, and bread dumplings. Since the price of pepper has come down significantly since the first century AD, go ahead and indulge!

Homeschooling? You can easily combine your science curriculum with dinner preparation. No, I am not speaking of the celebrated mummified chicken experiment—although, can you even claim you're homeschooling if you've never done that one?[15] Rather, I am thinking of a particular recipe, which is really edible and adds the benefit of a nature walk as the first step—milk-fed snails. Fit for the table of aristocrats and senators such as Varro and Pliny the Younger, this dish can also grace your table now—but only if you can gather enough snails nearby. Simply start by directing your children to collect as many snails as possible, keeping in mind that the serving portion is about three per person. Then soak the snails for a day or two in pure milk (or a milk porridge), making sure that they do not drown in the liquid. That's the tricky part!

One important warning, as we update the snail recipe from the Roman

13. Apuleius, *De Re Coquinaria*, book 8, trans. Joseph Dommers Vehling (Walter M. Hill, 1936). The text is also online on LacusCurtius, accessed March 6, 2025, https://penelope.uchicago.edu/Thayer/E/Roman/Texts/Apicius/8*.html.

14. Beyond Meat, accessed March 6, 2025, https://www.beyondmeat.com/en-US/.

15. For instructions, see "How to Mummify a Chicken," A One-Room Schoolhouse, accessed April 3, 2025, https://aoneroomschoolhouse.com/how-to-mummify-a-chicken/.

world to the present: We now know that some snails are the carrier of parasitic worms that cause schistosomiasis. Do not consume raw snails! But once they are sufficiently plumped up in the milk porridge, you can fry them in an oil of your choice. Serve with a side salad and bread for a complete meal. Additionally, Apicius recommends a wine sauce for the snails and naturally more wine for the meal itself. So, you can decide just how authentic you would like this meal to be for the younger crowd in your household. And, before you ask: No, this recipe has not been tested with dairy-free milk, so it is unclear how well it may turn out when substituting oat milk or almond milk for soaking the snails. I certainly would be interested in knowing how this dish might work with alternative milk!

Mentioning dairy-free milk does lead us to an important next point: Some households, including mine, have to contend with special dietary needs such as sensitivities to dairy, gluten, soy, and more. Thankfully, yet again, the Romans have plenty of ideas for you. How about some beets and green vegetables of your choice, gently roasted after boiling with some cumin and pepper? And if you are looking for allergy-friendly condiments as alternatives to the ever-popular soy sauce, you do not have far to look. Garum is sure to meet your needs! Its preparation process, while lengthy, is ultimately forgiving. Simply start by allowing some fish guts of your choice to ferment in brine. How long? Well, you can use neighbors' complaints about the smell as a guideline—but fermentation typically takes a few months. Then mix what's left with a liquid of your choice. Olive oil is the traditional option, but avocado oil is worth trying out as well. Serve garum as a condiment for any food. Especially try it on your roasted dormouse or scrambled eggs!

Last but not least, although we are leaving winter in the rear-view mirror, plenty of colds and other viruses are still going around. Thankfully, before there was chicken soup, there was cabbage soup. As Cato the Elder, the staunch archconservative politician of the Roman Republic, noted, no problem in life cannot be cured by some boiled cabbage. Except Carthage—it had to be destroyed. Try this dish and see if you agree!

Perhaps I should end this recipe romp with a disclaimer about some of the more exotic dishes: I don't actually feed my children snails (raw or even cooked) or dormice (wild-caught or home-raised). And I've never mummified a chicken. Please don't take my homeschooling license away!

Nevertheless, I hope that this quick frolic has shown just how many Roman recipes we have—and how diverse recipe books can be, not only in content but in literary form. We give authority to cookbooks and other manuals precisely because of their genre: We pick up these books because we expect to follow what they say on their topic.[16]

What the Absences Are Telling Us

A good historian looks not only at what is present in the historical evidence but also at what is absent—because the absences reveal important clues about a society and its values. Greeks and Romans wrote handbooks on so many topics for which we still have manuals and how-to guidebooks today, but they were silent on one important subject: the care of people.

You will readily find manuals today on how to care for children, the elderly, and those sick with particular chronic illnesses. However, no such manuals existed in antiquity until the rise of Christianity. For instance, we find that such leaders of the early church as Tertullian and Cyprian first wrote manuals of care for women. When these manuals first appeared, they displayed a love for the weak and demonstrated the Christians' conviction—in contrast to the pagans around them—that God loves everyone so believers must care for everyone.

God's Handbook

The book of Leviticus is an interminable slog for modern readers. What do we do with all of these rules, lists, requirements, and bizarre dietary laws—animals with hooves cloven (good) versus not (nope); those who chew their cud (good) versus not (avoid); or small animals that scurry along the ground

16. For a discussion of the power that genre specifically gives towards words employed in their intended circumstances, see the discussion of genre and power in Andrew Judd, *Modern Genre Theory* (Zondervan Academic, 2024), 43–64.

(that's a BIG no)? The confused modern reader might feel her eyes getting crossed as she stumbles over each regulation. Fortunately, we have one helpful starting point in considering such commands: We can recognize their genre.

Indeed, Leviticus is another example of that familiar genre of ancient manuals and handbooks. It uniquely combines multiple different sorts of handbooks into one scroll: clothing, marriage, household, religion, and cooking, as well as other topics, all collide. However, the book's authorship has ultimate significance. Tradition ascribes Leviticus to Moses, and through him directly to God. This reminds us that some handbooks are more authoritative and powerful than others. Fail to follow the instructions of a recipe, and perhaps you'll ruin dinner. Fail to follow God, and you'll ruin your life.

In contrast, Jesus's teachings complicate the list-laden glory of Leviticus. He reminds us that while God's words are powerful, the Word that became flesh is the true source of all power—indeed, the lists of Leviticus ultimately point to that Word. This was a difficult concept to understand for observers in Jesus's own day, since they were used to hearing words of power from a very different realm—Roman politics. We enter into that realm in the next chapter.

Recommendations for Further Reading

Apicius, *Cookery and Dining in Imperial Rome.* Edited and translated by Joseph Dommers Vehling. Dover, 1977.

Hippocratic Writings. Translated by J. Chadwick, W. N. Mann, I. M. Lonie, and E. T. Withington. Penguin Books, 1983.

Whitehead, David. *Aineias the Tactician: How to Survive Under Siege.* 2nd ed. Bristol Classical Press, 2002.

Questions for Discussion and Reflection

1. What kinds of manuals or handbooks do you use most often? What are the features of such manuals today, and what do we learn from them about our society?
2. Which of the manuals discussed in this chapter did you find the most surprising, intriguing, or unexpected? Why?
3. If you were to write your own manual or handbook to a topic, what would it be about? If you are feeling particularly adventurous, consider planning out your manual or even begin writing it.

CHAPTER

Cicero, Caesar, and Political Rhetoric in the Roman Republic

> By heavens, Senators, it is difficult to imagine where on earth we can be, or what sort of a system of government is ours, or what kind of a city we inhabit, when there are men sitting here among ourselves, in this most solemn and dignified of all the world's assemblies, who are actually plotting the destruction of every single one of us, and of all Rome, and of everything upon the face of the earth! I, the consul, am gazing upon them now; they are taking part in this national debate.[1]

In Rome You Can Be a New Man

It's an age-old story. A talented guy from a small town is eager to get away, stretch his wings, live the exciting big-city life, and become somebody instead of nobody. The problem is, dad can only finance things so far. Besides, this ambitious youth needs one particular thing more than anything else: connections. Networking! So what can this plucky upstart do, whether in the 70s BC or in the AD 2020s? Become a lawyer, of course.

Born in 106 BC in the small town of Arpinum, seventy miles from

1. Cicero, *First Oration Against Lucius Sergius Catilina*, in Cicero, *Selected Political Speeches*, trans. Michael Grant (Penguin Classics, 1989), 80.

Rome, Marcus Tullius Cicero, the greatest orator of the Roman Republic and (some have argued) all of Roman history, received the best education available in philosophy and rhetoric. He won his very first legal cases. Cicero continually ascended through the ranks, winning election to the Roman senate in 75 BC and buoying his reputation through more legal victories, particularly in his 70 BC prosecution of Verres.

Gaius Verres, a prominent Roman politician, had served as the governor of Sicily from 73 BC to 71 BC. During his tenure, he extorted bribes and shamelessly pillaged the province, bringing home an incredible amount of both cash and priceless art. To be fair, all Roman politicians, who had to finance their own electoral efforts (yes, really!), treated such plum political appointments as a get-rich scheme. Still, this extortion could be done respectably without attracting excessive attention to its sleaziness—and Verres crossed that line. Still, as a senior statesman, Verres had the support of a much more prominent lawyer speaking in his defense. No matter—Cicero pulled no punches and painted such a dire picture of Verres's crimes that he achieved an unexpected victory, making an immortal name for himself.

Overnight recognized as the greatest orator of his day, Cicero became powerful simply on the merit of his words. Ultimately, in the year 64 BC he was elected as one of the following year's two consuls—the chief annually elected office in the Roman Republic. Despite Cicero's impressive reputation, his victory was still surprising because in spite of all his achievements he was still a *novus homo*—a new man. This term, referring to a politician who was the first in his family to achieve a consulship, is telling. Very few men ever managed to pull off what Cicero had done. Indeed, the consulship, a coveted position at the top of the narrowing pyramid of elected offices to which one had to win election in strict order, was generally the purview of the oldest and most prestigious patrician families in Rome.[2]

One scion of such a family, Lucius Sergius Catilina (in English usually called Catiline), lost in the same election and did not take Cicero's victory well. Still, he figured he would give it another shot in the next election. When Catiline failed yet again to win a consulship for the following year in 63 BC, he was done playing nice. He formed an elaborate conspiracy with

2. For a survey of the history of the Roman Republic, I recommend Harriet Flower, *Roman Republics* (Princeton University Press, 2009), and Mary Beard, *SPQR: A History of Ancient Rome* (Liveright, 2015).

several other disgruntled aristocrats and senators who also felt like they were being displaced from political success by such upstarts as Cicero. More people also joined in, who likely just sought to make trouble for trouble's sake. Their plan? To assassinate Cicero and a bunch of other senators and take over the Republic by force.

Ancient historians have really hit the jackpot with the documentation of this conspiracy. We have Cicero's series of political attack speeches against Catiline—the four Catilinarian orations. We also have a monograph about the conspiracy from the contemporary historian and senator Sallust. Included in Sallust's narrative are the senatorial speeches from a trial after Catiline had finally been defeated. The question under debate: What to do with the conspirators? Caesar and Cato the Younger—two of the most prominent political figures of that day—delivered their opposing opinions, respectively, for cautiously jailing the conspirators or for executing them outright. We see here Roman liberals and conservatives—the Populares and Optimates—facing off each other in earnest. We'll come back shortly to this conspiracy in connection with Cicero's rhetorical art. For the moment, though, the main point is: Cicero's career—particularly the 63 BC Catiline episode—teaches us so much about the power of words in driving Roman politics. Along every step of the way and during every day in the Roman political sphere, people had to persuade other politicians and voters of their ideas while craftily using verbal subterfuge to knock down their opponents.

"Sticks and stones may break my bones, but words shall never hurt me," an English-language saying goes. No Roman—or, really, no resident of the ancient world—would ever have said this.

Little Brother Gives Advice: Running for Office the Roman Way

Sometime in the first century AD in the city of Pompeii, a graffiti artist endorsed a candidate running for local office with the best recommendation possible: "He makes good bread."[3] This endorsement is relatable; competent

3. Translation mine. The Latin states: "panem bonum fert," which can also be translated as "He offers good bread." For the text and images of the inscription, see Richard A. LaFleur, *Scribblers, Sculptors, and Scribes: A Companion to* Wheelock's Latin *and Other Introductory Textbooks* (Collins References, 2010), 182.

local professionals are treasured by those who know them and use their services.

I lived in a small town in Georgia for thirteen years. When I moved there and was looking for a dentist, a colleague recommended someone who was then serving on the city council. My colleague mused that since the dentist in question kept getting reelected, this presumably also reflected well on his *bona fides* at his day job. After staying with that excellent dentist for the entire thirteen years, I can confirm that my colleague's logic was correct. No one polices competence on the job and in local politics better than inhabitants of a small town.

However, vetting quality candidates gets infinitely trickier as we grow further removed from them. And the process of campaigning on a state or national level today takes on a commensurately different dimension for these candidates. Simply relying on one's famed baked goods or dentistry competence no longer cuts it when campaigning in elections where millions vote, as opposed to just a few thousand. So, what is the best way to approach electioneering in this environment?

Quintus Tullius Cicero, the younger and lesser-known brother of our new man, Marcus Tullius Cicero, once wrote a letter to his brother in the form of a short manual on running for office. Quintus's letter was written in 64 BC, the same year as his big brother was contending for the consulship. While Quintus ostensibly addressed his letter specifically to his brother, we need to keep in mind that Roman politicians regularly published their letters—Marcus Tullius Cicero certainly did. Thus, Quintus likely also intended to inform a larger audience. His manual is a treasure trove of information, revealing what some Romans thought about the process of campaigning and how they thought someone might prevail. But this advice manual strikingly spends as much time to consider the voters as it devotes to the politicians running for office. What is its key to winning elections? Understanding correctly the utterly depraved character of both voters and politicians, while playing up one's own rare virtue.

"Running for office can be divided into two kinds of activity: securing the support of your friends and winning over the general public," the younger Cicero outlines by way of an overall argument.[4] But who are these

4. Quintus Tullius Cicero, *How to Win an Election: An Ancient Guide for Modern Politicians*, trans.

friends? Anyone who can benefit you, so see how you might turn everyone you meet into a friend. Promise everything to everyone, albeit within reason: "The most important part of your campaign is to bring hope to people and a feeling of goodwill toward you. On the other hand, you should not make specific pledges either to the Senate or the people. Stick to vague generalities. Tell the Senate you will maintain its traditional power and privileges. Let the business community and wealthy citizens know that you are for stability and peace."[5]

But promises and flattering your most important (meaning, ahem, wealthiest) supporters cannot be your only election strategy. No less important, Quintus reminds us, is a well-run smear campaign against your competitors. Sure, this might sound sleazy—yet it is not only appropriate but expected in politics. It is also perfectly within reason to attack not just the candidate's own character, but that of his wife or parents or other relatives. Quintus was not exaggerating; much of his advice is confirmed by the political graffiti in places like Pompeii. You could even insult your opponent's supporters, as one Pompeiian political graffito did: "The late night drinkers all ask you to elect Marcus Cerrinius Vatia as aedile."[6] Presumably, this campaign-ad-style notice on a public wall was not meant to be an actual endorsement of the candidate in question!

Thankfully, most of the time one's competitors are guaranteed to provide plenty of fodder for such negative publicity just by living their best lives. But, then, the voters themselves are not necessarily much better. As Quintus observes with remarkable frankness, "Our city is a cesspool of humanity, a place of deceit, plots, and vice of every imaginable kind. Anywhere you turn you will see arrogance, stubbornness, malevolence, pride, and hatred."[7] And there we have it: morally flawed people running for office, seeking to be elected by a "cesspool of humanity."

Presenting all of his advice matter-of-factly, at the end the junior Cicero expressed his utmost confidence that his older brother had all the necessary qualifications to overcome his competition. In particular, he observed that

Philip Freeman (Princeton University Press, 2012), 27.

5. Quintus Tullius Cicero, *How to Win an Election*, 79.
6. For a discussion of this graffito, see Philip Freeman, "The Attack Ad, Pompeii-Style," *New York Times*, August 30, 2012, https://archive.nytimes.com/campaignstops.blogs.nytimes.com/2012/08/30/the-attack-ad-pompeii-style/.
7. Quintus Tullius Cicero, *How to Win an Election*, 81.

Marcus was the rare candidate with no scandal attached to his name. So, it turns out, there are real benefits to being a boring nerd. (I can confirm and heartily second this from my own life!) Marcus Tullius Cicero indeed prevailed and, as I previously noted, was elected one of the consuls for 63 BC.

If we limit and end the story here, solid advice has prevailed and the candidate with the squeaky-clean record has won the top political office in a tough race filled with more nobly born candidates possessing significantly worse character flaws. Such a story would be heartening, as it would confirm the power of the democratic process in securing stability even through contentious and scandal-ridden elections. In other words, such a story would comfort our own present political distresses. Most of all, we would really like to forget the whole "cesspool of humanity" characterization which actually groups together as one not just the general public but also the politicians themselves. Yet Roman history, just like the history of our own democracy, does not allow us to forget the deeply flawed nature of all people. If we want a feel-good story, we will not find it in the world of Roman Republican politics.

Ultimately, Quintus Cicero's advice manual only further highlights the instability of national campaigns and elections. But the key antagonist in politics is not the politicians nor the voters, those "late-night drinkers" who support our least favorite candidates. Instead, this enemy is lodged safely within ourselves—the greatest enemy of the orderly and democratic national political process is the deeply flawed and selfish nature that we all possess and bring with us to every season of elections. The conspiracy led by Catiline that unexpectedly came to define Marcus Tullius Cicero's consulship is a case in point. We now delve deeper into its details and implications.

Cicero Confronts a Conspiracy

One otherwise ordinary day, a group of armed insurrectionists led by a disgruntled candidate who had failed to win the recent election for chief political office planned to assassinate the leader of the state. They then intended to storm the senate house, assassinate multiple senators, and install their leader, thus redeemed, in what they saw as his rightful position of political authority. The date I am speaking of is, of course, November 7, 63 BC.

Yes, this conspiracy nearly toppled the Republic! So declared one of the chief targets of the coup, consul Marcus Tullius Cicero. Since antiquity Cicero's four Catilinarian orations have been among the most widely known works of Roman literature. Cicero reveals in these speeches intimate details about the conspiracy, its leaders, and their aim of taking the Republic by force. His description of the conspirators' character is no less powerful—only deeply selfish, perverse, and merciless people could orchestrate such a plan. Their earlier life had been no better; Cicero is only too happy to supply reports of their lifelong debauchery and selfishness. His charge is clear: Catiline and his fellow conspirators were rotten to the core.

However, Cicero's very rhetorical talent raised questions for some people. Was Catiline's scheme a true conspiracy? Or was the narrative of a grand conspiracy itself a hoax, a smaller crisis blown out of proportion by the overeager Cicero? So wondered some of Cicero's opponents in later years. In 58 BC, the plebeian tribune Publius Clodius Pulcher led the charge in turning public opinion against Cicero, whose acts as consul to suppress the Catilinarian conspiracy would eventually lead to a temporary exile from Rome. But what if Clodius, the debonair aristocrat-turned-plebeian aedile (an elected city manager), was asking the wrong question? What if the real question is not whether the events in question involved a conspiracy or a hoax but rather what both the events and the controversies around them reveal about the health of a republic? In this spirit, Cicero famously proclaimed early in his first Catilinarian oration, *O tempora, o mores!* ("Oh, times! Oh, customs!").

The Roman Republic had not been well for a long time, concluded the historian Sallust, writing about the conspiracy of Catiline two decades later in the late 40s BC. His work appeared in the wake of another conspiracy: the assassination of Julius Caesar during a meeting of the senate on the Ides of March of 44 BC, which effectively ended the Roman Republic. Sallust, once a promising politician and senator himself, turned to writing history as a consolation, a type of therapy, and an occupation to pass time after his political career had ended in disgrace. In the process he invented the subgenre of a monograph about a single war, writing two such works: one about the conspiracy of Catiline, which Cicero suppressed so controversially, and another about the war with Jugurtha, the ally-turned-rogue king of Numidia in northern Africa.

Both works express deep nostalgia for the bygone glory days of the Republic. The Roman character used to be so noble, Sallust laments—but look at it now! Sallust blames the debasement of the Roman character for the fall of the Republic through which he felt he was living. With the hindsight of historical knowledge, we can confirm that he was not wrong. Around the time when Sallust was quietly sitting at home, writing about the conspiracy of Catiline, Cicero met his end as part of the proscriptions of 43 BC. A proscription was a list of enemies of the state who could be killed on sight by anyone. The killer could then claim part of the victim's estate as compensation.

Proscribed by Mark Antony for writing a series of fourteen virulent *Philippics* against him, Cicero was captured and beheaded while attempting to flee into yet another exile. Per Antony's request, Cicero's head and hands were nailed to the rostra, the official location at which Republican politicians once addressed the people. Antony's wife Fulvia then stabbed Cicero's tongue, which he had employed so powerfully against her husband, with her hairpin. Few other visuals so vividly symbolize the end of the Republic and the power of words it once afforded its politicians.

The Roman *Cursus Honorum* (Ladder of Offices)

As you think about Roman Republican politics, recognize how extraordinarily competitive it was. Imagine a pyramid, with the office of consul (two elected annually) at the top. Every man in the Roman Republic wanted to be consul, and everyone who had previously been consul (e.g., Caesar in 59 BC) wanted to keep winning additional consulships in the future. But the ladder of offices (nicknamed the *cursus honorum*) to the top of the pyramid was difficult to scale, since each successive elected office had fewer openings to accommodate the rush of aspirants.

Making matters even more competitive, each former consul also wanted another supreme prize—the triumph. Awarded only for the most extraordinary of military victories, a triumph was the prize that one's great-great-grandchildren would still be talking about. Such an honor would have literal recognition and remembrance for future generations through the proud display of the victor's mask in the entrance hall of his family home.

Caesar's Gaul and the Political Power of Journalism

While Cicero fought his way through the chain of events which would culminate in his ignominious end, another man's meteoric rise to power upended the already tottering Roman Republic. (Someone recently remarked to me that meteoric rise always implies a no less dramatic end, and this was certainly true in this man's case.) This man was a friend of the politician-turned-historian Sallust, who recorded him giving a speech urging the senators to go easy on the Catilinarian conspirators and not execute them without a proper trial. He was also at least as noble as Catiline, tracing his family directly back to the founding of Rome and the goddess Venus. Not too shabby, as far as ancestries go. We know him today as Caesar.

Born in 100 BC, Gaius Julius Caesar was effectively a contemporary of Cicero—just six years his junior. The two men lived a parallel life of sorts, somehow always finding each other on the opposite side of every political matter and issue under debate. Nevertheless, both men had one thing in common: They found themselves ambitiously seeking the consulship. But while Cicero, the new man, had to claw his way to the top of Roman politics with his rhetorical talent, the blue-blooded Caesar was able to leverage his aristocratic family connections to attain the top office of Roman religion—*pontifex maximus*. He could also call upon his own rhetorical abilities, along with his acclaimed military acumen.

From 58 to 50 BC, Caesar was on assignment in Gaul, tasked with pacifying Rome's perceived longtime enemy. The fear honestly seems more historic than realistic at that point, but the memories of both the Gallic sack of Rome around 390 BC and later invasions from Gaul into Roman territory died hard. At the end of his history of the Jugurthine War, Sallust could wistfully remark that against all other enemies the Romans fought for imperialist expansion and the glory of victory, but against the Gauls they always fought for survival.[8]

Still, even if Sallust's dramatic description wasn't quite true on this point, Caesar had something to work with here—and he exploited it to the hilt. However, it was difficult to gain the award of a Roman triumph. One had to win a major and decisive victory, killing at least five thousand enemies, and obtain a final affirmation from the Roman senate. So, how did Caesar stack the deck in his favor of not only winning another consulship in the future but also gaining a triumph? Rightly worried in an age that had no social media nor modern communications that his absence from Rome would keep all his accomplishments outside the public eye, Caesar relied on the power of written words. He wrote highly literary campaign notes—the genre of *commentarii*—and published them in installments in Rome. Written in clear and simple yet elegant prose, Caesar's *Gallic War* has been—and remains—a staple for intermediate Latin students for centuries. To this day, if you begin Latin with a study of mostly just grammar for the first two or three years (in middle school or high school) or a single year (in college), your next step will very likely be Caesar.

Eight years of campaigning is a long time. Caesar's narrative consists of somewhat formulaic episodes: The Romans come across the Gauls or some related tribe; they engage; and they prevail. In one of the book's most striking moments, the famous 52 BC siege of Alesia, memories of the Trojan siege are evoked. But while the Greeks needed a full decade to besiege Troy and could only win by trickery, Caesar's experienced troops need a mere two weeks to bring the well-fortified town down. Caesar's military prowess is unquestionably impressive. And yet our modern eye, conditioned to abhor violence and genocide by two thousand years of Christianity, views Caesar's narrative of his campaigns as jarring and at times excessive—just like Homer's epics—in its glorification of blood-strewn battlefields.

In Homer we met heroes and wanted to sympathize with them, yet we also knew that the literal price of heroism was piling up the bodies of enemy warriors. Nevertheless, sometimes Homer gave us a glimpse of sadness for such violence, showing admiration for both Greeks and Trojans at various

8. Sallust, *Jugurthine War*, chapter 114.

points. No such ambivalence exists in Caesar's writing: He uses the full force of his simple narrative style to chronicle the Roman slaughter of the Gauls at every possible opportunity.

This brilliant ploy—akin to modern-day war journalism—worked. Caesar's "war in words" (as classicist Andrew Riggsby described it) kept his achievements in the public eye, even though he was away from his target audiences for nearly a decade.[9] His homecoming from Gaul caused a civil war between his supporters and those of his former colleague Gnaeus Pompey—fertile material for another campaign journal, *The Civil War*. After vanquishing all of his enemies in further civil wars, Caesar finally celebrated a quadruple triumph in 46 BC, which also commemorated his victory in Gaul. For a brief moment, perhaps he really felt that he was at the top of the world—but just two years later, he was dead.[10] How foolish and vain are the hearts of men!

In Christ You Can Be a New Man (or Woman)

The powerful writing of the Roman Republic's leading politicians allowed them to win election after election. The extreme pressure-cooker that was Rome in the first century BC required such skills for all who wanted to advance. And the few who made it to the top, even for a minute, assured themselves that the promises of the system were true—in Rome, one truly could be a new man. But then the crash came. At the end, the success which Cicero and Caesar and so many of their contemporaries attained through their mighty words teaches us that earthly awards—military success, political success, literary success—can only grant people fleeting joy.

So, why read these men's words now as Christians? Because they are powerful—and beautiful. Yet the source of the beauty they reflect—as well as our ability to appreciate it—does not stem from anything the Romans fully understood. The new man that everyone aspired to be in Rome was ultimately power-hungry and self-centered, willing to sacrifice all things (and all people) to achieve his goals. As believers, we know that this is not the way.

---

9. Andrew M. Riggsby, *Caesar in Gaul and Rome: War in Words* (University of Texas Press, 2006).
10. Barry Strauss, *The Death of Caesar: The Story of History's Most Famous Assassination* (Simon & Schuster, 2015).

Nevertheless, the idea of becoming a new man (or woman) is powerful for Christians today, in a very personal rather than political context. When we say that in Christ one is made new (2 Corinthians 5:17 and Ephesians 4:24), we testify to the power of conversion and of the Holy Spirit's work in the Christian's life. We are referring to the Word that became flesh, who can make each of us into a new being whose desire for beauty reflects this same desire in the maker of all things beautiful and true.

The longing we feel, like Cicero, to be a "new man"—to make something new and better out of ourselves—is yet another symptom of the God-shaped void in our world-weary souls. But God's promises to make us new in Christ offer a redemption not contingent on any earthly victory we may win. The most powerful words of all are those God speaks over every believer: "You are my beloved son or daughter."

Recommendations for Further Reading

Caesar, *The Civil War of Caesar*. Translated by Jane P. Gardner. Penguin Classics, 1976.

Caesar, *The Conquest of Gaul*. Translated by S. A. Handford. Penguin Classics, 1983.

Cicero, *Selected Political Speeches*. Translated by Michael Grant. Penguin Classics, 1989.

Sallust, *Catiline's War, The Jugurthine War, Histories*. Translated by A. J. Woodman. Penguin Classics, 2008.

Questions for Discussion and Reflection

1. Why do you think the idea of being a "new man" or "new woman" is so appealing to people? Have you ever struggled with this desire to remake yourself? What is Christ's answer to this desire?

2. What do we learn from Cicero's and Caesar's careers about words of power and the power of words in the late Roman Republic?
3. Can you think of a political speech in more recent history that has had great and (perhaps) lasting power? Why was it so powerful? If it has also had lasting power, why do you think its fame has endured?

CHAPTER

Ovid and the Rhetoric of Love

There's this ancient wood—no axe has thinned it for ages,
It might well be some spirit's home.
At its centre, a sacred spring, an arched limestone grotto,
And sweet birdsong all around.
While I was strolling here, through an overwoven
Dapple of shade, and wondering just what task
My Muse should embark on next, there appeared before me
Elegy, perfumed hair caught up in a knot,
And short—I think—in one foot: good figure, nice dress, a loving
Expression.[1]

That's Amore!

Years ago, my now-husband snail-mailed me a four-page-long letter, typed in a small font and single spaced. Its goal? To persuade me to go on a first date with him. But it was more than just that—which is why he needed to write so many words. In that letter, he explained his motives. He wanted us to embark on a serious courtship, all with an eye toward exploring the possibility of marriage. He spared no argument in this process. He listed qualities in me that he appreciated or admired. He talked about how much he valued our conversations and friendship. He noted his own desire to

1. Ovid, *Amores*, in Ovid, *The Erotic Poems*, trans. Peter Green (Penguin Classics, 1983), 3.1:1–10.

continue growing spiritually, and he admitted his hope to be one day a kind and godly husband and father.

Since I just referred to this man as "my now-husband," obviously the letter—epic in more ways than one—worked. How could it not? Its arguments were wonderful, and the impressive length of the missive added further heft to back up the quality of these arguments. In an age of abbreviated text messages, a long snail-mail letter stands out even more than in ages past. When are powerful words especially necessary? The main areas of life that readily come to mind when we think of how important rhetoric and persuasion can be are the ones we have considered so far: words of power and the power of words in the courtroom, in teaching (especially in writing and through manuals and handbooks), and in political rhetoric of various sorts. But what about the realm of romance?

My husband's letter is a modern reminder of a phenomenon that poets and letter writers have known for millennia. The crooner Dean Martin once famously declared that love is sparked when the pizza-like moon smacks you in the eye ("That's Amore," 1953). In real life, though, the moon needs a lot of help. The art of rhetoric contains much power to either facilitate or destroy romance. In particular, rhetoric can be especially destructive to romance when selfishly used. We learn this important lesson from the myriad ill-fated romances in literature and history, ancient and modern alike. Just think back to the story Euripides tells in his tragedy *Medea*. There is also an entire genre of dysfunctional love affairs: the Roman elegy.

As we think about Aristotle's breakdown of rhetoric into the three elements of *logos*, *pathos*, and *ethos*, we can see how different the realm of love is from the other areas. In the courtroom, one hopes that the *logos*—a high quality argument with excellent proofs—will prevail, even though both *pathos* and *ethos* can contribute. But the other two elements will always supersede *logos* in love. What do I mean by this?

To go back to my husband's epic letter, I can assure you that even if his letter had been much shorter, I still would have happily gone on the date with him. Why? Because I really liked him and was hoping that he would ask me out sometime soon. So, it was not about the letter presenting the absolute best possible proofs and therefore persuading a neutral audience. Rather, I was already interested in its writer. I was happy to read his words and be persuaded by them. Really, all he had to do to successfully employ *pathos* was write to me. Just about any method of asking me out would likely have worked—even a text. However, let me give a quick word to anyone taking notes on how to woo a future spouse: A letter is a tangible artifact. I still have my husband's letter! A text would eventually have gotten lost in the shuffle of all these years and phone changes.

This raises the question about a converse scenario: What if the recipient isn't as enthused about getting the letter? That is the question which Augustan poets investigated in greater detail than the writers of any other period of Roman literature. After all, literature has its own fads and fashions. In the age of Augustus, the first Roman emperor, who ruled in some capacity from 31 BC to his death in AD 14, the genre of Roman love elegy flourished, along with many other arts.[2] But it wasn't the happy, fuzzy kind of love poetry. The tales of mythological and real-life failed romance in the writings of the Augustan poets repeatedly show the limits of *logos* when the other party has no interest in romantic advances. But these poems also show that the success of rhetoric could sometimes still enable a very miserable romance in which one or both parties suffered.

What is elegy? It was characterized by both its subject (love) and poetic meter. Epic poetry since the days of Homer was written in dactylic hexameter—six measures per line of poetry. Each measure was either a dactyl (one long syllable followed by two short ones) or a spondee (two long syllables). In a wink to epic, elegy was written in elegiac couplets: units of two lines. The first line was the usual six measures, but the second one was just five. This causes clearly defined couplets—like couples holding hands. This is why the poet Ovid opens his *Amores* (*Loves*) by describing Cupid stopping by and cutting off the final measure from every other line. This story illustrates the connection of such poetry to epic—it really is almost epic in style and language, but not quite. Love isn't the subject of epics—war is. But just as the world of ancient epics was filled with gods, so Ovid's reference to Cupid also emphasizes the involvement of the fickle and unpredictable gods of love—Cupid, especially, but Venus, too—in the affairs of the heart and the poetry about them.

Ovid is arguably the most famous of the Augustan love poets, but

2. For an overview of Augustan art and culture, see Karl Galinsky, *Augustan Culture* (Princeton University Press, 1998), and Paul Zanker, *The Power of Images in the Age of Augustus*, trans. Alan Shapiro (University of Michigan Press, 1990).

he was only one of a larger group that also included such other poets as Propertius, Tibullus, and Sulpicia (yes, a rare woman poet whose work survived!). But their writing on love has little in common with my husband's sweet and practical letter. For them, love was about illicit fun in the here and now, for as long (or as little) as it could last. And while this love resulted in a lot of technically excellent poetry, it was certainly not going to lead to marriage. Instead, it all began—and mostly ended—with the art of seduction.

The Rhetoric of Seduction: Ovid Teaches the Art of Love

The year after Julius Caesar met his demise during that fateful senate meeting, the future poet Publius Ovidius Naso was born in the small town of Sulmona, outside of Rome. As we think back to the life trajectory of Cicero, we can imagine Ovid's well-to-do parents having similar aspirations for their son: the best rhetorical education that money could buy, to be followed by a career in law (a profession that relied on rhetorical prowess), leveraging success in the legal realm to enter Roman politics.

Rome, as everyone by this time knew, was where new men were made, so Ovid's parents planned for him to move there. But, as all parents know, not all talented kids meet their parents' dreams for their careers. Yes, Ovid did move to Rome. But unlike Cicero, who wrote political prose for business and dabbled in poetry for pleasure (terrible poetry, according to his contemporaries), Ovid ultimately blew off all political aspirations, fell in with the artsy bohemian crowd, and focused on writing love poetry. In the turbulent political world of late first-century BC Rome, perhaps that was actually better for one's health.

Ovid knew the art of seduction well and had the credentials to prove it. Before turning thirty, he had already been married three times and had two divorces under his belt. And then there is the mysterious—and possibly fictional—Corinna. A torrid affair with her partly propels Ovid's *Amores*, a series of rather racy forty-nine poems initially published in five books but known to us as a second edition of three books. But even when occasionally complaining that Corinna was ignoring him, or was overly demanding (for time, gifts, attention, etc.), Ovid also sometimes notes that he isn't above seeing other girls while dating her. What's the fun in fidelity, after all?

Instead, he'd rather brag about his conquests in very crude terms. Ovid isn't above kissing and telling. Quite the opposite: He relishes the opportunity.

When reading these poems, we can imagine Ovid as an immature emo youth of a very modern sort who lives in his parents' basement, mooches meals and snacks off them, plays the dating scene, and refuses to get a job, all while he tries to catch a break in his writing career. Perhaps this vision is not too far off, although Ovid's parents were wealthy, and set up marriage after marriage for their delinquent son. He did eventually find a wealthy patron for his poetry—the age of Augustus was prime time for that! Maybe we shouldn't feel excessively sorry for Ovid. His first-person accounts, whether meant to be real or fictional, are decidedly unlikable. The dramatic tell-all style he employs isn't far from trashy modern reality TV. And so, just like modern celebrities who parlay their romantic dysfunctions into lucrative book deals, Ovid used his own dysfunctional romances to write a guide to seduction—an epic poem in three books entitled *The Art of Love*.

If you are a Roman man, Ovid notes, the world is your oyster. You are in full control, so just set your eye on a prize (that happens to be a woman) and pursue it. The theater, the circus, and the beach at Baiae (near Naples) are all great spots to pick up a woman. All you have to do is identify your prey and then try moving close—very close, as in, touching her "by accident" close. Indeed, the crowds in the theater even make it easy to get into her personal space, since you have a convenient excuse for drawing near. Additional advice includes male grooming, good pick-up lines for an initial encounter, and then more advice about how to talk to your girlfriend once she actually is a girlfriend—for instance, always flatter her no matter what shape she is (too fat? too thin?).

At last, when you're victorious, like a military general on a battlefield, you can set up your own trophy to celebrate. Ovid proudly concludes Book 2 of *The Art of Love* with this boast:

> As great as Podalirius was among the Achaeans
> For his healing arts, or Achilles for his strength,
> Or Nestor in counsel, or Calchas as prophet, or Ajax
> In arms, or Automedon as charioteer,
> So great am I at the love-game. Sing my praises, declare me
> Your prophet and poet, young men: let my name

Be broadcast world-wide. As Vulcan made arms for Achilles,
So have I done for you: then use
My gift, as he did, to conquer! And when you've brought down your
Amazon, write on the trophy *Ovid was my guide*.[3]

The trophy in ancient military custom was a tree or a similar object set up on the battlefield by the victorious side. It was then decorated with battle spoils—the stripped-off armor of the defeated. Applying this concept to love, we see Ovid the victorious general despoiling his lovers, one after the other, in his *Amores*. We can also bring in a visual reference here. When celebrating their victories on coins, triumphant generals often displayed the defeated conquered land as a woman, disheveled and partly undressed.

Yet Ovid's women aren't just maidens to be captured and despoiled. Sometimes he does hope that they'll also take the initiative. And so, while he addresses the first two books of *The Art of Love* to men, he devotes the third and concluding book for women, including such helpful tips as how to sneak out past one's guardian. Climbing out the window to go see one's good-for-nothing paramour is actually not just for modern highschoolers in the movies. But what about those times when the knowledge of all the best tricks and ploys still fails to attain success? Ovid also thought about this. After all, ancient mythology was filled with such stories.

When Rhetoric Fails

A man went for a nice walk in the woods. He came across a pond. Ah, so refreshing on a hot summer day! He did what we all might do—perhaps dipped a toe, stretched out on the shore for a rest, and then leaned over to get a drink of the cool water. But things take an unexpected turn here. He saw in the water . . . a very handsome man looking back at him. Immediately, as Dean Martin might say, the pizza-like moon hit his eye. It was certainly amore! He could do nothing but stay where he was, mooning over the gorgeous mute apparition which he had fallen so desperately in love with at

3. Ovid, *The Art of Love*, in Ovid, *The Erotic Poems*, trans. Peter Green (Penguin Classics, 1983), 2:734–744 (emphasis original).

first sight. He spoke words of affection, sparing no rhetorical device that he thought might persuade his beloved to love him back. Nothing worked—the handsome stranger remained where he was, mute as ever, doing nothing but looking back at the first man. Eventually, the man withered and died.

This is the famous myth of Narcissus, whose vanity caused him to famously fall in love with his own reflection—that's who the mysterious stranger in the pond was, of course. No wonder that rhetoric failed here. This situation is meant to be absurd, yet it turns tragic. Narcissus withers away from his unrequited love with his own reflection and turns into a flower—this metamorphosis making him the perfect subject for Ovid's epic of many such transformations, *Metamorphoses*.

But narcissistic though Narcissus was, his story of unrequited love and failed rhetoric is intertwined with another's. It all started with the punishment of a nymph, Echo, who did not inform Juno, the queen of the gods, of her husband Jupiter's indiscretions. And so Juno cursed Echo: She could not say anything original anymore but could only repeat the words of others. Thus, when Echo fell in love with Narcissus, all she could do was repeat his own words back to him. Repulsed, he fled, cruelly rejecting her. As her body wasted away from grief, eventually only her voice—an echo—remained, living forever. Echo's fellow nymphs then asked the goddess of revenge, Nemesis, to curse Narcissus, ultimately leading to his own tragedy and transformation.

Many may dream of a relationship with a beloved who is a "yes" woman—who does nothing but agree and repeat one's words. Yet this rhetoric only disgusted Narcissus, who did not wish to hear his own words repeated back at him by a woman he did not love. His punishment for mistreating Echo—falling in love with his own reflection, which looks like him but cannot speak to him at all—is ominously symmetrical.

In the case of prolific authors like Ovid, it is striking to read multiple books and consider how they connect and illuminate each other. In Ovid's work, taken as a body, obvious connections emerge between the abusive relationship advice he offers in *The Art of Love* and the mythological tales of dysfunctional, exploitative, and at times downright horrifying love affairs that he gathers in his *Metamorphoses*. This epic's transformations are mostly of victims of love-gone-wrong from their human shape into trees, streams, stars, birds of the air, or beasts of the land.

As I read *Metamorphoses* and see its many stories of outright rape and abuse, I suspect that perhaps Ovid was not necessarily approving of the abusive relationships he describes in *The Art of Love*. However, it is hard to be sure about this—and some of Ovid's original readers felt the same way. Busting the neat categories we have in our modern minds, *The Art of Love* belongs to the didactic genre—similar to the instructional manuals and handbooks we considered in chapter 10. Sure, most handbooks have always been in prose, but the Roman world did have some poetic handbooks. For instance, an older contemporary of Ovid, the Epicurean philosopher Lucretius, wrote a didactic poem about the nature of the universe from his philosophical perspective, *On the Nature of Things*. Ovid himself wrote another didactic poem on women's makeup, *The Cosmetics of Women*, as well as another poem of a more serious nature on the Roman religious calendar, *Fasti*. The didactic genre increases ambiguity: Is this a joke, or is he serious? Ancient readers loved *The Art of Love*, but some were apparently as confused as we are. One person particularly puzzled about Ovid's aims in this work was the emperor Augustus himself.

Augustus had made improving public morality and, especially, increasing marriage and childbearing rates among Rome's aristocracy key policy issues during his rule. Unfortunately, his laws, which provided incentives for those who got married and had at least three children and penalties for those who didn't, did not achieve the desired effect. Making matters worse, Augustus's own daughter, Julia, had been caught in adultery. Angry and filled with grief, he exiled her to a small island for the rest of her life.[4]

Therefore, there were apparently ample reasons why, by the time Ovid published *The Art of Love*, Augustus was in no mood to laugh about seduction and extramarital affairs or tolerate a popular writer who seemed to be educating the Roman public in the anti-virtues. In AD 8, Augustus exiled Ovid to the remote city of Tomi on the Black Sea. Devastated, Ovid wrote a series of mournful poems to Augustus, *Tristia* (*Sorrows*), begging for a recall, yet to no avail. He died there ten years later.

Ovid's writing on love reminds us that there are multiple ways to measure the power of words. Audiences also matter in this calculus, for our

4. For an analysis of these complex dynamics in the Age of Augustus, see Kristina Milnor, *Gender, Domesticity, and the Age of Augustus: Inventing Private Life* (Oxford University Press, 2006).

words can reach multiple audiences. However, some of them may be less thrilled to read these words than others. And so, on one level Ovid's writing on love succeeded: Many Romans read him. Even better, he continues to be read now, over two thousand years after his death. Yet the very skill that made him so convincing in his art earned him banishment.

The Elegies of Sulpicia

An unexpected surprise is preserved in the manuscripts of Tibullus, an Augustan elegiac poet: six poems by Sulpicia, an aristocratic woman. These poems, all of them in the first person, describe her love affair with one Cerinthus. Presumably this was not his real name, but she was following the tradition we see in the male elegiac poets of giving a pseudonym to one's love interest.

Sulpicia's poems are surprisingly bold and not what one might have expected from a Roman woman in the age of Augustus—she is eager to spend time with Cerinthus and is jealous of his possible other liaisons. Most of all, her work opens the fascinating possibility that Roman women did write love poetry—yet much of it has not survived due to the accidents of survival. Writers like Sulpicia remind us of an important rule: Absence of evidence is not necessarily evidence of absence.

The Ultimate Love Affair: God and the Soul

The pre-Christian Roman world was undoubtedly a cruel place. As we read the works of Ovid and other Augustan love poets, we cannot help but see just how much more cruel this world could be to women than men. Women felt objectified and exploited, whereas the men felt in charge, using powerful rhetoric to seduce, conquer, and then move on, adding the realm of love to their trophies of Homeric-style victories. Since Ovid repeatedly likens the realm of love to the battlefield, we must remember that the battlefield always has winners and losers. It claims some as victims to crown others as heroes. Alas, the calculus on love's battlefield, as Ovid presents it, seems misogynistic to an extreme.

This ethic was baked into the pre-Christian worldview. In his book *From Shame to Sin: The Christian Transformation of Sexual Morality in Late Antiquity*, historian Kyle Harper explains the difference that Christianity made. Instead of accepting the status quo, the Christians from the beginning held both men and women to the same sexual ethic, condemning the view of love that Ovid held to. If all believers were image-bearers, treasured in God's eyes, and needed to live out this identity, then not only was sexual exploitation off the table but new possibilities were on the table. Among them was the option of lifelong unwed celibacy, with an eye to serving Christ.[5]

But an important question remains: How do we talk about romantic love as Christians? Medieval French writers thought about this question a great deal. In the twelfth century, Bernard of Clairvaux wrote a commentary on the most romantic and, some might say, the most scandalous book of the Bible—the Song of Songs. How many sermons in your churchgoing life have you heard on this book? I'll wait while you count. Still, Bernard's interest in this book might not sound too odd—except that he was a monk. Why would a monk, someone celibate for life, be writing about romance? For Bernard, the answer was simple: It was about the love of God. He believed that the ultimate love affair in which believers engage is the purest and most beautiful of all: the affair of God with the soul. Bernard had this vision in mind as he exegeted the Song of Songs, seeing that book as something much greater than just a story of a king romancing his bride.

The Middle Ages was a time when many were looking for this deeper transcendent meaning, finding it not only in Scripture but also in secular pagan texts. Two centuries after Bernard, an anonymous writer embarked on an ambitious project which we know as *The Moralized Ovid*.[6] A commentary on Ovid's *Metamorphoses*, it does for Ovid's work what Bernard did for the Song of Songs—finding a deeply Christ-rooted meaning and application in every single myth, story, and abusive transformation. This seems

---

5. Kyle Harper, *From Shame to Sin: The Christian Transformation of Sexual Morality in Late Antiquity* (Harvard University Press, 2016).
6. For an English translation, see *The Medieval French Ovide moralisé*, ed. and trans. K. Sarah-Jane Murray and Matthieu Boyd (Boydell & Brewer, 2023).

fitting to say, even though it may feel like a cliché: The greatest transformation we achieve is in Christ. So, medieval French writers remind us that there is more than one way to read a text. When we read writers like Ovid, who seem wholly opposed to what we would term virtue, we should remember that words have power to interpret and redeem other words, especially in the light of the most powerful word of all—the Word that became flesh.

At the same time, the medieval readings of authors like Ovid remind us of an instinctive urge of premodern writers and readers to do something that sadly seems to have gotten pushed out in modern education: shaping our character in the virtues through reading. Books offer us role models for good or ill, teaching us through stories about what it means to live a virtuous or a sinful life, as well as what the virtues even are. This was, for Greeks and Romans alike, a key purpose of both epic poems and of historical texts. Reading for us, just like for them, is never solely for the sake of entertainment, even though this can be valuable. Rather, reading books also opens us up to be changed, molded, and shaped to be better people or citizens. That is the clear goal of certain genres of Roman literature, to which we next turn.

Recommendations for Further Reading

Ovid, *The Erotic Poems*. Translated by Peter Green. Penguin Classics, 2004.

Ovid, *Metamorphoses*. Translated by Stephanie McCarter. Penguin Classics, 2023.

Questions for Discussion and Reflection

1. How do the Roman elegiac poets portray love? Why are the relationships they write about ultimately so unsatisfying and frustrating, even by their own admission?
2. For singles: If your future spouse wrote you a letter, what would you like it to tell you? What kinds of words would you find the

most reassuring and encouraging? For married people: If you have such a letter or communication, how did it assure you of your spouse's love?

3. How might we read Ovid and the other Roman elegiac poets as Christians today? What kind of models for reading do we get from the medieval writers who took it upon themselves to rewrite and reinterpret these earlier classics?

PART

Heroes and Role Models

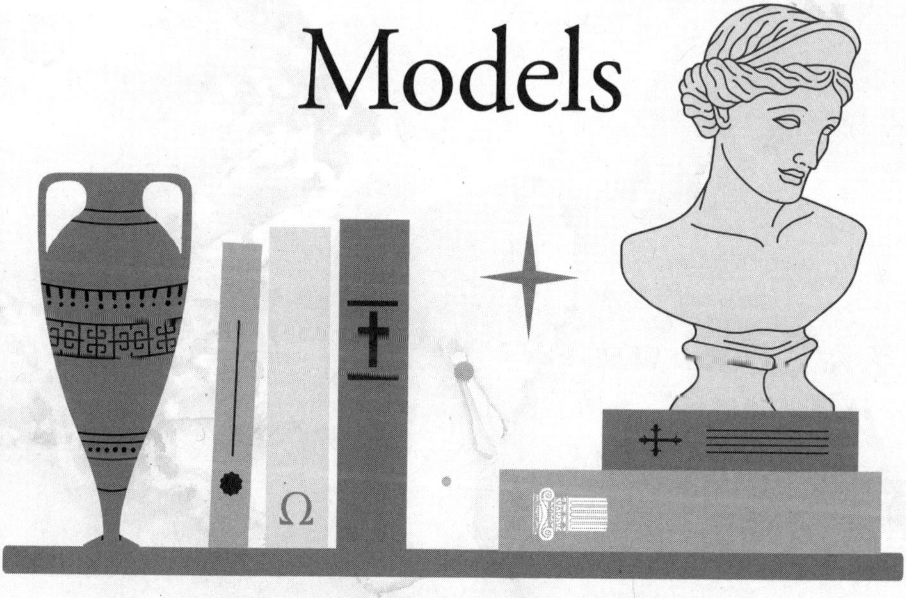

CHAPTER

Cato, Livy, and Exemplarity in the Roman Republic

> The Punic commander advances in the country of Sicily in the first Carthaginian war to meet the Roman army; he is the first to occupy the hills and the favourable positions. The Roman soldiers, as is natural in the situation, enter the area, which was open to trickery and destruction. A tribune comes to the consul and explains to him that annihilation is imminent, as the place is unsuitable and the enemy are on all sides.[1]

History, Anonymous

On a fine April day in the mid-eighth century BC, Romulus killed his twin brother Remus in a dispute over a new settlement they were building in the marshes by the shallow Tiber River. This village didn't look like much at first—and in some versions, Romulus murdered Remus precisely because Remus was making fun of how unimpressive the upstart walls looked. But this little settlement would grow up to become a metropolis—and empire—with a rich history. Yet it would take another six hundred years from that April day for a Roman to write the first-ever history of Rome in Latin.

1. Excerpt from Cato the Elder, *Origines*, in Michael von Albrecht, *Masters of Roman Prose: From Cato to Apuleius*, trans. Neil Adkin (Francis Cairns, 1989), 22.

In the mid-second century BC, Marcus Porcius Cato, the staunch conservative who had dominated Roman politics over the preceding half-century, turned to the final large-scale project of his long and tumultuous life—*Origines* (*Origins*), a history of Rome from its foundation to his time. By the way, he also left us some great cabbage recipes in his treatise *On Agriculture*, all part of burnishing his public image as a proper traditionalist Roman, upholding conservative values. If working the land and growing cabbages was good enough for the heroic Cincinnatus, it was certainly good enough for Cato!

Alas, only one lengthy fragment of *Origines* survives. It does give a good idea of Cato's approach. Sure, Greek models of great historical writing abounded, going back to the days of Herodotus and Thucydides. But Cato had built his entire career on emphasizing the importance of doing everything as a proper Roman ought—including using Latin exclusively for all communications. Just how far did he take this principle? When meeting with Greek ambassadors, despite being fluent in Greek (as all educated Romans were), Cato insisted on speaking in Latin and using a translator. He was certainly not a subtle guy!

Cato applied the same principle of thumbing his nose at all things Greek to his history. In the fragment that survives, he shares an episode of the First Punic War (264–241 BC). The Carthaginians managed to surprise and surround the Roman army somewhere in Sicily. However, a brave Roman tribune comes up with a solution to save the day. He offers to lead a detachment of four hundred soldiers and charge up a nearby hill to occupy it. The enemy will surely attack these four hundred and will slaughter them all. But this diversion will offer just enough distraction for the rest of the Roman army to escape safely and live to fight another day.

Sure enough, things go exactly according to plan, except that the tribune alone miraculously survives the attack and goes on to serve Rome with distinction. Cato suggests that this is divine intervention showing that the gods reward such heroism on Rome's behalf by giving further opportunities for the hero to do similar deeds.

If a certain famous episode in Herodotus's history comes to your mind as you read about this event, you are not mistaken. Yes, the Battle of Thermopylae in 480 BC was where three hundred Spartans heroically stood their ground at a narrow mountain pass. While they were all cut down at the end, they delayed the Persian army long enough for the rest of the Greeks to mobilize. Cato himself would like you to recall this episode, one of the most famous in all of Herodotus and, really, all of Greek history. But he insists that he is emphatically not imitating it. Nothing could be further from the truth:

> But in the evaluation of the same good deed there is a very big difference, depending on the place. The Spartan Leonidas accomplished a similar thing at Thermopylae—and because of his achievements all Greece bestowed on him gratitude and honours in abundance and exalted him with memorials of his glorious deed; with pictures, statues, honorific inscriptions, historical accounts and in other ways they gave expression to their profound gratitude for this deed of his; but for the military tribune there remained only small praise for his deeds, although he had after all done the same thing and rescued the situation for Rome.[2]

Of course, the Romans one-up the Spartans here. Instead of three hundred Spartans, meet four hundred Romans. But there is more. The Spartans fought for glory—and Leonidas especially received the lion's share of that glory as their leader and king. By contrast, the Romans, including the brave tribune, simply fought for Rome. Any Roman would do likewise.

And so, we arrive at the most innovative and unique aspect of Cato's history. Perhaps you noticed it already: There are no names! Who was this brave tribune? Cato isn't telling us.

Many today say (usually condescendingly) that history is just names and dates. But Cato's history had neither: We simply get episodes in sequence, anchored in time by the description of a notable historical event (e.g., the First Punic War). The individuals are identified only by their titles—consul, centurion, or, as in this case, military tribune. What is the point of such a history? For Cato, it is about giving all the glory to Rome rather than to individual Romans. And so, instead of glorifying the accomplishments of individuals (as, he hints, Greek history did), Cato is glorifying Rome and the accomplishments of Romans in general. In the process, his history becomes a powerful and inspiring example for future Romans.

2. Cato the Elder, *Origines*, 22–23.

Homer's epics and Herodotus's *Histories* celebrated heroes. But this is not Sparta; this is Rome. The heroes here are Romans first—or, at least, so Cato dreamed. In the end, his approach to writing history didn't become an example that anyone else followed. And yet the broader goal of Cato's history—to make virtuous Roman men and women by showing them examples of the virtues to imitate—continued. Rome's historians deliberately wrote exemplary histories.

Virtues and Examples

A brief word about, well, words. The term "example" in English doesn't have the force that "exemplum" does in Latin. It's one thing for me to encourage my eight-year-old to be a good example to his five-year-old sister by, say, not complaining about dinner and thereby guaranteeing that she also won't touch the maligned dish. But what about examples that inspire one to become a better person—to do something heroic? Maybe more heroic than trying three bites of Mom's lasagna?

For Romans like Cato and, a little over a century later, Livy, exemplarity was the point of history. The term "exemplum" recurs frequently in Livy, emphasizing to his original audiences why they ought to read his works and remember the stories of famous men and women in them. Not only could they admire such people, but they could try to be more like them.[3] Imitation is not just the sincerest form of flattery; it is the outright goal. Indeed, the best imitation grows into emulation—trying to not just copy one's role models but also outdo them. We talk about the virtues being "caught, not taught," and that is the general principle at hand. But, again, in a larger and cosmic sense, the virtues are more than just a self-improvement project because they aim to point us somewhere beyond our lives here and now.

For Christians, such talk of imitating the virtues of one's role models should remind us of the medieval Latin concept of *imitatio Christi*. This refers to the practice of individuals (real or literary) imitating Christ in some aspect of their life or behavior. It is used especially in describing sacrificial suffering. Every believer is called to imitate Christ, and this is an obvious emphasis in the literary lives of saints and martyrs.

---

3. Jane Chaplin, *Livy's Exemplary History* (Oxford University Press, 2000).

However, both Greeks and Romans revolved this idea of imitation around their own culture heroes—famous generals. So, *imitatio Alexandri*, for instance, refers to the common desire of all generals following Alexander the Great to imitate him. But in spite of all these differences in values between *imitatio Christi* and *imitatio Alexandri*, the same principle of the instructional use of history applies. The kind of history resulting from this goal looks a bit different from the historical writing we expect today.

Did your high school or college history class ever ask you to focus on the moral lessons you can learn from your historical study? Did it ask you to select a role model from history, whose virtues you yourself can imitate going forward? If not, your experience is perfectly normal. That is simply not the goal most modern historians aim to reach in their study of history.

Modern historical research emphasizes uncovering new sources and information to document previously unknown or misunderstood developments and events of the past. In other words, history's primary purpose seeks to emphasize science and discovery. In fact, many modern historians are outspoken in their dislike of seeking heroes in history—and they do have a point. Given the fallen nature of humanity, we know that there was only one individual who lived a perfect human life. He was not Alexander nor Caesar. And so the few modern histories that do openly look for heroes become flattened and inaccurate in their representation of the past—as well as the present. In any case, history has become a science in the modern university—not exactly like, say, chemistry, but still a respectable science with its own research methods and best practices.

Nevertheless, maybe we are the poorer for no longer seeking examples in our academic historical studies (although we still see the continued success of popular-level history and biographies which seek to inspire or motivate general audiences). But do consider again how the Romans looked at history. Roman historians saw the primary purpose of history as making their readers better people—better citizens, better Romans, and better warriors. In other words, exemplary history aimed to shape the character of both readers and hearers in the virtues of Roman citizenship. This included both men and women (although the latter technically weren't citizens)—and so role models were available for both.

Furthermore, while the term *virtus* (from which our modern "virtue" derives) literally means "manliness" and usually referred to battlefield courage of the Homeric variety, we see Roman pagan historians often using it to describe the actions of exemplary women.[4] And so, long before *virtus* became Christianized into something more akin to our modern concept of virtue, it was already undergoing a shift in the writings of Roman historians.

The cliché stereotype that ancient history, and especially Roman history, is that just the study of "dead white men" is all too common. But Livy's inclusion of women as prominent examples of the virtues in his history challenges this assumption and suggests that while Roman women were certainly disadvantaged in myriad ways, their character mattered to Roman society no less than the character of Roman men. On some occasions, even, the women's virtues apparently set the needed example for the men.

The Cardinal Virtues

The virtues that come up in the Roman historians as ideals for all Romans to follow are not new. We initially saw them in Homer, and then learned how Plato and Aristotle further developed their importance to cultivate the good character of individuals. In the Middle Ages, they would be considered the cardinal virtues—since they preceded Christianity, both pagans and Christians could claim them. These virtues are justice, prudence, temperance, and fortitude. Faith, hope, and love would join them later as theological or heavenly Christian virtues. For now, our story in this chapter considers a world that recognized and privileged the cardinal virtues, even if it did not have a clear term for them.

Lucretia: The Roman Bathsheba

The story sounds familiar in some respects. A member of the royal family, enthralled with the beauty of a married woman in his city, secretly raped

4. For an analysis of this term in the Roman Republic, see Miles McDonnell, *Roman Manliness:* Virtus *and the Roman Republic* (Cambridge University Press, 2006).

her while her husband was away on a military campaign. However, events in this case turned out differently than what we may remember from the Bible.

Instead of keeping the secret, as Bathsheba did after her encounter with David, this woman immediately summoned her father and husband, asking them to also bring witnesses. When they arrived, she told them about the rape, bemoaning the dishonor that it had brought upon her. Asking the men in her family to avenge this crime if they are "real men," she promptly committed suicide, proclaiming that no woman in the future would use her as an example of tolerating such dishonor. There it is—the *exemplum* or example that the Roman historian Livy presents for all Roman wives. We see that an honorable Roman wife needs to take action to preserve both her honor and that of her family. If her life is the cost of retaining honor, so be it.

This horrific tale is the rape of Lucretia by Sextus Tarquinius, one of the sons of the seventh and final king of Rome. It is one of the most famous episodes from Livy's *Ab Urbe Condita*, a history of Rome from the city's founding to the Augustan age, and it offers intriguing parallels to the story of Bathsheba. But instead of relying on God's restoration of justice, the men themselves bear the burden of administering justice on Lucretia's behalf.

Lucretia brilliantly models all four of the cardinal virtues. She has a desire for justice—which she demands the men to execute on her behalf. She displays prudence (wisdom) in wisely assembling the men most likely to follow through with this pursuit of justice. Livy describes her temperance—quietly spinning wool at home while her husband was absent on his campaign—as the quality that ironically attracted the evil Tarquin to rape her. Finally, her fortitude (bravery) leads her to kill herself rather than live in dishonor. Such a suicide—with a dagger, no less—is a hero's death.

Lucretia's dramatic suicide spurs revenge and revolution. Lucius Junius Brutus, who came as a witness with Lucretia's husband, picks up the bloody knife with which she had killed herself and uses it as a visual symbol to incite an aristocratic revolution against the king. The last king of Rome is promptly expelled from the city, elections are speedily held, and the first two consuls of what is now the Roman Republic are elected: Brutus and—believe it or not—Lucretia's widower, Tarquinius Collatinus. The latter's very name suggests that he is also a relative of the royal family, but Livy chooses to let that awkward detail slide by without comment until a bit later.

But there is more to consider. After all, while the wrongdoer is punished in the Roman story, the only person who, as far as we hear, actually dies as a result of the wrongdoing is Lucretia. While we think of her as the victim, in the Roman context even Lucretia herself apparently was not sure that she was a victim. If asked whether this was adultery or rape, Lucretia—and at least some Roman audiences—would possibly not have seen the difference. And so, while demanding revenge on Sextus Tarquinius, Lucretia considers her dishonor worthy of punishment by death, a penalty that sometimes applied to adultery in the Roman world. The Roman framework allows no redemption for her suffering. Without the heavenly virtues of faith, hope, and love, only revenge is left.

As we consider how Bathsheba's story turns out in contrast with the story of Lucretia, we see God's care, provision, and sorrow for the hurting and the oppressed. God cares about justice for victims like Bathsheba and does not overlook the disruptions of justice that sin wreaks upon the world. And, specifically, God doesn't demand from Bathsheba the kind of horrific penalty that Lucretia exacted upon herself, because his mercy rests on all who suffer.

Of course we know this, but the original Roman audiences didn't. They instead saw this episode as a tale of heroic feminine virtue spurring men into action. Left unsaid is this question: If the kings were so evil and corrupt, why didn't the Romans overthrow them earlier? Indeed, that is the shameful implication here. It took a woman to convict the men and tell them to do the right thing—"If you are men."

Cloelia: The Exemplary *Virtus* of Roman Women

Not long after the Romans expelled the king and installed the Republic, the Etruscans, led by King Porsinna, attacked the tiny state. They must have hoped for an easy victory, but the conflict hardened into a stalemate. Eventually the Etruscans requested hostages, whom the Romans had to surrender to maintain a temporary peace. These hostages were a group of young Roman men and women, presumably of aristocratic birth, and they were held at the Etruscan camp right across the Tiber from Rome proper. This location will prove significant.[5]

---

5. Livy tells this story in *History of Rome*, 2.13.5–11.

One of the hostages, a young woman named Cloelia, displayed considerable pluck and leadership skills. Livy tells us that she, along with a band of other female hostages, managed to deceive the guards. How? It is unclear. Perhaps they orchestrate a distraction of some sort. At any rate, a group of young women plunge into the Tiber and swim across the river back to Rome, as enemy arrows and javelins dramatically rain all around them. Miraculously, they all make it back to safety—no one is lost.

Yet again, we see the cardinal virtues in action. Cloelia leads with impressive fortitude and inspires the other women who follow her. Unlike most male military leaders, she doesn't lose any of her followers in the escape. Her successful planning, including a ruse of some sort, showed prudence—a discerning kind of wisdom in a difficult situation. Her virtues impress even Porsinna.

Porsinna doesn't care about the other hostages who escaped, but he demands that the Romans restore Cloelia to his custody. Once she is returned, however, he frees her as a reward for her bravery. Furthermore, he allows her to choose additional hostages to take back to Rome with her. Showing her prudence again, Cloelia asks to free some of the young men. Livy explains that this was a sage choice, as it showed Cloelia's recognition that these men were in potential danger while in custody. Perhaps they were being treated more harshly than the women. Besides, Rome needed them in its army.

Lucretia's virtues inspired Roman men to do something important that perhaps they should have done earlier—fight for their freedom and overthrow the tyrannical king. On the other hand, Cloelia's virtues inspire not only the Romans (due to her preservation of the other women who swam across the river with her), but also the Etruscans. The virtue of one Roman woman became an *exemplum* fit to inspire a foreign king.

On a Beach in Greece

The Aegean beach vacation seemed perfect at first, a welcome respite from the hard labor that they knew loomed ahead. But as the days of waiting turned into weeks, the vacation turned into a nightmare from which they could not escape. Their walks on the beach, so magical at first and a glorious leisure, were now just one mindless activity to feel like they were doing something to keep busy.

This strange scene comes from a second-century BC tragedy, *Iphigenia*, by the leading Roman poet of the day, Ennius, a contemporary of our friend Cato the Elder. Only fragments from this tragedy survive, and the most famous of those is a mournful speech delivered by the chorus of Greek soldiers stuck on this gorgeous beach, remarking on the paradoxical aimlessness yet necessity of continuing to pace from one area of the beach to another.

Writers of the Roman Republic adapted many Greek myths into their own tragedies, and *Iphigenia*, whose plot is set right before the Trojan War, was no exception. But discussions of complex Roman cultural values and, at times, crises of the day were at the core of these plays. And so, stranded on this lovely beach while waiting for favorable winds so they could sail to Troy, this chorus of Greek soldiers echoes such Roman Republican politicians as Cato who bemoaned the excess of *otium*—the Roman term for leisure.

Otium—the diametric opposite of *negotium*, the state of being busy, on task, or at work—was held to be the ideal state of existence in Roman society, for this leisurely state of being was essential for philosophical reflection, writing, and any meaningful life of the mind. But, as the Greek soldier chorus notes, too much of a good thing nullifies its original goodness. What about a life defined by an excess of *negotium*, instead? If an excess of free time is problematic, is an excess of busyness any better? This question is not a merely theoretical issue; it has significant implications for the shaping of character in the virtues. We become what we think, what we do, and what we value.

But this conflict between leisure and busyness at the forefront of the beach episode is not the key to resolving the problem. After all, the problem is caused by an absence of something—or, rather, someone—who should be there, but isn't. This story, in effect, is the opposite of the tale of the heroic tribune that Cato tells in his *Origines*.

All soldiers are used to following orders from a commander. In Ennius's tragedy, however, no one is at hand to lead them or to set an example of virtue in the moment. Instead, they aimlessly follow each other, setting an example of futility in the absence of good leadership and good role models. The message is clear: The absence of good examples to follow can be deeply destructive to a society.

This lesson was not lost. A century and a half after Ennius, the emperor Augustus fully agreed. He accordingly commissioned Vergil, the leading poet of the day, to craft a Roman national epic. This tale would not only imitate but would downright rival the Homeric epics. In the process, it would craft the quintessential Roman hero as the best *exemplum* for all Roman men—pious Aeneas.

Recommendations for Further Reading

Livy, *The Early History of Rome, Books I-V.* Translated by Aubrey de Sélincourt. Penguin Classics, 2002.

Livy, *The War with Hannibal, Books 21–30.* Translated by Aubrey de Sélincourt. Penguin Classics, 1965.

Questions for Discussion and Reflection

1. What do you think about Cato's experimental approach to history? Try to retell a story from American history without using any names. How does it change your view of the familiar history to leave out the names?
2. What virtues do we see in the stories of women that Livy tells? Can you think of any additional virtues or heroic qualities in these stories beyond those discussed in this chapter? How does reading these stories as a Christian shape your perspective on them?
3. To what extent do you find yourself relying on examples in your life? Who are your role models, and how have they become your role models?

CHAPTER

Vergil's Exemplary Romans[1]

I'll begin to sing of what keeps the wheat fields happy,
under what stars to plough the earth, and fasten vines to elms,
what care the oxen need, what tending cattle require,
Maecenas, and how much skill's required for the thrifty bees.[2]

Restoring the Golden Age

A few years ago, when we still lived in Georgia, I planted a small garden in my yard. Since the earth under the thin carpet of grass—mostly wild onions, to be honest—was all exhausted clay, I bought a few bags of real dirt all jazzed up with Miracle-Gro. I wasn't sure how all of this would work, but I knew the basics: You stick some seeds in this dirt in the spring once night frost is no longer a danger and you try to remember to occasionally water and weed the soil. Eventually, some green edible stuff will sprout, keeping the family supplied with zucchini and radishes all summer long.

The experiment sort of worked during this first year. The radishes were anemic and mostly grew green tops. We used them for salad—it was not the best, but we felt that we were eating the work of our hands. At least the zucchini and squash lived up to expectations, producing abundantly until fall. But in the second year, a worm got into the soil and all the zucchini

1. You will find some modern authors spelling Vergil as "Virgil," with an "i" instead of an "e." Both spellings are acceptable, but "Vergil" is closer to the Latin "Vergilius."
2. Vergil, *Georgics* 1.1–4, trans. A. S. Kline, Poetry in Translation, accessed March 6, 2025, https://www.poetryintranslation.com/PITBR/Latin/VirgilGeorgicsI.php.

and squash wilted. I suddenly understood how the original Jonah (not my middle son—his namesake) felt when his beloved plant died.

In the third year, I tried planting okra, hearing how well this native African plant does in the Georgia heat. Then we went on a two-week family vacation and I forgot that I had even planted anything. Imagine my surprise later that summer when massive okra plants actually flourished in my tiny garden, producing gorgeous pods that are so delightful when sautéed in some olive oil with a little bit (or a lot) of garlic.

I think of the description of the garden of Eden in Genesis 2. It flourished—it just did. The curse of the fall made farming and gardening the hard work that they are today. Long before Christ, ancient mythology also had similar stories—tales of a long-gone time of effortless flourishing for all living things. Ancient writers were convinced that there had once been a golden age of mankind. During this time, as the Greek poet Hesiod reflected (and as we discussed in chapter 2), people were close to the gods, plants flowered without requiring much care, and diseases stayed away, allowing people to live much longer and more enjoyable lives. Romans additionally connected this golden age with their god Saturn, who ensured the flourishing of peace and agriculture.

Over half a millennium after Hesiod, an ambitious Roman politician made the restoration of the golden age of mankind the focus of his political image. To be fair, much restoration seemed to be needed in the broken Republic of his day. Like all politicians, he knew that he was certainly the right man for the job.

After a century of steadily escalating political instability and outright violence in the Roman Republic, Julius Caesar's grandnephew and adopted heir somehow emerged as the last man standing in 31 BC, when he defeated Mark Antony and Cleopatra in the Battle of Actium. But the resulting peace was initially uneasy. Over the ensuing decades until his death in AD 14, Augustus carved out a new and unprecedented degree of power for himself. Today we call him Rome's first emperor—but during his lifetime he actually went by the more demure title of *princeps*, first citizen. In this capacity, he embarked on restoring the Golden Age of Saturn in Rome. But how to do it?

This political underpinning is crucial for understanding the Augustan literary boom. Great art can flourish more easily in a time of peace and stability, especially when patronage exists. Since many Augustan writers were not independently wealthy, they needed patrons. Additionally, Augustus was, we could say, the original culture warrior.

What is a subtle way to effect political and social change in a society under stress? Augustus understood that changing the culture was key to making his desired changes "stick." And changing the culture meant, in this case, promoting the message of restoring peace, joy, and flourishing—of people, of nature, and of Rome. And so the Augustan propaganda focused on all things beautiful—having public gardens and festivals all around Rome, commissioning new art to beautify the city, and subsidizing a whole cadre of poets and prose writers. Augustus also threw regular public feasts, because (it turns out) people of all ages and in all periods of human history have appreciated a free lunch.

This is the age of elegiac poets like Ovid, Propertius, and Tibullus; the satirist Horace; and the astrologer poet Manilius. On the prose side of things, this is also the age of the historian Livy, the famed architect Vitruvius, and many more writers who were famous during their day but are now largely forgotten. Indeed, there was no shortage of great writing during the Age of Augustus. But if we had to name one great poet who overshadowed all his contemporaries, Vergil would be preeminent.

Augustus was not a very likable guy, but he knew the value of beautiful words in renewing culture and the spirits of people worn down by decades of civil war and political instability. In writing stunning poetry to please Augustus, earn a salary, and encourage the Roman people all in one fell swoop, Vergil's first choice of topic in his poetry does not seem political at first glance: farming. It's just about loving the land, working it, and seeing it flourish again. And yet ever present under the surface are the reminders of the civil wars that were still in living memory. Vergil repeatedly reminds his readers that only Augustus maintains this peace that in turn allows the humble bees to do their work again.[3] But more Romans need to grow in the virtues that will allow them to support the state in various ways. Thus, the Roman state needs role models—those examples that Livy also wrote about in his history.

---

3. A more recent novel by a Ukrainian writer, Andrey Kurkov's *Grey Bees* (Deep Vellum, 2018), gets at this same theme. It focuses on the plight of a Ukrainian beekeeper who worries for his bees, since they are creatures who do not understand war.

Of Men and Bees

Go to the ant, you sluggard;
    consider its ways and be wise!
It has no commander,
    no overseer or ruler,
yet it stores its provisions in summer
    and gathers its food at harvest.[4]

So wrote Solomon in his Proverbs to encourage the people of Israel, but it could just as easily have been written by Vergil in late first-century BC Rome to inspire the Age of Augustus. The wise ant, Solomon notes, is a wonderful role model of industriousness for people, who might be tempted to be lazy when the weather is nice. But the easy-come fruits of summer should not lull one into relaxing. Without storing away provisions for winter—without hard work all summer long—one will starve. The agricultural life is an annual cycle that predictably repeats—or, better, renews itself—year after year. By necessity it also conditions people in a number of virtues. Like it or not, hard work from which people cannot escape has that effect on them.

Vergil opens his agricultural epic poem *Georgics* on a similar note, with an ode to bees and the agricultural life:

> I'll begin to sing of what keeps the wheat fields happy,
> under what stars to plough the earth, and fasten vines to elms,
> what care the oxen need, what tending cattle require,
> Maecenas, and how much skill's required for the thrifty bees.[5]

The bees are hard workers, but the farmer must also labor to support them if he is to profit from their labor. Therein lies the value of both the bees and the farmers as role models for Augustus's new golden age.

It is quietly normal and glorious to write beautiful epic poetry on some of the most mundane of actions—ploughing the wheat fields, tending grape vines, caring for beasts of burden and dairy cattle, and keeping bees. The

4. Proverbs 6:6–8.
5. Vergil, *Georgics* 1.1–4.

ideal farm was entirely self-sufficient—able to produce everything needed for life. We see such a farm in action in the *Georgics*: It produces its own bread and wine side by side with its own meat, dairy, and honey. Interestingly, this poem is not the work of a farmer! Vergil is a voluntary exile from the world of farming. He is now an urban poet who waxes eloquent over the life of a farmer to his patron, Maecenas, who is an urban (and urbane) wealthy businessman.

But the bees are also natural poets and thus fitting companions to Vergil's work. They produce their own steady rhythmic music as they go about their work. They cannot stop their steady buzzing any more than they can stop making honey. In this regard, they are no different from the poet, who also cannot stop creating verse. And so, in the first book of this strange mix of matter-of-fact farming advice dispensed in epic language and meter, Vergil presents an overview of the agricultural year. An astute reader will recall Hesiod's *Works and Days*, in addition to Proverbs. The advice revolves around seasons of the year and the many tasks that must be done during each season. In the second book of *Georgics* Vergil turns to viticulture, while the third book considers care of livestock.

We gain an important perspective from knowing that while the poem has a didactic feel, Vergil's audiences were fellow well-to-do urban dwellers, appreciators of poetry but only admiring farming from afar. The farmers he lauds were too busy taking care of their land. Besides (and perhaps even more significant), a full generation before Vergil, much of Italy had already been taken over by wealthy senators and speculators buying up small farms to consolidate their own massive estates. The small farmers of the mid-Republic were long gone, displaced into cities and replaced by slave labor working the large-scale farms belonging to absentee landlords. But Vergil is in the midst of this loud absence, still praising farmers. His work seems to suggest that role models do not have to be real—they just have to inspire.

The independent small farmer, self-sufficient in all his needs, is a creature more legend than reality in the age of Vergil and Augustus. His ideal as painted in poetry echoes modern tradlife more than actual farming life in any historical period. In reality, he is vulnerable—subject to natural forces over which he has no control. Indeed, *Georgics* concludes with a vivid and visceral description of a plague that once devastated the cattle and also threatened the farmer himself. All this work is necessary—one cannot do without it. But doing it all is still no guarantee of success, either—yet failure may be costly.

Ultimately, *Georgics* ends on a note of despair. Even Augustus can only do so much to restore a true golden age. Plagues will still happen, even under the rule of the self-proclaimed prince of peace—who, of course, wasn't the real Prince of Peace. These plagues will befall any good farmers who are left. But then, plagues also happen to poets. Death spares no one—yet the bee doesn't care. Despair will get you nowhere. Besides, there is too much work still left to do. The ant agrees.

The Ploughman's Lunch

Also attributed to Vergil (but unlikely to have been written by him) is a curious shorter poem, less epic in scope—just 142 lines—about a garlic-cheese paste dish, *moretum*, often translated as "The Ploughman's Lunch." This poem describes the hard work of the farmer leading up to lunch, and includes the preparation of said lunch with ingredients on hand—fresh (and, needless to say, homemade) goat cheese, greens from the farm, lots and lots of garlic, salt, olive oil, and vinegar.

I have previously prepared a version of this recipe myself, relying on modern ingredients. It has a strong flavor on its own but goes well over hardboiled eggs or bread. I was reminded that the Romans consumed massive amounts of garlic—a useful natural antibiotic in the days of pre-modern medicine.

"I Sing of Arms and a Man"

A graffito survives near a doorway to a private residential building in the Roman city of Pompeii. It is an incomplete hexameter line of poetry: *fullones ululam ego cano*—"I sing of fullers and the owl."[6] Our vandal graffiti artist

6. Fullers were laundry professionals—most people did not do laundry at home in the Roman world. For a picture of this graffito and other information on fullers and their businesses, see "The fulleries (*fullonicae*)," Ostia, accessed April 3, 2025, https://www.ostia-antica.org/dict/topics/fullones/intro.htm.

appears to have been not only a man of fine humor but also someone who had at least some pretense at literary education. The house owner had every right to be annoyed, but we can laugh at the artist's wit. We're not the ones stuck with a defaced wall!

This graffito is clearly a spoof on the most famous line in all of Roman poetry. Even the barely literate knew this line, as its prevalence in other graffiti and inscriptions around the Roman world attests. This is the opening of Vergil's *Aeneid*: *Arma virumque cano*—"I sing of arms and a man."

After writing two large-scale poetry collections on the virtues of agriculture—*Eclogues* and *Georgics*—Vergil spent the final decade of his life composing (on commission from Augustus) what would become Rome's national epic, its *Iliad* and *Odyssey* all in one. His subject? The mythical hero Aeneas, a Trojan prince who is a minor character in the *Iliad*. In Roman lore, Aeneas dramatically escaped from burning Troy, sailed to Italy, and became the founder of Rome. Sort of—to be precise, he founded the city (Lavinium) that would found another city (Alba Longa) that would ultimately found Rome. I realize that it's confusing when you spell all this out.

To be fair, this patchworked explanation wasn't so important to the Romans. It mattered most that Aeneas was the ancestor of Romulus, Rome's founder, which gave the Romans a direct line back to Homer. Sure, the Greeks won the Trojan War in the Homeric epics. But through the myth of Aeneas the Romans got the last word—and the best Homeric hero of all. Move over, Achilles. Sure, Aeneas wasn't the Best of the Achaeans. He wasn't even the Best of the Trojans—that title belonged to Hector. But he was the First of the Romans.

As the First of the Romans, living in the shadow of a prophecy whose fulfillment he will not get to see, Aeneas is the Roman hero and *exemplum* par excellence. But of what is he an example? He certainly is a military hero, a great example of the Roman *virtus* as martial glory—and *arma* (military arms) is the first word of the epic about him. Yet the epithet Vergil repeatedly uses for Aeneas is nonmilitary—unlike the epithets that Homer uses for heroes (e.g., swift-footed, he of the shining helmet, godlike, lord of men). Instead, Vergil calls Aeneas *pius Aeneas*.

What does *pius* mean, and why use it, as opposed to more Homeric options that Vergil could have selected? The English "pious" is not a commonly used term, although you may be more familiar with its noun form—piety. "Piety" in English means devotion to God. It describes a life ruled by religious obedience. The same is true in Vergil's Latin—except, of course, with one significant difference: The religious obedience is to the pagan gods rather than to Christ.

The Romans from their earliest days believed in the *pax deorum*: A peace with the gods that served as a sort of social contract between them and the Romans. So long as the Romans worshipped them correctly and reverently, the gods would protect the Romans. But the gods punished any disrespect from people. That punishment could take the form of military disaster, plagues, or famine. In such a system, piety becomes a key feature of heroes and role models.[7] A leader who is pious and who can mediate between the nation and the gods can strengthen the fragile peace with the gods. After all, as we know from mythology, the gods are quick to take offense. And so, Vergil wrote his Roman national epic to give us the tale of divine provision—and human obedience or piety—in the founding of Rome.

Divine Provision

Readers in antiquity were already describing the first six books of the *Aeneid* as Vergil's *Odyssey* and the second six books as his *Iliad*. It is a strange beginning—storm and shipwreck, *Odyssey* style. The storm is caused by the wrath of Juno, the queen of the gods, who likes the Greeks but abhors the Trojans. But through divine provision—most notably the patronage of Venus, the goddess of love who also happens to be Aeneas's mom—the Trojans crash as safely as possible on the shore of North Africa. Venus gets her other son, Cupid, to make the queen of the place, Dido, fall in love with Aeneas. Thus, divine provision for him in this place is assured.

So what is this place where the Trojans crashed? It turns out to be none other than Carthage, Rome's most dreaded enemy. The Romans had fought three brutal wars against Carthage before finally razing the city to the ground for good in 146 BC. But at this point, during the mythical times right after the Trojan War, Carthage is merely under construction and supervised by the capable eye of Queen Dido.

---

7. For a survey of Roman religion and the specific differences between Roman religious beliefs and those of Christians, see Nijay Gupta, *Strange Religion: How the First Christians Were Weird, Dangerous, and Compelling* (Brazos Press, 2024).

The audiences learn what happened before the shipwreck through Aeneas's conversations with Dido. He tells her in vivid detail how Troy was sacked through the ruse of the Trojan Horse, narrating the atrocities that befell the city as Greeks spared no one. Over four centuries later, that part of the *Aeneid* came vividly to Augustine's mind as he reflected on the Gothic sack of Rome in AD 410.

Aeneas had miraculously escaped the burning city of Troy, along with some others. Dramatically, he fled while carrying his aged father Anchises (who clutched the household gods) on his back and holding his young son's hand. Aeneas's wife, Creusa, was supposed to be walking behind him, but after escaping from the city he discovered that he had lost her. Honestly, this part of the narrative has always rankled me; why did he not make sure she was safe? Creusa's ghost eventually appeared to him, offering a prophecy: The gods have ordained that Aeneas will reach Italy, found a great nation, and get a new wife there. Convenient!

Perhaps after hearing this tale and the prominent role of prophecies looming therein, Dido should have adopted some caution. Instead, book four of the epic, a self-standing episode, is the story of her tragic romance with Aeneas. Dido tries to convince him to remain in Carthage, and he is apparently happy to stay. Who wouldn't prefer stability to an uncertain voyage, after all? Alas, the gods order Aeneas to leave. Worried about Dido's reaction, he and his men quietly load their ships and sneak away in the night. Devastated, Dido kills herself with the sword Aeneas had left behind. As she slowly dies, she curses him:

> Our shores will clash, weapons and seas collide.
> My curse is war for Trojans and their children.[8]

This curse, Vergil's audiences knew, was the Punic Wars. Here is Roman history interwoven into the epic, suggesting divine control over these centuries of events leading up to the present—the time of Augustus. Indeed, in book six Aeneas descends to the underworld to consult his dead father. By way of encouragement for Aeneas as he prepares to face the struggles and war ahead, Anchises parades in front of him the glories of Rome's future. He

8. Vergil, *The Aeneid*, trans. Sarah Ruden (Yale University Press, 2008), 4.628–29.

names all the heroes into the age of Augustus, even including the nephew of Augustus, Marcellus, for whose untimely youthful death the entire underworld also weeps. Vergil clearly knew which side his bread was buttered on when he included this scene to console the mourning *princeps*.

The poem's final five books are devoted to the war in Italy, which Aeneas is not eager to fight but cannot avoid. Yet again pious Aeneas is simply doing what the gods command, even though it viscerally pains him. Vergil gives his audiences a real Roman *Iliad* here, with stunning poetic battle sequences along with new heroes and villains. And, like the Trojan War, this war is also over a woman—Lavinia, the princess who was supposed to marry the local prince Turnus but is now fated to marry Aeneas.

The poem concludes with a dramatic duel of Aeneas and Turnus. Looking upon the wounded Turnus surrendering at his feet, Aeneas momentarily feels compassion even for this enemy. But then he notices the belt that Turnus had earlier stripped from Aeneas's young ally Pallas:

> Aeneas stared—the spoils commemorated
> His wild grief, and he burned with hideous rage.
> "Will you escape, in loot from one of mine?
> It's Pallas who's now stabbing you, to offer
> Your vicious blood in payment for your crime."
> Incensed, he thrust the sword through Turnus' chest.
> His enemy's body soon grew cold and helpless,
> While the indignant soul flew down to Hades.[9]

Homer's *Iliad* had begun with the rage of Achilles and ended with the funeral of Patroclus, whose death Aeneas had avenged. Vergil's *Aeneid* ends with the rage of Aeneas. Pious Aeneas is pious to the end, avenging his friend just as the Romans asserted they did in their alliances.

But was this the ending Vergil had in mind? We cannot know for sure. Vergil was a notorious perfectionist. Composing on average just one line of poetry per day, he was not satisfied with the state of his epic. On his deathbed he ordered it to be burned, but Augustus overruled him. The *Aeneid*

9. Vergil, *Aeneid* 12.945–52.

was quickly published and became an immediate sensation throughout the Roman world. Through public recitations and its extensive use in education from the very day of publication, it became an instant classic in every sense of the term and earned a place of honor even in graffiti.

Awaiting the Messiah

Vergil's audiences did get the glorious Roman epic to buoy their spirits in the Augustan Age and beyond. But beautiful as the *Aeneid* is, something is missing. There is much suffering, but is the founding of Rome a proper goal for all this pain and brutality? It just doesn't feel adequate or redemptive. Isn't there more to life than suffering through war and atrocities just so you can get to the Age of Augustus, with its pretty temples and occasional free public lunches?

Vergil apparently also wondered about this. In his poem *Eclogue* 4, he tells a tale not about the golden age of Augustus but of a different one yet to come. It will be the age when justice reigns, and it will all begin in nature. Goats will herd themselves home to be milked, poisonous snakes and plants will die off, and sheep will turn their wool into all the colors of the rainbow to assist spinners. But who will bring about such an age? A certain child, a mere babe.

Vergil died in 19 BC, before Christ's birth, but in this poem we see a transcendent longing stronger than elsewhere in his poetry. It expresses a conviction that the present world is not the only world there is. We realize that this baby is an *exemplum* even more powerful than Aeneas. While Aeneas, the model of piety, obeyed the gods and founded Rome, this baby will restore a cosmic peace. Earthly heroes will never be perfect. Thankfully, there is one who was and is and forever more will be.

By Late Antiquity, Christians were interpreting this eclogue as prophesying the birth of Christ. They dubbed it the "Messianic Eclogue," a title that became firmly established during the Middle Ages. The work's longing for a savior coming to earth in the form of a mere child redeemed and transformed Vergil himself in the eyes of his Christian readers. Vergil, as Dante was convinced over 1,300 years later, knew things others did not.

Recommendations for Further Reading

Vergil, *The Aeneid.* Translated by Sarah Ruden. Yale University Press, 2008 and 2021 (revised edition).

Vergil, *The Aeneid.* Translated by Robert Fagles. Penguin Classics, 2010.

Vergil, *The Aeneid.* Translated by Shadi Bartsch. Random House, 2021.

Virgil, *The Eclogues and the Georgics.* Translated by C. Day Lewis. Oxford World's Classics, 2009.

Questions for Discussion and Reflection

1. What is *pax deorum*? Why is it so important for our understanding of the Roman literary imagination?
2. What are Aeneas's main virtues in Vergil's *Aeneid*? What kind of a hero is Aeneas, and what do we learn about the Romans from his presentation as the ideal Roman?
3. Why is Vergil so interested in agriculture? What similarities do we see between his agricultural writings and the teachings on agriculture and work in the book of Proverbs?

CHAPTER

Tacitus on How to Be a Good Man Under a Bad Emperor

> So long as he was a subject, he seemed too great a man to be one, and by common consent possessed the makings of a ruler—had he never ruled.[1]

Qualifications: On Paper vs. Reality

In 1968, Richard Nixon capped a very successful decades-long political career with his election to the presidency. Brilliant in all he had done—including a stint as vice president under Dwight Eisenhower—he seemed a true golden boy. A successful first term as president followed, during which he ended (to much applause) the American involvement in Vietnam. Four years later, he easily won reelection for a second term—by a massive margin. Then came Watergate. His reputation in tatters, Nixon ignominiously resigned to avoid impeachment, avoiding jail only because of his successor Gerald Ford's pardon.

It has become a cliché to talk about qualifications on paper as opposed to reality. Nixon's story applies here, but this scenario has a long history—especially in politics. The first-century Roman historian Tacitus noted this same contrast in a particularly poignant description of Galba, emperor for just six months from June AD 68 to January AD 69: Galba, quipped

1. Tacitus, *The Histories*, trans. Kenneth Wellesley (Penguin Classics, 1995), 46.

Tacitus, would have been a great emperor had he never ruled. Ouch! Both Tacitus's writings and American presidential history show that all too often the "on paper" qualifications we have in mind involve tangible credentials like education, family and social status, and experience.

Impeccable credentials aren't bad criteria. Someone in charge of a corporation or an empire or a university needs to be knowledgeable. Experience is also helpful. Qualifications for a position of responsibility matter, because they show that the individual has the right preparation to be able to do the job and handle the unexpected crises that invariably come with it. But Tacitus notes that another key ingredient was missing in Galba, and people did not realize this until it was too late: character. That same ingredient, Americans learned to their chagrin during the Watergate scandal, was also missing in Nixon.

Too often, as another cliché goes, power corrupts. And power specifically corrupts character. Virtuous individuals are always vulnerable to power's erosion of their qualities. But power will only make things much, much worse for someone utterly lacking in virtues. In discussing the four different emperors who successively ruled Rome in AD 69, Tacitus observes about the last one, Vespasian: "He alone—unlike all the emperors before him—changed for the better."[2]

Tacitus would know. Born ca. AD 55, he would have been a teenager in AD 69, the tumultuous Year of the Four Emperors which plunged the entire empire into civil war and crisis. It all started in June of AD 68, when the unstable emperor Nero committed suicide, certain that he was about to be overthrown (which was probably true).[3] Galba, proclaimed emperor by the Praetorian Guard, stayed in power until January of AD 69, when Otho won the favor of the Guard. The soldiers promptly assassinated Galba and installed Otho. But the army in Germany had simultaneously declared its own commander, Vitellius, emperor.

The armies of Vitellius and Otho clashed in the First Battle of Bedriacum (also known as the First Battle of Cremona) in April of AD 69. Otho committed suicide and Vitellius took power. However, elsewhere the armies of Vespasian, who had been engaged this entire time in the Jewish

---

2. Tacitus, *The Histories*, 47.

3. However, some modern historians have tried to rehabilitate Nero a bit—for instance, Edward Champlin, *Nero* (Belknap Press, 2005).

War, also proclaimed him emperor. Vespasian left his son Titus in charge of besieging Jerusalem and returned to Italy. In December, he defeated Vitellius in the Second Battle of Bedriacum (or the Second Battle of Cremona) and established a new imperial dynasty—the Flavians.

If you found this super-fast race through the Year of the Four Emperors a bit whiplash-inducing, imagine having to live through it all, as teenaged Tacitus did. Admittedly, without modern communication methods the spread of information was only as fast as the speed of a horse carrying messengers and letters. We also do not know if Tacitus grew up in Italy, but he may not have—in the late AD 70s he married the daughter of Gnaeus Julius Agricola, a senator from Gallia Narbonensis (in today's southern France).

In typical Roman fashion, Tacitus trained as an orator and eventually entered politics. It is funny to think about his nickname—Tacitus, meaning "quiet." Maybe in person he was taciturn, but not in his writing! His historical works include the *Annals*, a year-by-year history of Rome from the death of Augustus (AD 14) to the death of Nero (AD 68). He continued that work with his *Histories*, which picked up where the *Annals* ended, and meant to cover everything until his present time. Alas, only the portion of the narrative about AD 68–69 survives. Tacitus also wrote shorter works: *Agricola*, a laudatory biography of his father-in-law; *Germania*, a treatise on the customs of German tribes which gives modern anthropologists really bad heartburn; and *Dialogue on Orators*, a survey of rhetorical styles and famous rhetoricians.

But Tacitus was, first and foremost, a career politician, and his experiences in politics undoubtedly shaped his writings. While Vespasian's new Flavian dynasty seemed to start on a good note, his son Titus died young after ruling for just two years (AD 79–81). Vespasian's younger son, Domitian, ended up being an emperor in the mold of Tiberius, Caligula, and Nero—vengeful, suspicious of everyone, and periodically launching purges. Everyone was relieved by his assassination in AD 96, which ushered in a period of relative stability. But those living through this era could not have known for sure that better times were imminent.

Writing under a friendlier emperor, Trajan (ruled AD 98–117), Tacitus looks back at that grimmer period of Roman history—the tumultuous rule of the Julio-Claudian dynasty, the cruel empire-wide civil wars of AD 69 that followed the suicide of Nero in AD 68, and the tyrannical rule of

Domitian (AD 81–96). Bad emperors, Tacitus knew, were common; good ones were the exception. And this raised an important question for a historian who cared about role models: How can one remain a virtuous man under bad emperors? What is the cost of such virtue? And why is a virtuous life—and a possible untimely death because of it—worthwhile in a world that has dramatically different values? The very few heroes in Tacitus's works are repeatedly men who put character and virtues first.

The Loyal Hero: Germanicus

To this day, the woods of the Teutoburg Forest are lovely, dark, and deep. However, what happened there over two thousand years ago was far from lovely. In AD 9, Arminius, a chieftain of a Germanic tribe who had previously served with distinction in the Roman army, lured three Roman legions—some fifteen thousand men, or close to ten percent of the Roman field force at the time—under the leadership of Publius Quinctilius Varus into the depths of the forest.

Surrounding the Romans in a narrow ravine where they could not maneuver, their numbers working against them, Arminius slaughtered them almost to a man. Varus and many of his fellow commanders, being proper Romans, opted for honorable battlefield suicide, falling on their swords. Only a few soldiers managed to escape in the chaos of the massacre. Somehow, they made it back to Rome to report what happened.[4] The magnitude of the loss, the greatest in the recent memory of the Roman state, was difficult to fathom. The emperor Augustus, in shock, declared public mourning. Roman expansion halted for the moment, and the Germanic provinces were henceforth classified as areas of trouble until at least the days of the emperor Marcus Aurelius in the late second century AD.

Tacitus does not directly cover the tragedy of Varus's lost legions, yet this generation-defining disaster looms over the early part of his narrative in the *Annals*—the part that has to do with the heroic young commander and nephew of the emperor Tiberius, Germanicus. In opening his *Annals*, a title reminding the reader that this history will go year by year in annalistic

---

4. Joanne Ball, *Publius Quinctilius Varus: The Man Who Lost Three Roman Legions in the Teutoburg Disaster* (Pen and Sword Military, 2023).

fashion, Tacitus first zooms through the preceding nearly eight hundred years of Roman history just to review the highlights. First there were kings, then a Republic. Eventually, Augustus stepped into a civil-war-induced power void and usurped power. Finally, upon Augustus's death, Tiberius came to power. Some thought that this moment could have been an occasion to revert back to the Republic, but it wasn't. Rather, rule by one man only became further solidified.

Tacitus firmly believed that there were important character implications of these developments for all Romans in this strange twilight zone where consuls were still elected each year, yet the Republic was no more: "Even most of the oldest generation had come into a world of civil wars. Practically no one had ever seen truly Republican government. The country had been transformed, and there was nothing left of the fine old Roman character. Political equality was a thing of the past; all eyes watched for imperial commands."[5]

Just like the Athenians once firmly believed that life under a democracy shaped one's soul in the democratic virtues, so did some Romans, including Tacitus, believe that life under the Republic shaped the souls of citizens to be more service-minded, sacrificial, and virtuous. Loyalty to the state mattered. By contrast, one-man rule only made everybody sycophants. To be under subjection to the whims of one man always left higher potential for the loss—rather than the gain—of virtues. Such is the nature of wanting to please one man who has near-absolute power.

However, one man was still left who, perhaps, exemplified those old Roman virtues. He was Germanicus. His father, Drusus, was the deceased—and more popular—younger brother of the emperor Tiberius. Some believed, Tacitus reports, that Drusus would have restored the Republic if he had lived, thus preventing Tiberius from continuing Augustus's imperial legacy. The son inherited his father's reputation and popularity wholesale.[6]

Germanicus's conduct, especially his camaraderie with his soldiers, shows a compassionate commander, devoted to serving the state and his own men. In one moving scene, Tacitus tells how Germanicus and his

5. Tacitus, *Annals*, trans. Michael Grant (Penguin Classics, 1996), 33.
6. Tacitus, *Annals*, 52.

troops visited the site of the Teutoburg Forest massacre, which had taken place some six years prior. The scene was grim:

> Germanicus conceived a desire to pay his last respects to these men and their general. Every soldier with him was overcome with pity when he thought of his relations and friends and reflected on the hazards of war and of human life . . . On the open ground were whitening bones, scattered where men had fled, heaped up where they had stood and fought back. Fragments of spears and of horses' limbs lay there—also human heads, fastened to tree-trunks. In groves nearby were the outlandish altars at which the Germans had massacred the Roman colonels and senior company-commanders.[7]

Germanicus learns that some among his troops had been there with Varus on that fateful day. They bear the indescribable burden of giving a battlefield tour to the rest.

Tacitus's emotion-laden narrative of Germanicus visiting a famous massacre site from six years earlier and burying the Roman soldiers who fell there leads us to notice an important detail: Here were Roman soldiers who had been left dishonored, unburied on the battlefield where they had fallen fighting for their country. And yet, until Germanicus had taken this task upon himself, no one had considered going there and burying them. Not Augustus, even though he mourned the loss of the legions. Not Tiberius, who had sent Germanicus to that general area with other tasks. Not the survivors, either.

Americans in Vietnam were renowned for taking care of their comrades-in-arms. Their loyalty to retrieving the bodies of those killed, not allowing them to be dishonored in death, was at times used against them by the enemy. But the idea of needing to grant an honorable burial to those who honorably fell, defending their country, was preeminent. People in the ancient world thought no less—we can recall the heroine of Sophocles's *Antigone* choosing to die rather than leave one of her brothers unburied. And so, we should be shocked to hear that under the rule of emperors the bodies of Romans slain in battle could be left for years, unburied and

7. Tacitus, *Annals*, 67.

uncared for. This says something about such rulers' character, just as it speaks volumes about their care for their people.

The Exemplary Vices of Emperors

We realize that emperors care only about their own honor. But good and virtuous men remain loyal to those they command and will give them due honor even in death. According to Tacitus, this care and desire to honor Roman soldiers who paid their lives for Rome distinguishes Germanicus from the other leaders all around. Such a desire to honor Romans whom he didn't personally know would have made Germanicus a good emperor, had he ever ruled.

In Tacitus's *Histories*, Galba earned the assessment as someone who would have been a great emperor had he never ruled. Germanicus, however, is the tragic hero of the *Annals*: the man who could have been a great emperor had he not tragically died so young. He fell victim to possibly poisoning or some other general evil scheme of Tiberius and his mother Livia, rumored to be the poison queen. Tacitus doesn't spare any gossip on these counts.

And yet Tacitus, a skeptic and realist, never fully buys into his own favorite's goodness. He wonders if sons really replicate their fathers' virtues. After all, a son of Germanicus did become emperor—Caligula, who earned his "little boot" nickname from his days as an adorable tyke accompanying his father on his travels and visits to military camps. But he was not a good emperor—not by a long stretch! Rather, true goodness clothes men who never have to exercise such great power but who are faithful and content with little. While Livy and Cato specialized in exemplary heroes, Tacitus specializes in exemplary villains. Most of the leaders he writes about are antiheroes—clear examples of what happens when someone utterly lacking a moral compass gains great power.

In the *Histories*, we meet not only the foolish Galba but also the luxuriously depraved emperor Otho, who seems to have cared most about his appearance and about pleasures of the body. He exemplifies pride and lust, two of the medieval seven deadly sins. And then we meet the extraordinary glutton emperor Vitellius, a sluggard unable to make effective military decisions. Sloth and gluttony are also among the seven deadly sins. All of these immoral leaders come to a bad end but make so many others also suffer in the process.

Tacitus sees the Roman Empire's environment as fertile ground for eroding the virtues—particularly in the leaders but not excluding their followers. And yet, as the example of Germanicus shows, some men still choose to pursue the virtues even at great cost to themselves. But perhaps the most striking heroes of Tacitus's writings are not Romans—rather, they are Britons. This decision speaks volumes in light of Tacitus's repeated emphasis on the erosion of Roman character under emperors.

The Virtuous Barbarians

Across the English Channel from Germany, where Germanicus had earned his nickname by pacifying the province, the Romans spent much of the first century AD trying to subdue Britain. Julius Caesar had first crossed the Channel, going to Britain twice while campaigning in Gaul in the 50s BC. The emperor Claudius (AD 41–54) then made a more concerted effort, but Britain remained a trouble spot. Then the revolt of Boudicca broke out during the reign of Nero.

In AD 61, angry over the abuses of Roman occupation (including the rape of her daughters), the warrior queen Boudicca and her tribe, the Iceni, took up arms against the invaders. Over the course of this revolt, Boudicca's army burned multiple Roman settlements, including Londinium (modern London), and wiped out an entire Roman legion—the Ninth. When the Roman commander Suetonius Paulinus finally managed to defeat her, his victory was considered a miracle and did nothing to dispel the mystique that has been attached to Boudicca's name ever since. For Tacitus, who briefly reports on her revolt, she is a heroine, a woman of virtue who is fighting for a just cause—freedom. In her speech to her troops before the final battle, per Tacitus's report, Boudicca declares:

> We British are used to woman commanders in war . . . I am descended from mighty men! But now I am not fighting for my kingdom and wealth. I am fighting as an ordinary person for my lost freedom, my bruised body, and my outraged daughters. Nowadays Roman rapacity does not even spare our bodies. Old people are killed, virgins raped. But the gods

> will grant us the vengeance we deserve! The Roman division which dared to fight is annihilated. The others cower in their camps, or watch for a chance to escape. They will never face even the din and roar of all our thousands, much less the shock of our onslaught. Consider how many of you are fighting—and why. Then you will win this battle, or perish. That is what I, a woman, plan to do!—let the men live in slavery if they will.[8]

Did Tacitus really hear Boudicca's speech? Probably not. And yet he considers Boudicca as a fitting person to state the obvious. She is not willing to live in slavery. But what about the Romans who are fighting her and who have accepted the rule of emperors over them? Their increasing brutality is only a symptom of the moral degradation to which their enslavement has led them.

Tacitus extols another standout barbarian hero in his *Agricola*: Calgacus. In AD 83, Calgacus leads the Britons into their final battle against the encroaching Romans, who are led by Tacitus's father-in-law Agricola. Shortly before their battle at the Graupian Mountain in what is now Scotland, Calgacus echoes Boudicca's alleged speech from two decades earlier:

> It is no use trying to escape their arrogance by submission or good behaviour. They have pillaged the world: when the land has nothing left for men who ravage everything, they scour the sea. If an enemy is rich, they are greedy, if he is poor, they crave glory. Neither East nor West can sate their appetite. They are the only people on earth to covet wealth and poverty with equal craving. They plunder, they butcher, they ravish, and call it by the lying name of "empire." They make a desert and call it "peace."[9]

Homeric heroes fought for glory, but Calgacus forces us to consider the point of the kind of fighting the Romans are doing. Where is the glory in greed and plunder? Is the Roman Empire good? Through this sympathetic barbarian, Tacitus not only raises this uncomfortable question but gives a no less uncomfortable answer: "They make a desert and call it 'peace.'" So this, Tacitus taunts, is what the famed *Pax Romana* (the Roman Peace) really is.

---

8. Tacitus, *Annals*, 330.
9. Tacitus, *Agricola and Germany*, trans. A. R. Birley (Oxford World's Classics, 1999), 22.

If, as the cliché hypothetically goes, a tree falls in the forest and no one sees it, did it really happen? Or, as Tacitus asks, if someone speaks the truth but no one harkens to it, is it still true? If someone speaks the truth but it makes no difference, does the truth matter at all? By writing these difficult episodes with Romans as villains rather than heroes, Tacitus clearly feels that speaking the truth matters. His skepticism over the use of his own writings pervasively comes through—but at least his own virtue as a truth-teller was secure.

The Virtuous Father-in-Law

In *Agricola*, Tacitus presents two heroes, both of them people of virtue. We have already considered the barbarian leader, the flashy Calgacus. But charismatic people aren't the only leaders to watch for in history or in real life. There is a reason Tacitus was so deeply impressed with his father-in-law Julius Agricola. In this biography, he describes with little fanfare the understated yet consistently principled life of Agricola, who played a leading role in restoring peace and stability in the province of Britain in the 70s and early 80s AD.

There is something significant about the life of quiet virtue—something remarkably un-Homeric and un-Roman. It is the value of cultivating virtue even when no one is watching. Paradoxically, the people who practice quiet virtue attract and satisfy others who seek peace.

Rooted Virtues in an Uprooted World

Six centuries before Boudicca exhorted her troops to fight for their freedom, Jewish exiles who had lost their fight for freedom sat by a foreign river and mourned:

> By the rivers of Babylon we sat and wept
>
> when we remembered Zion.

There on the poplars
    we hung our harps,
for there our captors asked us for songs,
    our tormentors demanded songs of joy;
    they said, "Sing us one of the songs of Zion!"

How can we sing the songs of the LORD
    while in a foreign land?[10]

Their response to exile makes sense—how could they not mourn? And yet this response forgets the cause of the exile. The story of the Old Testament is about God's people rebelling, over and over again, and God calling them back to repentance, over and over again. Exile followed centuries of largely unheeded prophetic warnings and admonitions. Consequently, the mourning of the exiles is the result of their ancestors' choice to reject God and the holiness to which he had called them. Furthermore, while the singers' own guilt is not mentioned in this psalm, the books of Jeremiah and Ezekiel highlight their personal complicity in these sins.

However, such tear-filled sorrow was not the only possible response to exile. Among these exiles was a young man, Daniel, whose story is prominently featured in the Old Testament as an example of spectacular faithfulness—even literally spectacular for all who beheld what Daniel and his friends went through. This story of Daniel is a tale of rooted virtues in an uprooted world.

For Daniel, a virtuous life is a life of obedience to God no matter where one may be, because a life with God is better than a life without him. With this conviction, he dares defy his captors on multiple occasions—such as in his insistence on eating a diet that would allow him to keep God's law and, later on, his insistence on continuing to pray to God even though King Darius's advisers had passed the law forbidding prayer to anyone but the king. Daniel earned his well-known trip to the lions' den for violating this latter law. Why did Daniel repeatedly risk his life, while so many Jews around him did not? Because he knew that God's promises were true. Daniel would have agreed with the psalmist:

10. Psalm 137:1–4.

Better is one day in your courts
    than a thousand elsewhere;
I would rather be a doorkeeper in the house of my God
    than dwell in the tents of the wicked.[11]

These are words of comfort for any who find themselves living under the rule of wicked leaders—as we all will at some point in our lives. Earthly rulers and bosses will always disappoint us, and we ought to not look to them as unconditionally perfect role models. Even more alarmingly, a virtuous life will not always give us rewards here. And yet, as Tacitus also saw, the virtuous life is its own reward.

But what does this even mean? Any answer to this question is incomplete without the knowledge of God. Thanks to God, we know that the virtuous life in the here-and-now is important because it prepares us for a perfect life with the perfect One. Our lives here shape us for eternity. Daniel knew this truth!

Recommendations for Further Reading

Tacitus, *Agricola and Germany*. Translated by A. R. Birley. Oxford World's Classics, 1999.

Tacitus, *The Annals of Imperial Rome*. Translated by Michael Grant. Penguin Classics, 1996.

Tacitus, *The Histories*. Translated by Kenneth Wellesley. Penguin Classics, 2009.

Questions for Discussion and Reflection

1. If you had to list the top five qualities of a virtuous political leader, what would they be? Why these five?

11. Psalm 84:10.

2. Describe someone you know—either personally or from a movie or a book—who is a Calgacus-style virtuous leader, and then describe another individual who is an Agricola-style virtuous leader. What do we learn from these differences about the nature of leadership?
3. How would you answer the question Tacitus investigates: Why should one strive to be a virtuous person, no matter who is in control of the government?

CHAPTER

Suetonius, Plutarch, and the Emperor's New Groove

Veni, vidi, vici.—I came, I saw, I conquered.[1]

Lives, Lies, and Limericks

In May 2023, *Library Journal* published a list of the biographies and memoirs of the year most in demand by libraries. Topping the list was *Spare*, Prince Harry's tell-all memoir.[2] A blend of self-pity, anger, and a whole lot of gossip and juicy tales about the British royal family, this book would have seemed surprisingly familiar and relatable to some readers in the Roman Empire. Sibling rivalry and strife? Check. Dysfunctional royal marriages mired in rumors of infidelity? Check. Endless worry over the line of succession? Check. Longing to protect one's reputation in spite of all of the above? Again, check.

The genre of biography (and, later, memoir) has always thrived, especially on the lives of the most famous people—especially royals. Sure, readers might expect to learn morals and lessons from such books. But the *sine qua non* of a good biography is entertainment. If some outrageous lies get mixed in with gossip—after all, *Fama* (Rumor) is described by Vergil as

1. Suetonius, *Divus Julius*, chapter 37. For the translation of this phrase, see Suetonius, "Julius Caesar," in *The Twelve Caesars*, trans. Robert Graves (Penguin Classics, 2007), 18.
2. "20 Best-Selling Biographies & Memoirs | The Most Sought-After Titles by Public Libraries," *Library Journal*, May 16, 2023, https://www.libraryjournal.com/story/may-2023-bestsellers-biography-and-memoir.

a monster of many ears, eyes, tongues, and lips—it only makes the results spicier.[3] And, let's face it: Readers of biography have always liked spice. For better or worse, emperors provided plenty of relish and zest in their biographies.

In the early second century AD, shortly after the time when Tacitus ("the quiet") started writing his historical works, another man with a similar nickname—Gaius Suetonius Tranquillus ("the calm" or "the peaceful")—began a historical and literary experiment of his own. Unlike Tacitus, who was interested in the year-by-year narrative of historical events, Suetonius went for a more sensational, gossipy, and even tabloid-style approach. One might call this an occupational hazard! A lifelong imperial secretary, Suetonius had a back seat to imperial drama right in the palace. Perhaps this bureaucrat's interest in writing these tales down was cathartic. Besides—as the timeless advice for writers goes—write what you know! And Suetonius obviously knew imperial gossip. He likely had access to more information than just about anyone else. All he had to do was quietly listen for decades—and then report.

Today, we are used to the genre of biographies of famous men and women. Indeed, biographies of royals, presidents, and generals regularly rise to the top of bestseller lists. But when Suetonius decided to develop the biographical genre, he was still doing something relatively new, especially in Latin. Sure, in the late Republic one Cornelius Nepos had written a series of short biographical sketches of famous men. And Tacitus had just published *Agricola*, the biography of his father-in-law.

But Suetonius's biographies are set apart from traditional historical books by his decision to thematically sum up emperors' lives by stories of virtues and vices rather than simply recounting lives from birth to death in a linear fashion. Additionally, Suetonius includes rumor and gossip in his exploration of virtues and vices, sometimes wondering aloud if a story is true for sure or is just juicy. If it meets the latter standard, he always proceeds to tell! He even writes down unsavory limerick-style songs; for example, he selects a few specimens from what appears to have been an unusually high number of ribald songs about Julius Caesar. Here are two songs that Caesar's soldiers sang at his triumph, according to Suetonius:

---

3. Vergil, *Aeneid*, trans. Theodore C. Williams (Houghton Mifflin, 1910), 4.173ff. The text is also online on the Perseus Digital Library, accessed March 6, 2025, https://www.perseus.tufts.edu/hopper/text?doc=Perseus%3Atext%3A1999.02.0054%3Abook%3D4%3Acard%3D173.

Gaul was brought to shame by Caesar;
By King Nicomedes, he.
Here comes Caesar, wreathed in triumph
For his Gallic victory!
Nicomedes wears no laurels,
Though the greatest of the three.

Home we bring our bald whoremonger;
Romans, lock your wives away!
All the bags of gold you lent him
Went his Gallic tarts to pay.[4]

Suggesting that perhaps the soldiers' bawdy ditties were rooted in some facts, Suetonius uses the intervening narrative between the two songs to list Caesar's alleged affairs. No real details; just names.

In proof that great minds think alike, while Suetonius was pursuing his project in Rome a Greek-speaking priest across the Ionian Sea in Delphi, Greece, was setting out on a similar experiment of his own. A prolific writer whose works (most of which don't survive) included philosophical books, collections of sayings, and short essays on a wide range of topics (including Egyptian religion and life in Sparta), Plutarch is best known today for his *Parallel Lives of Famous Greeks and Romans.*

"How might we best perceive and understand the virtues and vices of famous men?" Plutarch wondered, just as Suetonius had done. His answer: by setting them in comparison and contrast with each other. And so he embarked on an ambitious project, creatively pairing biographies of Greeks and Romans. For example, he compared the Athenian mythical founder Theseus with the Roman founder Romulus, the legendary general Alexander the Great with Rome's military legend Julius Caesar, and the famous Athenian orator Demosthenes with the likewise famous Roman orator Cicero.

Both Suetonius and Plutarch thought something was notable about putting renowned individuals front and center in the story of a period and place. What do we learn from their lives? What do we learn from their less famous actions—not just the way they won battles or elections but how they

4. Suetonius, "Julius Caesar," 24–25.

treated their wives, mothers, and children or what they liked for breakfast? Those details may seem decidedly insignificant in the grand scheme of history, but they tell us much about an individual. Of course, the subject of each of Plutarch's biographies is not just any individual but one exceptional in some way.

There's Something About Caesar

When my youngest daughter was just two years old, she would often boldly march into her teenage oldest brother's room and command him to do whatever came to her mind at the moment: wake up, clean his room, or read to her. He would frequently unquestioningly obey her, although he regularly resisted orders from all others in the family. Only after the fact would he comment pensively: Why do I take orders from a toddler?

The Romans called this phenomenon *auctoritas*—that ambiguous *je-ne-sais-quoi* quality which a few people possess, even if they technically have no official title or authority. Consequently others obey them, even though they are not entirely sure why. "There's just something about Caesar," we could say. And there was certainly something like this about each of the famous generals or politicians that Suetonius and Plutarch examine in their biographies.

It is no coincidence that Suetonius and Plutarch lived and wrote at a period in the late first and early second centuries AD when emperors were clearly here to stay and the Republic was never coming back. Thus, this was the time to wonder: Just how did perfectly ordinary men manage to accumulate such power? This question was particularly significant for Augustus, whom historians consider the first real emperor. How did a man whose only titles were *princeps* (first citizen) and *pater patriae* (father of the fatherland) manage to rule an empire?

The answer, one might say, was the emperor's mystique. Or, his "groove," if you will. Again, it is something unexplainable, special, a star quality, or whatever you want to call it. Suetonius and Plutarch were certain that the emperors had this mystique. But Plutarch believed that other famous leaders, long before the days of emperors, also possessed this quality. People are complicated, and sometimes straightforward history that emphasizes big events overlooks the moral character of individuals who shaped these events.

Sure, famous generals like Alexander and Caesar won a lot of battles and conquered plentiful territories, but who were they, really? In the process of considering this question about famous individuals, Plutarch directs his readers to self-examination.

Plutarch cautions us to distinguish history and biography in the introduction to his pair of biographies of Alexander and Caesar:

> I am writing biography, not history, and the truth is that the most brilliant exploits often tell us nothing of the virtues or vices of the men who performed them, while on the other hand a chance remark or a joke may reveal far more of a man's character than the mere feat of winning battles in which thousands fall, or of marshalling great armies, or laying siege to cities. When a portrait painter sets out to create a likeness, he relies above all upon the face and the expression of the eyes and pays less attention to the other parts of the body: in the same way, it is my task to dwell upon those actions which illuminate the workings of the soul, and by this means to create a portrait of each man's life. I leave the story of his greatest struggles and achievements to be told by others.[5]

Fine, Plutarch. Yeah, we know: You're no Herodotus or Thucydides, and you sort of have a chip on your shoulder about it. To be fair, so has every historian since Herodotus, Thucydides included. But you're attempting to sell biography as better than history. In fact, Plutarch seems to suggest that biography's emphasizing the virtues and vices of individuals much more overtly teaches its readers something that history had indeed aimed to do. History just got sidetracked from that aim of offering us great examples of virtues and vices by having to chronicle all those other pesky events such as battles and sieges.

Plutarch's portrait analogy only drives his point further home, recalling Thucydides's statement about his own approach to speeches in his history.[6] We are thus reminded that history and biography are art no less than science. The careful reader can take many things away: The biographers never talk about "the workings of the soul" of great men just for entertainment's

---

5. Plutarch, "Alexander," in Plutarch, *The Age of Alexander: Nine Greek Lives*, trans. Ian Scott-Kilvert (Penguin Classics, 1973), 252.
6. See chapter 4.

sake. If famous men of the past—both Greeks and Romans—have parallel lives, we surely all still lead parallel lives with other individuals who faced similar struggles, dilemmas, and temptations. Our decisions may not make or break empires, but they do form us and those around us. Furthermore, as Christians we can note extraordinary sin in these lives of famous men yet also a correspondingly extraordinary potential for repentance and redemption. Such is the nature of grace.

But one aspect of these biographies might appear jarring to the modern reader: All of the biographies that Suetonius and Plutarch wrote were, of course, about men. I say "of course," because these were biographies of emperors and famous rulers and generals—all occupations that were only available to men in the ancient world.

We could reply in frustration by writing off these authors and their heroes as a bunch of unruly misogynists. But I hope we don't. There is value in trying to understand writers from another time, place, and culture on their own terms—even while agreeing that we do not need to replicate them. Here is how I put this issue to my students over the years: As historians, we must understand our historical subjects. We never owe them complete or partial agreement. But we do owe them understanding. Indeed, understanding is perhaps all the more crucial in those instances when we don't agree with our sources.

And so, we come back to the reality of Suetonius's and Plutarch's exclusively male subjects, the reality of an age comprising male-only politicians and leaders. However, this does not mean that Suetonius and Plutarch were uninterested per se in women's virtues and vices or their stories. In fact, both writers give prominent places in their biographies to the mothers, wives, and daughters of their principal subjects. Plutarch also explored women's virtues in more detail elsewhere, such as in his essay "The Bravery of Women." In the end, while the rulers—and, therefore, all men—form the subject of these biographies, the moral formation of all individuals, men and women alike, unquestionably mattered to these Classical authors, as it should to us.

Best Death in Eveningwear

Years ago, one of my professors was running a few minutes late to a graduate seminar on Classical Greece. Naturally, we found a good way to entertain ourselves—cue a beauty pageant of late fifth-century BC Greek leaders, most of them subjects of Plutarch's biographies. Just imagine pitting Pericles versus Nicias versus Alcibiades versus Lysander versus Thucydides. Who would win?

As befits a proper beauty pageant, we put on both a talent category and a swimsuit competition. Thucydides was initially in the lead, but then came the most difficult category of all: best death in eveningwear. The Athenian playboy Alcibiades—the one man that all men and women in Athens desired (as Plutarch tells us)—won this contest easily, accumulating in the process enough points to win the overall pageant.

Alcibiades was unquestionably extraordinarily talented and beautiful, as Plutarch admits. Socrates did have a moderating influence on him for a time, calling him to humility. But this restraint seemed to be temporary, as we gather from story after story of Alcibiades instigating fights over the least provocation or Alcibiades partying too hard and getting into trouble for things done while drunk. Alcibiades consequently goes into exile and causes more problems over time. He belatedly learns that it is not enough to be smarter and more handsome and more noble-born than anyone else. Virtue still matters.

While we may occasionally find Alcibiades's story amusing, the vices of this most charismatic man of late fifth-century Athens are fully on display in the story of his life. This brilliant man ended up switching sides repeatedly during the Peloponnesian War—joining the side of Sparta when exiled from Athens, then joining Athens again when exiled from Sparta, and so on. In the end he dies ignominiously in exile, shot with arrows while dashing out of a burning house possibly ignited as payback by the family of yet another respectable woman he had seduced—or perhaps by his political enemies, who finally caught up to him. This decidedly scandalous matter-of-fact episode closes Plutarch's account of Alcibiades' life. Every time I read about the incredible gifts that Alcibiades had and the ways in which he misused them, I cannot help but think: "What a waste!" Indeed, Plutarch wants us to take away such a conclusion from the life of this tragic hero turned villain. Over the course of his life, he learned . . . absolutely nothing. Nothing but vice!

But then, think of how many people we know today that this profligate trajectory can describe—whether celebrities or politicians or, more soberingly, friends and loved ones. Indeed, the pursuit of the virtuous life challenges us to consider this question: If all our decisions and actions shape us, how do we want to be formed deep down? It is difficult to learn one's lesson from foolish decisions and misfortunes, but the book of Proverbs repeatedly reminds us that this makes a key distinction between a wise man and a fool. A wise man learns: ideally from the mistakes of others, but, in the worst case, from his own mistakes as well.[7]

Plutarch paired Alcibiades with a lesser-known figure from early Roman history—one Coriolanus, whom we know best today because of Shakespeare's tragedy. Both Plutarch and, later, Shakespeare were fascinated by the promise of this great general—someone so talented, with such potential for greatness! And yet pride becomes his downfall. Unwilling to play along with the plebeians, Coriolanus gets himself exiled. That same pride, then, leads him to ally himself with the Volsci—Rome's enemies—thus fighting against his own home state.

Plutarch sees in Coriolanus someone who is misled. He suspects that Rome's own early view of the virtues that matter is partially at fault:

> We must remember that the Romans of those days prized above all else the kind of virtue which finds its expression in warlike and military achievements. We have an interesting piece of evidence for this in the fact that there is only one word in the Latin vocabulary which signifies virtue, and its meaning is *manly valour*: thus the Romans made courage stand for virtue in all its aspects, although it only denotes one of them.[8]

Plutarch suggests a warning for us here: How do we define virtue? What is true virtue? We must also consider a no less important corresponding question: What is vice?

Ironically, the Roman definition of virtue that Plutarch criticizes is remarkably Homeric. We saw Achilles, Ajax, Hector, and other heroes of the *Iliad* also place military achievements above all else. But things didn't turn out so well for them, either. Plutarch is asking questions of transcendent importance here. A priest of the pagan gods in Delphi, he could only feel

7. For example, Proverbs 14:16 and Proverbs 21:11.
8. Plutarch, "Coriolanus," in Plutarch, *The Makers of Rome: Nine Lives*, trans. Ian Scott-Kilvert (Penguin Classics, 1965), 16 (emphasis original).

that something was wrong—but he never found the answer he was looking for. Some of his contemporaries, however, did.

The Gospels as Biography

It is no small task to write the biography of God, but, in a way, the four Gospel accounts in the New Testament are doing this, using multiple genres to encompass this daunting task. In the process, we find yet again this question: "Who is good?" The answer, as Jesus reminds us, is: "God alone." And yet this does not mean that pursuing the virtues is outdated or somehow unnecessary for believers. Rather, Jesus repeatedly reminds believers that God alone is holy and such holiness has deep implications for us.

Ultimately, the doctrine of the adoption of believers offers good news for us as we look to grow in the virtues. Through Christ we have been adopted as God's beloved children, heirs not only to the glorious promises of God's kingdom but also to the qualities of Christ through the process of sanctification. And so, unlike biographies of emperors or generals, the Gospels are biographies that call us all to holy living.

Christians Reading Pagans: Looking for Role Models

In reading Suetonius's and Plutarch's catalogs of virtues and vices of famous leaders of the ancient world, especially of Roman emperors, we get ample reminders that there is nothing new under the sun. Imperfect men have been in power for a long time. Likewise, the temptation to vice over virtue has been a challenge for all people, but especially for those with power.

Thus, perhaps the most salient conclusion emerging from the genre of biographies is the negative impact of leadership positions on men who could have been great but whose souls were corrupted by power and a lack of accountability. This warning was particularly clear to writers living in the age of emperors, since Suetonius and Plutarch had so many notorious examples to draw from. They conclude that there is no good emperor, just as at an earlier time the Old Testament prophets could conclude that there was no good earthly king.

Still, biographies continue to fascinate us because we want to find heroes, even if they are flawed. We all want someone to look up to. Children from birth are mimetic—they imitate parents, siblings, and anyone else they see. The same is true with adults. We always seek examples of people whom we can imitate—or disregard. After all, the stories of antiheroes steer us away from particular destructive courses of action. Over the last few chapters, we have traced this fascination with positive and negative examples in Greek and Roman writers, including the Roman historians, the epics of Vergil, and finally the biographers of the early Roman Empire.

We can learn a lot about a culture's values from seeing who its heroes are. In the ancient world before Christianity, these heroes were always famous politicians and generals—an overlapping category, for to be one was always to be the other. Only after the rise of Christianity do we see different sorts of heroes arise: the meek, the lowly, and the ones willing to die for their faith. The rise of these new heroes correspondingly changes the genre of biography.

The genre of the various acts of Christian martyrs is firmly established by the early fourth century, when the church historian Eusebius worked hard to compile them into a single work—which, alas, does not survive. Of course, stories of martyrdom go back earlier—consider the Gospels, which tell of Jesus's passion, and Acts, where we learn about the martyrdom of Stephen. And then there were the many early stories of female martyrs. For instance, we know the story of Perpetua and Felicity because Perpetua kept her own prison journal while awaiting execution—and it survived.

In these new biographies, we see the rise of a new sort of culture hero, one that looks nothing like the glorious Homeric heroes, handsome and aristocratic Athenian generals, or powerful Roman emperors. Instead, the new heroes of these martyrdom accounts are weak men and (so often!) women, far from beautiful at times and enslaved or poor in some cases. In a nutshell, they all fail to live up to the traditional Roman definition of virtue—*virtus*, that hypermasculine definition of virtue as military valor that Plutarch also criticizes. And yet the example of these new culture heroes and heroines tantalized those who heard or read their stories of martyrdom.

This is, one could say, a remarkable mystery. Why would thousands of men and women from all walks of life in the Roman Empire hear the stories of these martyrs, or possibly even see their martyrdom in person, and then choose to follow Christ, the one for whom these martyrs died such gruesome, horrific deaths? Shouldn't the human fight-or-flight impulse tilt firmly toward flight from danger? Maybe. But Jesus's teaching that the key to gaining true life is to let go of this current life clearly caught on time and again, offering an example worth imitating.[9] Those who embraced these new culture heroes, instead of obeying the natural impulse to flee from danger, found the truth to be more valuable than their earthly life and safety.

In my first book, *Cultural Christians in the Early Church*, I argue that the allure of culture somehow always finds ways to infiltrate the best of intentions.[10] And yet we cannot deny that in the midst of their culture's subconscious influence, which they often could not fully articulate or notice for themselves, the early Christians still wanted to follow heroes who showed what it was like to be in this world but not of it.

Recommendations for Further Reading

Plutarch, *The Age of Alexander: Nine Greek Lives*. Translated by Ian Scott-Kilvert. Penguin Classics, 2012.

Plutarch, *Fall of the Roman Republic: Six Lives*. Translated by Rex Warner. Penguin Classics, 2005.

Plutarch, *Makers of Rome: Nine Lives*. Translated by Ian Scott-Kilvert. Penguin Classics, 1965.

Plutarch, *The Rise and Fall of Athens: Nine Greek Lives*. Translated by Ian Scott-Kilvert. Penguin Classics, 2024.

Suetonius, *The Twelve Caesars*. Translated by Robert Graves. Penguin Classics, 2007.

9. See, for example, Matthew 10:39 and Matthew 16:25.
10. Nadya Williams, *Cultural Christians in the Early Church: A Historical and Practical Introduction to Christians in the Greco-Roman World* (Zondervan Academic, 2023).

Questions for Discussion and Reflection

1. What were Suetonius's aims in writing biographies of emperors? Why do people still read biographies for entertainment?
2. What are some differences between Suetonius's project and Plutarch's? Which one do you find more appealing, and why?
3. If you were to write someone's biography, of whom would it be? Why? What characteristics—virtues, vices, decisions—would you emphasize in telling this person's life?

PART

Virtues and Vices in the Age of Anxiety

CHAPTER

Apuleius and Marcus Aurelius Consider the Soul

> Let your every action, word, and thought be those of one who could depart from life at any moment. But taking your leave of the human race is nothing to be feared, if the gods exist; for they would not involve you in anything bad.[1]

Two Philosophers Walk into an Empire

This section header isn't a joke—it is serious business. It revolves around the most important question of all: Why are we here? And the "here" isn't just the Roman Empire; we're talking about something more serious and existential in scope. The question could be rephrased as that most cliché of all questions that people have always pursued even before the term or discipline of philosophy even existed: What is the meaning of life?

Let us set the stage. It was the height of the *Pax Romana*, that great age of prosperity and relative peace in the Roman Empire stretching from the days of Augustus, the first emperor, to the chaotic Crisis of the Third Century. But two unfortunate travelers saw that the stitches in the seemingly strong fabric of the empire already could not hold. Their misadventures in war and in provincial travel, respectively, showed that the

1. Marcus Aurelius, *Meditations*, trans. Robin Hard (Oxford World's Classics, 2011), 12.

perceived successes of this "happiest age of man" (as the eighteenth-century British historian Edward Gibbon dubbed it) were merely a veneer—and not a strong one.[2] A world of abject misery was bubbling just underneath the shiny marble-like surface of the empire's edifice. But the everyday physical suffering of the residents of that world, filled with so many varieties of casual disregard for human life and dignity, was nothing compared to the unfulfilled spiritual longings of their souls.

What is the nature of the soul dwelling within each human body? And what is the relationship of the soul to the body? The pre-Christian Greeks and Romans thought much about these questions, even though their answers ran up against the limits of pagan theology. Nevertheless, many of them were firmly convinced that a soul—some sort of intangible spiritual portion—inhabited the physical body.

One of the most famous of these explorations in ancient philosophy is the "Myth of Er" episode in book 10 of Plato's *Republic*. Er is a soldier killed in battle—a common enough occurrence in the ancient world. His soul descends to the underworld, but is sent back with a message of warning to the living. Miraculously restored to life on the day of his intended funeral, Er relays a message: The underworld is a place where people will certainly receive their just deserts. The wicked are punished while the righteous are rewarded.

This is a straightforward answer to a difficult question, and comes with a nicely tied bow! And yet the simplest answer is not always the correct answer. This message, in its simplistic form that is misunderstood by some even today as the gospel, still did not satisfy many of the ancient polytheists. What else might the soul long for? Times of stress make these questions and quests for greater meaning all the more urgent as despair sets in. And this is where we meet our two philosophers, writing on the edges of the Roman Empire as crisis looms.

The glorious *Pax Romana* that the rule of Augustus inaugurated involved relative peace around the empire for a solid century and a half, only interrupted by the turbulent AD 69 Year of the Four Emperors. But in the second half of the second century AD, some threads began to visibly unravel. The Marcomannic Wars with invading Germanic tribes sparked in AD 166 and

2. Mary Beard, *SPQR: A History of Ancient Rome* (Liveright, 2015), 401–3.

dragged on until AD 180, encompassing much of the rule of the emperor Marcus Aurelius. Additionally, other pressures were simmering right under the surface, waiting to explode in earnest in the third century AD.

However, that crisis is still a few decades into the future in the moment we discuss. For now, there is just a general feeling of unease that things are about to fall apart, so everyone is waiting for the other shoe to drop. What does this mean for those living in that time? In response, our two philosophers, who never met in real life, do what they know best: They write. They give us a window into this period of transition in the Roman Empire—a transition from the golden age of the *Pax Romana* to the tumultuous age of anxiety that begins in their lifetime but will long outlive them. This age will continue in fits and spurts until the end of the Roman Empire and into the period that we now call the European Middle Ages. We will focus on their stories in this chapter—but our first order of business, as at any good party, is introductions.

The Philosopher Emperor and the Suspected Magician

In a tent somewhere within a forest of what we know today as Germany, an emperor dictates ideas to his secretary at the end of yet another busy campaign day. He is tired, and the cold of the German winter is wearing down his body. His tent, while significantly more spacious and glamorous than the cramped shared tents of the common soldiers, is decidedly far from comfortable. But Marcus Aurelius seems able to dismiss the cold and any other discomforts. Although he has spent much of his life at war, battle is the last thing on his mind at the close of this day. Instead, he is thinking about the meaning of life.

Marcus Aurelius is an unusual man for this job. Previous Roman commanders dreamed of victories and martial glory—but not this one. Instead, while succumbing to his fate and duty—the emperor must lead his troops on the campaign!—he cares most about his ideas, which he painstakingly compiles into a remarkably relatable book that has endured for over two millennia. His *Meditations* has been a continuous bestseller on Amazon (the online store, not the horseback-riding archer warrior ladies) in the twenty-first century.

The *Meditations* will further popularize the philosophy of stoicism, a relentless project of self-improvement that strives toward moral excellence for the sake of moral excellence. After all, being a good person is a worthy reward in and of itself, even (or maybe especially!) in a disintegrating world. In other words, Marcus Aurelius exhorts each man and woman to become one's own anchor in the face of crisis.

Meanwhile, across the Roman Empire in North Africa, another philosopher is hard at work, hoping to fulfill his dream of making philosophy his day job and not just a hobby to pursue in the margins. This is Apuleius from Madauros, and we first see him on trial, pleading for his life and reputation. Accused of using magic to influence a wealthy elderly widow (and the mother of his old school friend—awkward!) to marry him, Apuleius gives a cheeky speech in his defense, arguing that his accusers are mistaken. He is no magician, don't worry! He's just a *philosophicus platonicus*, a philosopher in the mode of Plato.

At first glance Apuleius's most famous work does not seem to be philosophical, although a close look proves otherwise. In fact, it is the only Roman novel written in Latin that entirely survives. Modern readers all too often assume that the novel is a modern genre, one that reflects our own dispositions, interests, and questions. But it isn't. Novels in both Greek and Latin flourished in the Roman Empire—many more survive in Greek than Latin, thanks to Egyptian papyri. Telling many stories of romances and road trips gone wrong, often thanks to being kidnapped by pirates, these novels explore big questions about the meaning of life in a time of uncertainty. These questions ultimately reflect their authors' search for the soul's redemption from this present suffering age of anxiety. They reflect the dominant desire in this age to ask difficult questions and not settle for easy answers. Analyzing the seen, they seek the unseen. Will they find it?

Marcus Aurelius on Vocation and Saving Yourself

Scholars of the ancient world share a longstanding joke that every research project must begin with Homer. As with so many jests, this one is largely true. The shadow of Homer extends far across the ancient world. Those Homeric values, especially the pursuit of epic-worthy martial glory, continued to motivate Greek and Roman rulers and generals for centuries. But

Marcus Aurelius stands out against such a background. Before Marcus wrote his *Meditations*, the most famous journals of a general written on campaign had been none other than Caesar's *Gallic War* and *Civil War*. Walking his readers back home in Rome through his campaigns, vividly describing battles and other successes, Caesar effectively made his own accessible *Iliad*, portraying himself as the Best of the Romans. We can imagine him in his tent, night after night, dictating the successful events of the day to his scribe.

However, two hundred and fifty years later, Caesar's striving seemed to be all vanity to Marcus Aurelius. Spending decades of his life on a war that had won him a fair degree of distinction, he felt the emptiness of such endeavors: "How swiftly all things vanish away, both the bodies themselves in the universe, and the memories of them in time."[3] The Homeric heroes and Caesar would have expressed astonishment at such sentiments.

Marcus Aurelius seems to be someone trapped—a philosopher imprisoned in the job of a general, a duty-bound emperor of a vast empire that he did not want to govern but felt that he must continue doing his best. All the while, he kept thinking about his soul—the foremost topic that keeps coming up over and over again in his writings. His military campaigns, successes, and victories do not take priority. Spending his days leading the Roman army into war, he wrote in the margins of his days about what he believed truly mattered. This predicament makes Marcus Aurelius's plight remarkably relatable to us, even though most of us likely do not while away our evenings writing meditations on the state of our soul. But we can certainly relate to the feeling of being trapped in a career or vocation that we did not choose or desire. Even worse, maybe we once loved our career but it has turned out very differently from what we expected.

This latter career scenario was my experience. After spending fifteen years as a professor, I walked away from academia when my job became something very different—mostly online, without in-person interactions with students. I felt trapped until I finally realized that walking away was really an option.[4] I used the word "soul-sucking" to describe what my job had become at that point. Marcus Aurelius would have understood. Unlike

3. Marcus Aurelius, *Meditations*, 13.
4. Nadya Williams, "Discerning Vocation: Walking Away from Academia," *Anxious Bench* (blog), Patheos, May 23, 2023, https://www.patheos.com/blogs/anxiousbench/2023/05/discerning-vocation-walking-away-from-academia/.

Marcus, however, I did have the luxury of being able to walk away. But even more significantly, unlike Marcus, I ultimately felt secure in my soul's love for God—and God's love for me. And this difference allows believers in Christ to find a peace that Marcus Aurelius could never attain.

What does it mean to love one's soul and prioritize its improvement and cultivation? Marcus Aurelius found that this meant turning inward. He continually enjoins his readers and himself to work harder, strive further, and demand more of your soul. Theologian Michael Horton tracks this answer throughout ancient pagan philosophical and religious ideals in his book *Shaman and Sage*.[5] Exemplified by such figures as Orpheus, shaman-like wise men in pagan antiquity tried to look deep within their souls, attaining some sort of enlightenment in the process. While ostensibly not writing about religion, Marcus Aurelius does use theological language in reflecting about his soul—in a way that later Neoplatonist philosophers such as Plotinus will develop further.

However, promises of salvation from within are empty, doomed to disappoint and only leaving us in further despair because we simply cannot save ourselves. Marcus Aurelius's contemporary Apuleius came to this exact conclusion in his own investigation of the same questions. Rather, salvation is found in external forces over which we have no control. What might these forces be? To find Apuleius's answer, we now turn to his novel, *Metamorphoses* or *The Golden Ass*.

Plotinus and Neoplatonism

What Plato did for early Greek philosophy, Plotinus did for its revival in the late Roman Empire. True, educated Greeks and Romans had been reading Plato for all this time, but Plotinus, a native of Egypt, picked up in the mid-third century AD where (one could say) Plato had left off six and a half centuries earlier.

5. Michael Horton, *Shaman and Sage: The Roots of "Spiritual but Not Religious" in Antiquity* (Eerdmans, 2024).

Plotinus's work survives as six *Enneads*—groupings of nine essays each, totaling fifty-four. Their topics revolve closely around different manifestations of goodness, truth, and beauty. While not a Christian, Plotinus was skeptical of traditional Greco-Roman polytheism and was interested in studying the soul. In the nineteenth century, scholars dubbed Plotinus and the philosophers who followed him as "Neoplatonists"—new Platonists, as opposed to the old ones who had studied with Plato and his students. We should not be surprised that some later Neoplatonists were Christians—for instance, both Origen and Augustine were influenced by Neoplatonism, even if they were not absolute adopters of the system.

A Donkey, a Princess, and the Perilous Journeys of the Soul

A young man, bored with his life and searching for excitement, takes a road trip. Visiting Thessaly, well-known in antiquity as the homeland of witchcraft, he gets much more excitement than he bargained for. Fascinated by tales of magic all around, Lucius the protagonist asks his new lover, the enslaved servant of a witch, to smear some magic ointment on his body. But things go terribly wrong here. While Lucius had expected to turn into an owl for a little while, he becomes, instead, an ass—literally, not figuratively. This mishap turns out to be more serious than he had anticipated, as the only antidote to the transformation was fresh roses administered internally, not topically. Alas, none were available late at night. But a night in the stable never hurt a donkey!

However, before dawn could bring the next day and the antidote, a band of robbers steal Lucius-donkey from the stable. The rest of Apuleius's masterpiece follows Lucius in his animal form as he experiences the worst that the underbelly of the Roman Empire could offer its human and animal subjects. Repeatedly traded, sold, bought, stolen, and beaten by all who own or merely meet him, Lucius the asinine narrator documents his troubles while awaiting the salvation that he fears may never come.

Apuleius seems to have called his novel *Metamorphoses*, but we know it better today by the title that one later reader—none other than Augustine—gave it: *The Golden Ass*. Interpreting the first-person narrative of this novel literally, Augustine took it to be Apuleius's memoirs. (And, yes, this should make Augustine even more lovable in your eyes!)

Augustine perhaps felt a certain kinship to this narrator, who understands the spiritual nature of his perilous journey at the end: In the eleventh and final book of the novel, the reader finds out that Lucius is saved by the mystical Egyptian goddess Isis. During her festival procession, she at last provides the roses he needs to be transformed back into his human body. But he does need to pay a price: He dedicates himself as her priest for the remainder of his life. Thus, as we instinctively know, redemption always has a cost. And in his new role as the chaste priest of Isis—a monk of sorts, if we use an anachronistic term—Lucius now looks back at his previous misfortunes. They were as much the fruit of his own sins—especially his excessive curiosity—as the result of the cruelty of fate and empire.

The novel's denouement shows the miraculous salvation of the body—the sort of security that no one could take for granted in the Roman Empire. As a priest of Isis, Lucius now lives a leisurely life of religious ceremonies and observance governed by various rules, many of which he is not allowed to reveal to the uninitiated. And yet a surprising tale nestled exactly in the middle of the novel, which Lucius overhears while yet a donkey, hints that perhaps salvation could be something more: something that involves deeper joy and security than simply a life of safety in the here-and-now. This tale, surprisingly emerging from the pen of Apuleius, the pagan writer who never knew Christ, shows his own awareness of the spiritual longings that were steadily drawing some of his contemporaries to the true faith.

As the tale goes, there once lived three princesses. The youngest of them is named Psyche—her very name means "the soul" in Greek. She is so beautiful that the people of the land compare her to Venus, the goddess of love and beauty. Worse yet, they begin to worship her as Venus, bringing offerings to her instead of to the goddess's temple. Jealousy was a key character feature of the pagan gods, so Venus unsurprisingly plotted her revenge. But something else happened, instead: Venus's son, Cupid, falls in love with Psyche and takes her to be his wife. He brings her to his palace in secret, while her disconsolate family believes she has been killed by the goddess.

But there is one condition—of course, there was; there always is!—Psyche can never see her husband's face nor know his true name.

All goes well for a while until Psyche goes back to visit her family, whom she has so dearly missed. Jealous of her happiness, her two sisters encourage her to learn the truth about her husband's identity. They are shocked to learn that she has never seen his face, suggesting to their impressionable sister that he could be a horrible monster. One night as her husband sleeps, Psyche lights a lamp and learns the truth of his divine and glorious identity, but at a terrible cost. Angered at her violation of the one command he had instilled upon her, Cupid immediately abandons her, afraid and pregnant. For the rest of the tale, Psyche must prove herself to Venus through a series of trials until she is happily reunited with Cupid. The tale concludes with a joyous celebration of their wedding, at which even Venus dances in celebration.

The divine characters of this story make it seem like a myth, the product of centuries of circulation in folklore and tradition. Indeed, this tale has made its way into modern anthologies of Greek and Roman myths. And yet experts emphasize that this story has no trace before Apuleius, suggesting that he made it all up. In other words, this is not a typical myth but rather the product of one man's thoughts, searching blindly in the darkness for something that he can feel but not see. How did Apuleius himself imagine this tale? In a novel that contains two miraculous stories of divine rescue—that of Lucius at the mercy of Isis at the end and that of Psyche's journey to salvation in the middle—it is difficult to believe that the writer himself was not searching for a deeper spiritual meaning. Furthermore, unlike Marcus Aurelius, who searched for the god within, Apuleius was convinced that we could not save ourselves.

Apuleius's tale, like so many of the greatest classics of pagan literature, reflects a greater truth than its author had realized. The search for that higher truth has fascinated Christian readers of his novel ever since. Beginning in Late Antiquity, some read the tale of Cupid and Psyche as an allegory about the love affair of the human soul with God. Psyche's trials to find Cupid were interpreted as the journey of the soul to find God. Writing in the early sixth century, Fulgentius the Mythographer retells the story as an allegory, depicting Psyche as Adam—the one who had been given every blessing but squandered it by disobedience. Like Adam,

Psyche was driven out of Paradise, the place of love, for her own faults. But, completing the story of the gospel, Psyche was restored to relationship with Christ at the end.[6]

An Oxford Don Responds

Is there yet more to this story, though? One British academic in the mid-twentieth century thought so. He was C. S. Lewis, an adult convert to Christianity who had held a lifelong fascination with pagan mythology—which features prominently in his conversion memoir *Surprised by Joy*.[7] Indeed, Lewis shared this captivation and deep knowledge of Greco-Roman mythology with many of the earliest converts to Christianity in the Roman world. After all, they too were immersed in the world of pagan gods and stories about them.

After his conversion Lewis still occasionally thought about the myths, and he returned later in life to the tale of Cupid and Psyche. However, unlike readers over the previous nearly two millennia, Lewis believed that the key to understanding this tale's deepest meaning lay not in the fate of Psyche but in that of her sisters. But no less significant for Lewis were the players whose role Apuleius had also considered vital in their presence but even more so in their absence: the pagan gods.

C. S. Lewis's stunning novel *Till We Have Faces* was his own favorite work. It is his response to Apuleius across time and space. A tale of sorrow and grief over what could have been, it shows Lewis's understanding of the mind of another writer. Lewis thought that Apuleius, in his brilliance and arrogance, could not understand perfectly something that seemed so clear in the tale he himself had told: The path to salvation lies in the rejection of the pagan gods.[8] In Lewis's retelling, we hear the story through a new narrator, one whom Apuleius himself had ignored: Psyche's older sister, Orual,

---

6. Fulgentius, *Mythologies*, trans. L. G. Whitbread (Ohio State University Press, 1971), 3.6. The text is also online at the Theoi Texts Library, accessed March 6, 2025, https://www.theoi.com/Text/FulgentiusMythologies2.html#23.
7. C. S. Lewis, *Surprised by Joy* (HarperOne, 2017).
8. In his brilliant but strange book on the philosophy of mind, *All Things Are Full of Gods: The Mysteries of Mind and Life* (Yale University Press, 2024), David Bentley Hart uses the deified Psyche—along with Cupid, Hephaestus, and Hermes—to present an elaborate imagined dialogue about the nature of knowledge, the mind, and the soul.

who lives her entire life in her sister's shadow. Wrestling with guilt over her betrayal of her sister, and angry with the pagan gods whose treachery—or, rather, absence—she so acutely feels in her own life, Orual feels deeply lost.

In the novel's dramatic denouement days before her death, Orual finally comes face to face with the long-lost Psyche in a vision. However, this Psyche looks like her earthly self yet also somehow different, glorified. At last, Orual understands: "Joy silenced me. And I thought I had now come to the highest, and to the utmost fullness of being which the human soul can contain. But now, what was this? . . . I knew that all this had been only a preparation. Some far greater matter was upon us." A loud voice of someone she does not see then declares: "You also are Psyche."[9]

Orual concludes: "I ended my first book with the words *no answer.* I know now, Lord, why you utter no answer. You are yourself the answer. Before your face questions die away."[10] "What if God is the answer?" C. S. Lewis gently nudges us to consider. What if the Sunday School answer to all questions—Jesus—is true? This changes everything.

Recommendations for Further Reading

Apuleius, *The Golden Ass*. Translated by P. G. Walsh. Oxford World's Classics, 2008.

Marcus Aurelius, *Meditations*. Translated by Gregory Hays. Modern Library, 2003.

Marcus Aurelius, *Meditations*. Translated by Robin Hard. Oxford World's Classics, 2011.

Questions for Discussion and Reflection

1. What stresses did people of Apuleius's age and the third century AD experience?

9. C. S. Lewis, *Till We Have Faces: A Novel of Cupid and Psyche* (Mariner Books, 2012), 306–8.
10. Lewis, *Till We Have Faces*, 308.

2. How do you define vocation? What vocational conflicts did Marcus Aurelius confront in his life? Have you experienced any vocational conflicts—a sense that you may be called to do something different than what you are doing? How might you resolve such a situation?
3. What emotions does the story of Psyche, as told by Apuleius, evoke? How are the changes that C. S. Lewis made to this story significant? What emotions come to the fore, instead? Think of another story from mythology or secular fiction—how might you retell it with Christian eyes? What difference does this change of perspective make?

CHAPTER

Three North African Converts Read the Pagan Classics

Take it and read, take it and read.[1]

Winners Write History?

A man in anguish is weeping in a garden, when he suddenly hears a child's voice emanating from somewhere close by: "Take it and read, take it and read." It's more poignant in Latin—just two words pronounced over and over in a singsong: *tolle lege, tolle lege.*

But there is no child in sight. Rather, I suspect that what we have here are God's two most famous words heard outside of Scripture. Heard by no one but their intended hearer, these words were meant to do just one thing: bring their hearer at last to Christ. And they did. So, at thirty-one years of age, Augustine of Hippo, a scholar and rebel who would go on to become one of the greatest theologians of all time, finally surrendered his life to Christ. I love dramatic stories of conversion. Don't you?

My husband grew up in a Christian home and never felt like he had an Augustine-style moment. A number of other lifelong Christians have described the same conundrum: It was strangely more difficult to know precisely when they were ready to make a public profession of their faith, as they had been in church every time the doors were open since they were

1. Augustine, *Confessions*, trans. R. S. Pine-Coffin (Penguin Classics, 1961), 177.

two days old. By contrast, I came to Christ at age thirty, and it felt dramatic, wild, and engulfing—think *Invasion of the Body Snatchers*, but good. Considering my family background, perhaps there was no other way it could have happened. I was born into a secular Jewish family in Russia back when the Soviet Union still existed, so the country's official religion was atheism. Then right before the Soviet Union collapsed, my family immigrated to Israel. When I was in high school, we moved to the U.S. for a year because of my dad's work. A year turned into a lot more, which is how, over a quarter-century later, we are still here.

I am not trying to give you whiplash in following the geographic and spiritual twists and turns of my early life. Rather, I am trying to explain why it would have felt so spectacular and unexpected for me, a secular Jew for three decades, to come to Christ at that point. Statistically speaking, the odds were minuscule. But God has been known to defeat much greater odds. Indeed, every conversion is a miracle, as Augustine's struggle to accept Christ shows. It sounds trite to bring miracles and conversions together in our day and age, when no lions in arenas loom in consequence of a public profession of faith, but here we are.

Of course lions did not loom for Augustine, either. His conversion came after the emperor Constantine had made Christianity respectable by endorsing it himself—first in the victorious battle that solidified his rule over the Roman Empire, and then by being baptized on his deathbed. However, lions were well-acquainted with plenty of earlier converts, particularly with those who came to Christ before the Edict of Milan in AD 313.

Winners write history—so the adage goes. In the case of some martyrs, this turned out to be truer than expected. In AD 202, a new Christian—still technically a catechumen and therefore not yet officially received into the faith—a young noble woman and a nursing mother named Perpetua, wrote a prison journal while awaiting martyrdom in Carthage. Together with her was an enslaved pregnant woman, Felicity. An anonymous editor would later take Perpetua's journal, add to it a moving eyewitness description of the two women's execution, and publish it. A mere woman's testimony of her faith thus became a bestseller.

Half a century later in that same city, a man who was born around the time of Perpetua's martyrdom himself came to Christ in middle age. Shortly after, he unexpectedly found himself thrust into a limelight he never sought, an appointment as bishop of Carthage. For a decade in this position (AD 248–258), he ministered to believers and their leaders near and far, writing letters, sermons, and treatises to encourage, answer questions, send some cash in times of need, and generally show Christ's love. At last, in AD 258 Cyprian willingly died a martyr's death, in his final words asking Christians in attendance to collect some money to bless his executioner. Over a century later, Augustine would consider Cyprian his chief influence.[2] The stories of these three converts appear at first glance so different. Perpetua, especially, is an outlier. What does a young nursing mother have in common with two of the most famous bishops and theologians of the early church? Can we even set Perpetua and her work on the same level as the brilliant and distinguished Augustine?

Yes, I think we can. Their writings put together give us valuable glimpses of how new converts to Christianity in the Roman world, both men and women, relied on the great pagan writers of the past in their own writing. In this, they did one thing that the pagans never imagined their works would be used to do: bring glory to Christ. In other words, the knowledge of the great pagan works and writers lent them the language, the themes, and at times the very words they used to express their joy for a new life in Christ. More specifically, as we read Perpetua, Cyprian, and Augustine and see their repurposing of themes in pagan classics to talk about their own walk in Christ, we find a desire for what would become known as the three heavenly virtues: faith, hope, and love.

Perpetua's Faith

Over a millennium before Perpetua's time, the legendary Achilles had to make a choice—according to his mother, the nymph Thetis, who relayed a message to him from the gods. He could live in obscurity to a ripe old age, or he could acquire immortal glory by dying a hero's death at Troy. Thetis knows what she would prefer Achilles to choose. But her son, the Best of the Achaeans, ever in pursuit of more glory and recognition, chose the opposite.

Perpetua was a member of the nobility, raised in a respectable pagan home. At some point (we don't know how or through whom), she came

2. Matthew Alan Gaumer, *Augustine's Cyprian: Authority in Roman Africa* (Brill, 2016).

to believe in Christ and began attending church services with other local Christians in Carthage, including Felicity, a slave in her household. During a local persecution of Christians in AD 202/3, both women found themselves first under surveillance, then arrested and imprisoned, and finally executed.[3] In her powerful prison journal, Perpetua documents all this—and more. She is vulnerable but confident throughout as different male authority figures confront her, demanding that she renounce her faith. After all, in the Roman world women were, with some exceptions (e.g., mothers of three children), subject to a male relative's authority—father, husband, or brother.

And so, the first man whom Perpetua likely defied is not mentioned—her husband is gone from her life before she begins her journal. The anonymous editor does note, to make clear her respectability, that she had been legally wed. She wasn't widowed—otherwise, the editor would surely have mentioned this. Such a notable absence, combined with the fact that she was living back in her father's house with an infant son before her arrest and imprisonment, leads us to a likely explanation: Her husband divorced her because of her conversion. If he had done so, he was merely the first in a string of men who had authority to demand her to renounce Christ. Then, as she reports, her father repeatedly exhorts her to abjure her faith. Finally, at her trial, the procurator—the highest Roman official in the province at the time—gives her one last chance. Given every opportunity to choose possibly a long life without Christ, she instead chooses a death that will lead her to glory with her Savior.

How Homeric! And yet the epic glory here is filtered through Perpetua's faith, which encourages her that there is something greater than life. Of course Achilles knew this too, as he chose epic glory over a long life. But we know that his glory is empty compared to the one Perpetua knew would be hers. Perpetua never mentions *kleos* ("renown" or "glory"), whereas Achilles was obsessed with it. Instead, in his introduction, the anonymous editor notes the importance of this story in bringing glory to God.

Interspersing her chronological narrative of events, which steadily draws closer to the day of execution that would come, Perpetua includes

---

3. For a full discussion of Perpetua and Felicity, see my book *Cultural Christians in the Early Church: A Historical and Practical Introduction to Christians in the Greco-Roman World* (Zondervan Academic, 2023), 83–104.

her visions, each one more striking and powerful than the last. These visions are remarkable, and she recognizes that they presage her martyrdom. But the third vision, on the night before her execution, is the most unusual. She narrates:

> I was stripped naked, and I became a man. . . . And I rose up into the air and began so to smite him [i.e., her opponent in the vision—a frightening-looking Egyptian] as though I trod not the earth. But when I saw that there was yet delay, I joined my hands, setting finger against finger of them. And I caught his head, and he fell upon his face; and I trod upon his head. And the people began to shout, and my helpers began to sing. And I went up to the master of gladiators and received the branch. And he kissed me and said to me: Daughter, peace be with you. And I began to go with glory to the gate called the Gate of Life.
>
> And I awoke; and I understood that I should fight, not with beasts but against the devil; but I knew that mine was the victory.
>
> Thus far I have written this, till the day before the games; but the deed of the games themselves let him write who will.[4]

So Perpetua concludes her journal. The duel in her vision sounds decidedly Homeric, as so many duels of gladiators in the Roman arena also were—they were based on one-to-one epic-style martial combats. Indeed, some gladiatorial shows and executions were staged as mythological reenactments.[5] More than that, in her fight for Christ in this vision, Perpetua is transformed into a man, an epic hero in the flesh. And just as the heroes of epic duels sometimes were granted temporary supernatural powers by the gods, so Perpetua is given the miraculous ability to fly in the arena, hitting her opponent from above.

Sounding remarkably calm and secure, Perpetua concludes her journal by interpreting her vision: This battle is spiritual, and she rests (and writes) secure in her coming victory. There is much else to discuss in this stunning

4. Perpetua, *The Passion of Saints Perpetua and Felicity*, trans. W. H. Shewring (Sheed and Ward, 1931). The text is also online at the Medieval Sourcebook, Fordham University, accessed March 3, 2025, https://sourcebooks.web.fordham.edu/source/perpetua.asp.
5. Kathleen Coleman, "Fatal Charades: Roman Executions Staged as Mythological Enactments," *Journal of Roman Studies* 80 (1990), 44–73.

short document—such as Perpetua's sacrifice of her motherhood, since her tender love for her son was still no match for her unwavering belief that she was called to martyrdom. But I perhaps most appreciate Perpetua's example of the heavenly virtue of faith. Never trite nor saccharine, her faith in God's love and provision for her is clear in a way that the Homeric heroes could never imagine—because their gods could never offer it.

Cyprian Teaches Love

A pagan rhetoric teacher turned Christian in middle age, Cyprian was an unlikely candidate for the role of bishop of Carthage, the most influential see in the Roman province of Africa. He would effectively be the head of the church in that region. And yet perhaps the congregants who surprisingly elected him as their bishop in AD 247/8 recognized something that we too can see in his writings nearly 1,800 years later. For everything Cyprian did, he did in love.

Love, as we saw earlier, was a central subject for several pagan writers. For instance, Plato's *Symposium*, one of the most renowned works of philosophy in antiquity, was a dialogue seeking to define love. What is love, anyway? How does it work? Why is it important? The different conversationalists we explored offered rather different definitions—like the one Aristophanes offered about the (originally) conjoined human beings. Jealous of their harmony, Zeus had separated them, and now they just go through life looking for the other half that will complete them. And then the Roman love poets intertangled their view of love with much dysfunction and disregard for human dignity. The love affairs glorified (or mourned) by the Roman elegists were decidedly earthly affairs, doomed to fall apart.

As a highly educated Roman rhetorician, Cyprian was familiar with all these attempts to describe love. Indeed, he was also teaching and ministering during the heyday of ancient romance novels such as Apuleius's *The Golden Ass*. Many more such works, written in Greek, were preserved in the Egyptian sands, showing us that the steamy romance novel is not even a modern genre after all.

But what is love for the Christians? Cyprian knew well that this is not just a theoretical question. In one of the most famous passages about love in all of the New Testament, Paul writes:

If I speak in the tongues of men or of angels, but do not have love, I am only a resounding gong or a clanging cymbal. If I have the gift of prophecy and can fathom all mysteries and all knowledge, and if I have a faith that can move mountains, but do not have love, I am nothing. If I give all I possess to the poor and give over my body to hardship that I may boast, but do not have love, I gain nothing.

Love is patient, love is kind. It does not envy, it does not boast, it is not proud. It does not dishonor others, it is not self-seeking, it is not easily angered, it keeps no record of wrongs. Love does not delight in evil but rejoices with the truth. It always protects, always trusts, always hopes, always perseveres.

Love never fails.[6]

In other words, love is the key prerequisite for the Christian life. As Paul makes clear, the oversimplification of Christianity as just "do some good deeds once in a while" will not fly. The heart also matters—you must have love for others! And not just any kind of love—it must be patient, kind, and all these other difficult attributes that we struggle to bring forth in loving our family members, much less people to whom we are not related or, worse yet, utter strangers. But one could say that Paul's exhortation still seems awfully theoretical.

One way to sum up the entirety of Cyprian's ministry, in word and in deed, is that he put the flesh of pastoral care on the skeleton that Paul had originally provided. Above all, Cyprian wrote about caring for others and loving them well—in word, deed, and cash. He saw that people have concrete needs in this physical world. It is no accident that Cyprian's earliest surviving treatise, "On Works and Alms," emphasized almsgiving as an act of love for other suffering Christians. Cyprian argued that faithful and loving believers had the opportunity to win the white crown of works as well as the red crown of martyrdom.

Cyprian's letters and treatises, which may have started their lives as sermons, offer yet more concrete examples of his emphasis. For example, the treatise "On Jealousy and Envy" urges believers to love one another genuinely and fully, opposing these contrary qualities as a departure from

6. 1 Corinthians 13:1–8.

the path to Christ. Additionally, "On the Dress of Virgins" is Cyprian's manifesto of pastoral care for female believers who have dedicated their virginity to Christ. He addresses the virgins themselves, urging them to love God more than themselves and their appearance (and their fancy dress). At the same time, he is showing the significance of pastoral care for one of the most vulnerable groups of people in the Roman Empire—women without the protection of a husband or another male relative.

If all of this sounds like the ordinary work of a pastor—shepherds take care of their sheep!—we need to remember its significant context. Cyprian's ministry fell right into the middle of a period of unprecedented political, economic, and military instability in the Roman Empire lasting from the assassination of the emperor Severus Alexander in AD 235 to the ascension of the emperor Diocletian in AD 284. Just imagine the instability of the United States in 2020—the political strife of the election, the economic difficulties, and a deadly pandemic. Now imagine 2020 dragging on for almost fifty years, exacerbating the social and political fissures we experienced. That was the Crisis of the Third Century in the Roman Empire.

In the middle of this crisis, for a decade Cyprian pastored and taught . . . just love. In his sermon "On Mortality," concerning the plague that was devastating the empire in the 250s, he simply exhorted the members of his congregation to not stop caring for the dead and the dying. Christians know where their security lies—in Jesus, whom we will see in heaven. Cyprian consequently said that Christians should not fear the worst of the sufferings in this earthly life. The familiar children's hymn beginning "Jesus loves me—this I know / For the Bible tells me so" long postdates Cyprian, of course. But I am convinced that had he ever heard it, he would have loved it.

The Power of Love

In his book *The Rise of Christianity: A Sociologist Reconsiders History,* Rodney Stark considers the reasons for the explosive growth of Christianity in the Roman Empire—from a tiny fraction of 1 percent of the population in the beginning of the third century to about 10 percent of the population by the century's end.[1] How in the world, Stark wonders, did Christianity grow so greatly in the period when the suffering of everyone in the empire was at its highest? Why would any outsider in this beleaguered gods-forsaken (as some pagans were convinced) empire want to convert to a bizarre "cult" that worshipped a crucified Messiah?[2] Because, Stark concludes, the Christians loved.

1. Rodney Stark, *The Rise of Christianity: A Sociologist Reconsiders History* (Princeton University Press, 2023).
2. For an overview of just how utterly strange Christianity was in comparison with everything that the Romans were familiar with, see Nijay Gupta, *Strange Religion: How the First Christians Were Weird, Dangerous, and Compelling* (Brazos Press, 2024).

Augustine Finds Hope

Years ago, I was asked to teach a freshman seminar that would involve readings on higher ed and train students in some basic how-to-college hacks. After thinking about what book to assign for the class to read and slowly discuss together, I settled on Augustine's *Confessions*. Many of the students had never even heard of Augustine before and found him a tough slog, but I stand by my decision. I think everyone got something from the overall experience and left the class knowing "how to college" better.

To be fair, education is not the main theme of Augustine's *Confessions*—his search for God is. Still, education is a key topic in this work because it was so central to Augustine's life. He received a rigorous education both in his native North Africa and in Italy. He then spent yet more time in the education world as a rhetoric teacher. A proud nerd-above-all-nerds, Augustine read more voraciously than most others in his day. Sure, he kept a lifelong chip on his shoulder over his failure to master the Greek language—but I humbly believe that he still made up for it.

Augustine's incredible knowledge of Greek and Roman literature (the former in Latin translation), philosophy, and history seamlessly permeates his writings. For example, the early portions of his monumental *City of God*, the magnum opus of his later life, is really a survey of pagan literature. But as we close this chapter, I want to turn to another instance in Augustine's writings and life story where he directly brought pagan literature to bear on his journey to God.

Shortly before describing his conversion, Augustine embarks on a meditative survey of Greco-Roman pagan literature that he has read. He describes not only what he found present in it but, more importantly, what he found missing. First and foremost, relying on the writings of such philosophers as Plato, Cicero, and Plotinus, he notes that their creation narratives and general visions of the divine are remarkably similar. Augustine had already read about the concept of God as the Word in pagan classics. He contends that even if it was presented somewhat differently, it was recognizable enough. But he straightaway adds that he did not find in those pagan works the tale of how people rejected God and, in reply, how God welcomes to his family all who believe.

Augustine continues, "In the same books I also read of the Word, God, that his *birth came not from human stock, not from nature's will or man's, but from God*. But I did not read in them that *the Word was made flesh and came to dwell among us*."[7] Likewise, Augustine adds, he had read in pagan books that God did not consider his divinity a supreme prize. And yet he still draws a contrast: He didn't find anything in pagan books about a God willing to sacrifice himself, take on the shape of man, die on a cross, and be resurrected. Nothing in these books speaks of the atonement—the need for God's sacrifice.

Most importantly of all, Augustine concludes, quoting from Matthew 11:29, he never found God's call in any pagan books: "*I am gentle and humble of heart; and you shall find rest for your souls.*"[8] In a world filled with cruel and power-hungry gods, able to punish an overly curious man by turning him into a donkey, these words of Jesus taught Augustine soul-saving hope.

When Christians Read the Pagans

Augustine found that the promises of Christ stand out all the more powerfully when contrasted with pagan myths and stories about gods and

7. Augustine, *Confessions*, 145 (emphasis original).
8. Augustine, *Confessions*, 145 (emphasis original).

men. Most of all, God's promise of rest for the weary soul finally soothes Augustine's beleaguered strivings. Not many pages later in the *Confessions* comes his final conversion—the moment of weeping in the garden and hearing the voice exhorting him to "take it and read."

I find Augustine's description of his conversion process very relatable. My high school track coach used to describe me as "all book sense and no common sense." He was not wrong. I think I've grown significantly in the commonsense department over the quarter century I've lived since high school—but book sense still comes most naturally to me. And so, when I began exploring Christianity at age thirty, I imitated what Augustine did: I read. I read apologetics in favor of Christianity and arguments against Christianity. I read books on a variety of aspects of Christian belief. But what finally "broke" me and led me to accept Christ? My reading of the Gospels.

When we read the pagan classics side by side with the Bible, especially the Gospels, something extraordinary happens. We are able to get closer to the world of the earliest converts to Christianity and can understand them better. In the process, we see why someone might turn their back on the cruelty of Zeus and seek the welcoming love of Christ. Thus, during our reading our own faith also grows. Whenever Christians ask me for reading recommendations besides the Bible, I invariably respond: Read the classics, from the pagans all the way to the moderns. This is why.

Recommendations for Further Reading

Augustine, *Confessions*. Translated by Henry Chadwick. Oxford University Press, 2009.

Augustine, *Confessions*. Translated by Sarah Ruden. Modern Library, 2018.

Augustine, *City of God*. Translated by Marcus Dods. Hendrickson Publishers, 2009.

Cyprian, *On Mortality*. Translated by Robert Ernest Wallis. In *Ante-Nicene Fathers* 5, edited by Alexander Roberts, James Donaldson, and A. Cleveland Coxe. Christian Literature,

1886. The text is also online at New Advent, accessed March 7, 2025, https://www.newadvent.org/fathers/050707.htm.

Cyprian, *On Works and Alms*. Translated by Robert Ernest Wallis. In *Ante-Nicene Fathers* 5, edited by Alexander Roberts, James Donaldson, and A. Cleveland Coxe. Christian Literature, 1886. The text is also online at New Advent, accessed March 7, 2025, https://www.newadvent.org/fathers/050708.htm.

Perpetua, *The Passion of Saints Perpetua and Felicity*. Translated by W. H. Shewring. Sheed and Ward, 1931. The text is also online at the Medieval Sourcebook, Fordham University, accessed March 7, 2025, https://sourcebooks.web.fordham.edu/source/perpetua.asp.

Questions for Discussion and Reflection

1. What about Perpetua's story do you find particularly unusual and memorable? How does she compare to the pagan heroes we've read about so far?
2. What is love, according to Cyprian? Why does such love matter?
3. How did Augustine finally come to know Christ? Why do such conversion stories matter?

CHAPTER

The Christian Vergil's Violent Virtues

Christ, you have always pitied the harsh agonies of human kind!
You are known for your Father's strength, but yours is one power
(for we worship one god under each name; yet not just one name,
since, Christ, you are God from the Father).
Tell us, my king, how the militias of our armed minds can
drive out the Sins
from the caverns of our souls.[1]

The Christian Vergil

In the early fifth century AD, at the same time as an aged Augustine was caring for his flock in North Africa's Hippo Regius and churning out sermons and treatises, a lesser-known poet across the empire in Spain was working on a new allegorical epic. This epic, *Psychomachia* or *The Battle of the Soul*, is a mere one thousand lines—barely more than a tenth of Vergil's *Aeneid*. But what it may seem to lack in length, it makes up for in innovation. Its violent subject matter would recall the martial epics of both Homer and Vergil, earning this author the title of the Christian Vergil.

Aurelius Clemens Prudentius is little known today, and that is a pity. In an age of anxiety and violent warlords around the Later Roman Empire,

1. Marc Mastrangelo, *Prudentius' Psychomachia* (Routledge, 2022), 33.

thinking of spiritual matters as war—an invisible mirror to what was so readily visible all around—seemed natural and familiar to both Prudentius and his readers. Of course, the concept of spiritual warfare has a rich theology that runs through the Bible—consider, for instance, the famous passage about the armor of God:

> Finally, be strong in the Lord and in his mighty power. Put on the full armor of God, so that you can take your stand against the devil's schemes. For our struggle is not against flesh and blood, but against the rulers, against the authorities, against the powers of this dark world and against the spiritual forces of evil in the heavenly realms. Therefore put on the full armor of God . . .[2]

We are not speaking of literal armor, and yet the imagery in this passage is just vivid enough to have inspired Christians from antiquity into modern society and its VBS curricula. It is tempting to imagine putting on real armor to fight real conflicts in the surrounding world.

And so, in writing this unusual epic, Prudentius entered into dialogue with a rich tradition of previous pagan and Christian writers—Ephesians 6 included. At the heart of this conversation was the spiritual formation of Christians, a process that would allow the virtues to defeat the vices within each believer's soul. How do we educate the soul to love the virtues? The answer, for Prudentius, can perhaps be best summarized in the language we can borrow from a Christian writer who lived two hundred years earlier, whom Prudentius himself occasionally referenced.[3]

"What Has Athens to Do with Jerusalem?"

The above question from the early third-century AD theologian Tertullian has become arguably his most famous saying—perhaps only surpassed in fame by his quip that "the blood of the martyrs is the seed of the church."[4]

---

2. Ephesians 6:10–13.
3. For example, see Marc Mastrangelo, *The Roman Self in Late Antiquity: Prudentius and the Poetics of the Soul* (Johns Hopkins University Press, 2008), 216, n. 59, and Cillian O'Hogan, *Prudentius and the Landscapes of Late Antiquity* (Oxford University Press, 2016), 136.
4. Portions of this chapter are adapted from my essay, "Why Athens and Jerusalem Still Need Each Other, and Why a Healthy Democracy Needs Both," *The Raised Hand*, November 29, 2023,

It is always risky to take famous quotations out of context. And yet these two statements, uttered in different contexts, readily reveal something about Tertullian and his worldview. First, no one has yet accused him of having a sunny disposition. For Tertullian, the glass wasn't half-full or half-empty—rather, the glass was broken, shattered, and destroyed beyond repair.

Second and relatedly, Tertullian believed that suffering well was a key testimony in the life of a Christian. Finally, third and most relevantly, Tertullian's question about Athens and Jerusalem is one of the earliest Christian expressions of concern about the learning that happens (and doesn't happen) at secular or downright pagan educational institutions and intellectual centers. Specifically, Tertullian's (and Prudentius's) concern was about ensuring that education involved growth in the virtues for every student.

Athens, for Tertullian and the rest of the Roman pagans and Christians of his day, stood for the centuries-long tradition of pagan educational excellence in philosophy, rhetoric, and everything else we might generally label today as the liberal arts. In 431 BC, over six hundred years earlier, we saw the Athenian democratic statesman Pericles boast about Athens: "We are the school of Hellas." His confidence was not excessive.

At its height, Athens was a city where philosophers and public intellectuals roamed the streets, engaging the public in intellectual debates and conversations (although some hearers resented how these haranguers took up their time). Over the centuries that followed the heyday of Athenian democracy, Athens's political influence steadily waned. Nevertheless, its reputation as the school of not just Greece but the entire Greco-Roman Mediterranean world was only rivaled by its most famous copycat—Alexandria. Athens was academia par excellence—all brain. But what is a brain without a heart and a soul? Jerusalem, by contrast, was the symbol of faith and true belief for Tertullian and his Christian conversationalists. Much as Athens was all brain, Jerusalem was all heart and soul—a city with a Temple-shaped void left in the Jewish and Christian imagination long after the Romans destroyed the Second Temple in AD 70.

Tertullian believed that you cannot simply reason your way into faith in Christ through the study of pagan philosophy and rhetoric. As with all educated men of his day, Tertullian was well-steeped in the pagan classics,

---

https://substack.com/home/post/p-139050377.

so his statement seems shocking at first glance. Here he is, using the very rhetorical training he has received from his Athenian-style education to argue against Christians needing to have such an education! However, that is not what he is doing. In asking his question, Tertullian is not calling Christians to reject education (including pagan learning) as unnecessary but rather to probe deeper. Just as the brain alone cannot bring someone to saving faith, neither can the heart and the soul alone ground one's faith with deep roots, leading to a flourishing life. Similarly, we can say, just going to college—relying on Athens—will not bring someone to saving faith in God.

But then, a life that relies on one's heart without meaningfully employing intellect is going to produce a shallow faith and an even shallower ethical compass. This possibility greatly concerned Tertullian. Two hundred years later, Prudentius was no less worried. What is the solution? Both Tertullian and Prudentius answered by emphasizing an education that cultivated the virtues.[5] Let us consider Tertullian's rhetorical question about Athens and Jerusalem. Does one need the other more? What is the best relationship between them, anyway?

Athens Needs Jerusalem

Pericles's Athens may have been the school of Hellas, but the history of the Athenian democracy in the decades following Pericles's statement clearly showed that knowledge and academic excellence on their own are dangerous. A democracy of educated citizens may not flourish but rather disintegrate into mob rule or oligarchic tyranny. Why? Because moral dilemmas arise, and intellectual and philosophical knowledge alone are insufficient for dealing with them.

In chapter 4, we considered a dramatized version of the diplomatic debate that took place in the Melian Dialogue episode of Thucydides's history of the Peloponnesian War. We find the Athenians utilizing excellent rhetorical arguments based on natural law: It is natural for those who are strong to get their way, and the weak have no choice but to submit. And so the Athenians act in accordance with this principle: They capture the city,

5. For reflections on the relevance of this kind of education in our age, see Kyle Hughes, *Teaching for Spiritual Formation: A Patristic Approach to Christian Education in a Convulsed Age* (Wipf and Stock, 2022).

kill all adult males, and sell all women and children into slavery. However, even Thucydides, a hardened military man and also an Athenian, was shocked by this casual cruelty and the utter lack of moral compass that the Athenians exhibited.

Things got worse. In 404 BC, after Athens surrendered to Sparta, an oligarchic revolution shook the city. With Sparta's support, the Thirty Tyrants installed themselves as masters of Athens. For eight months a regime of bloodletting, a veritable reign of terror, convulsed the city, which had already been traumatized by the prolonged preceding war. Who was chief among the Thirty, the most bloodthirsty of them all? Socrates's student, Critias.

As Socrates's students debated matters like the ideal state, the nature of virtue, and what makes something or someone good, they apparently learned to argue well, articulate their ideas brilliantly, and acquire all other skills required for securing political power. However, they did not learn ethics or compassion. Socrates's students were renowned as brilliant. They had received an excellent education. But lacking genuine character formation in the virtues, some of them turned that education against fellow citizens, overthrowing their democracy and ruthlessly killing anyone who opposed them. After all, selfishness and desire for power are the only impulses that do not have to be learned—they are inbuilt.

This sad example of Athens—and many others—are important reminders for us today, as we also are prone to idealize education as the filling up of a brain with all the right knowledge and methods. Learning outcomes for secular schools at all levels emphasize specific skills and knowledge points. For instance, students will learn about a particular topic or figure out how to solve a particular type of problem. This kind of education isn't bad, but it just isn't complete because it leaves no tools for addressing moral dilemmas. And yet moral dilemmas that demand ethical thinking are the defining characteristic of our age, just as they were in the Athenian democracy. Knowledge without ethics is dangerous. Just knowing how to argue a case well may win the case, but if we care about justice we should know that some victories require our soul as their price.

And so, the history of Athens—even though it was the "school of Hellas"—reminds us that knowledge and superb education without the virtues—without character formation—is at best neutral and at worst downright dangerous. Such an education merely renders the morally rootless person a danger to self and others, having no tools for resisting the cruelty, moral ambiguity, and anxiety of our age.

Character formation in the virtues is key for the good life, not just for individuals but also for the whole society—and let's not forget our democracy here. But where do our ethics come from? Where do our knowledge and valuing of virtues come from? While echoes of the virtues come through in some pagan writers, they only see through a mirror dimly. The pagan religious traditions could hand down rules—for instance, the gods hated blood pollution, so murder was certainly bad. But these traditions could not provide for true, genuine transformation of character beyond just getting someone to follow the rules. They could not explain why—to use the example of murder again—something was so bad. In the pagan imagination, such things had nothing to do with humans and everything to do with the arbitrary preferences of the pagan gods and the desire to keep general order in community.

Thus, I contend that this need for character formation in the virtues clearly shows that Athens needs Jerusalem. Without Christ, there is no clear declaration of the preciousness of each and every human life—because every single person is made in the image of God. Without the understanding of humanity's preciousness in God's eyes, the Athenians' conduct at Melos can be considered perfectly natural—in accordance with nature, as they themselves claimed. So, sometimes we can best see what is most needed by its absence. Mercy, love, and compassion for others are essential virtues for building a functional home, community, and a society of citizens willing to cooperate with each other and occasionally sacrifice their own interests for those of the larger whole.

It is tempting for the strong to behave toward the weak as the Athenians did toward the Melians—focusing on self-interest without cultivating compassion for others. But we should recognize how morally bankrupt such conduct is and condemn the consequent warping of our own souls which would occur. But then the question naturally follows: Does character formation—this education in the virtues for citizens—really even need education of another sort? In other words, we have just established that Athens needs Jerusalem. But does Jerusalem really need Athens?

This question elicited much debate in Late Antiquity, when such thinkers as Jerome encouraged giving up pagan literature in favor of reading the Bible and sacred books alone. In a letter to a friend, Jerome describes his dysfunctional addiction to reading Cicero (yes, really) and recounts a vision from the Lord that accused him of being a Ciceronian rather than a Christian. Convicted that his interest in pagan rhetoric was a sin, Jerome at one point decided to give it up cold turkey, effectively proclaiming that Christians have no business ever reading pagans.[6]

I have also occasionally heard people express such a view today—that Christians only need to read the Bible. But we need to know why this is not a good idea! Just like Athens needs Jerusalem, so does Jerusalem need Athens.

Jerusalem Needs Athens: Prudentius and the Epic of Virtues

While Athens without Jerusalem is dangerously unmoored from ethics and love for fellow human beings, Jerusalem without Athens is ignorant of the physical and spiritual dangers of this world. Jerusalem offers grounding for the soul and the heart, but intellectual development is also an integral part of this spiritual formation.

Christian intellectuals in Late Antiquity—from Tertullian to Cyprian and Ambrose and Augustine—were aware of this important connection. In their writing about spiritual matters, they leaned on the lengthy tradition of pagan learning, including not only rhetoric and philosophy and history but also timelessly beautiful literature. They employed all of this in the service of educating Christian citizens in the virtues. Let us now return to Prudentius and his battle for the soul.

Psychomachia (i.e., the battle within/for the soul) describes in vividly graphic and violent detail the epic battle that surpasses all other epic battles: the battle of virtues and vices within the soul of every Christian. In writing this poem, Prudentius was consciously interjecting himself into the tradition of epic poetry going back to Homer. He was also aware of his role as an educator—the bringer of Athens to Jerusalem. After all, the greatest

6. Jerome, "Letter 22 to Eustochium," in *St. Jerome: Letters and Select Works*, trans. W. H. Fremantle, *Nicene and Post-Nicene Church Fathers* 2/6, ed. Philip Schaff and Henry Wace (Christian Literature Company, 1893), 35–36. The text cited is also online at Early Church Texts, accessed March 6, 2025, https://earlychurchtexts.com/public/jerome_letter_22_ciceronian_or_christian.htm.

and most beautiful works of literature in the ancient world were meant to inspire, teach virtues, and form good citizens.

In fact, we can draw a fairly direct line of epic tradition connecting Prudentius back to earlier models whose influence his audiences would have readily recognized. To briefly sum them up, Homer's *Iliad* produced an unforgettable set of heroes, especially Achilles, the Best of the Achaeans. These heroes all competed for excellence on the battlefield by killing other heroes in grotesquely bloody duels. Drawing on this Homeric model, the Roman poet Vergil produced Rome's most famous epic poem—the *Aeneid*, describing the flight of the hero Aeneas from the burning city of Troy to Italy, where he would found a new Troy.

Vergil depicts Aeneas as a model warrior and hero. He is pious—respectful of the pagan gods, including his mom Venus, the goddess of love. In addition, he demonstrates *virtus*—the Latin term that literally means "manliness" or "bravery." But the early Christians eventually transformed this term into virtue as we know it—meaning something heroic off the battlefield, imbued with more spiritual implications.

This shifting meaning of *virtus* corresponds to the different nature of heroes that Christianity produced. While the heroes of pagan epics were men—to a man—who won glory through the slaughter of other heroes on the battlefield, Christianity afforded a new path to heroic glory through martyrdom. These martyrs, the new heroes of this revolutionary movement, were often weak—young nursing mothers, teenage girls, slaves, and defenseless old men. And yet, through heroic martyrdom and through their suffering that offered the blood which became the "seed of the church" that Tertullian spoke of, they won glory to rival or surpass the glory of Achilles or Aeneas.

Prudentius takes this long and full history to heart in devising his epic. The heroes are no longer mighty men who kill other guys on the battlefield but rather virtues that defeat sins to the applause of the glorious martyrs of the church. Just watch Faith drop-kick Paganism on the head, or Good Works strangle Greed with dramatic abandon, or Patience bravely (and patiently) overwhelm Anger. The same dramatic duels for which earlier pagan epics have been known are harnessed to describe these duels of the virtues against the vices. But there is more—Prudentius's epic straddles genres. While clearly a martial epic, it is also a didactic poem seeking to educate.

Research on good pedagogical practices over the past couple of decades has emphasized the importance of storytelling. Certain parts of the brain are activated by stories, and we better retain information presented to us as stories than as simply a list of facts.[7] Prudentius's didactic poem follows this same wisdom. It is one thing to list the virtues and vices to students and say: Do this, not that. But that would be boring and forgettable, even if true. Instead, Prudentius needed to harness all of the previous rhetorical and intellectual tradition of Athens in the service of the good, the beautiful, and the true in order to tell these stories of virtue and vice more engagingly. In this way, pagan epic in the service of Jerusalem becomes a redeemed tool of education for the soul. With his poetic experiment, Prudentius brings Athens and Jerusalem together in a particularly obvious and highly entertaining way. He shows that a rich spiritual life blossoms when combined with a virtuous life of the mind that is spent in pursuit of good and beautiful things—like edifying poetry.

Prudentius admittedly did not become as big a hit as maybe he had hoped—and I will refrain here from casting any judgment on the quality of his poetry. At any rate, even though he tried to write himself into the same tradition as Homer and Vergil, you may have never heard of him before reading this chapter—and it is just as likely that you have heard of Homer and Vergil before reading this book. That is okay. Nevertheless, Prudentius's example reminds us of the important work that educators do, whether their names become immortalized in history or not. Forming souls through education in the virtues is certainly a weighty responsibility.

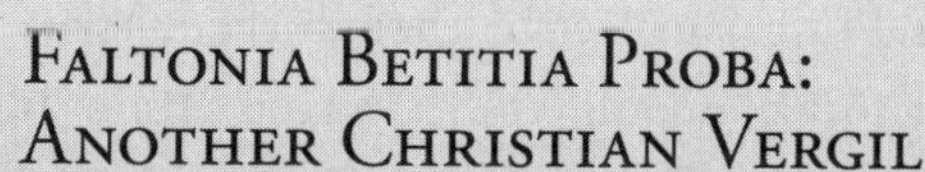

Faltonia Betitia Proba: Another Christian Vergil

Prudentius is not the only late Roman poet to imitate Vergil. Rivaling him for the title of the Christian Vergil is an aristocratic woman, Faltonia Betitia Proba, who lived and

7. Theologian Michael Horton presents a similar argument in *Covenant and Eschatology: The Divine Drama* (Westminster John Knox Press, 2002).

wrote almost a century earlier than Prudentius. Her 694-line *Vergilian Cento Concerning the Glory of Christ* is worth reading despite its comparative lack of adrenaline.[1]

While Prudentius wrote his own poetry, Proba reworked actual verses from Vergil's *Aeneid* into her epic about Christ. Thence the title of her work contains the word *cento*, which means "patchwork." This term describes poetry created from other poets' work—but the result is distinctly her own.

1. For a concise introduction to Proba, see Adam Renberg, "Mothers of the Church: Faltonia Betitia Proba," *Anxious Bench*, July 15, 2024, https://www.patheos.com/blogs/anxiousbench/2024/07/mothers-of-the-church-faltonia-betitia-proba/. For a more comprehensive and academic introduction, see Sigrid Schottenius Cullhed, *Proba the Prophet: The Christian Vergilian Cento of Faltonia Betitia Proba* (Brill, 2015).

The Virtues as Heroes

Ultimately, Prudentius's epic has a rather simplistic plot: All we get is the duels of each virtue opposite a corresponding vice. Although the victory of the virtues is dramatic, the story is done there. The good guys defeat the bad guys in this tale, assuring the audiences, who lived in an age of turmoil and anxiety—the epic was published ca. 405, just a handful of years before the vicious sack of Rome by the Goths in 410—that all will be well even if it doesn't quite look like this at present.

But as we reflect on the meaning of this allegorical battle, we can consider an obvious additional matter: Although the allegory reassures the audience that the victory of good over evil in God's realm is guaranteed, it also demands action from its readers. To understand these demands, let us turn to the description of the armor of God in Ephesians 6:13–17, which more overtly teaches us something important about agency in these duels:

> Therefore put on the full armor of God, so that when the day of evil comes, you may be able to stand your ground, and after you have done everything, to stand. Stand firm then, with the belt of truth buckled around your waist, with the breastplate of righteousness in place, and

with your feet fitted with the readiness that comes from the gospel of peace. In addition to all this, take up the shield of faith, with which you can extinguish all the flaming arrows of the evil one. Take the helmet of salvation and the sword of the Spirit, which is the word of God.

No people are in sight in Prudentius's epic—the personified virtues simply battle it out. But as ancient readers knew—and as we also ought to remember—virtues don't exist on their own in real life. We must do our part to clothe our souls with them—through our life in Christ. And that is also Prudentius's point, of course—the larger battle is happening within and for each of our souls. But the address to Christ that opens *Psychomachia*—quoted at the beginning of this chapter—reminds the reader that our Lord is ultimately in control. Pagan epics always opened with an address to a divinity who would bless the poet's work, inspiring him to say beautiful and true things. Christ serves this purpose here for Prudentius.

With this reminder of Christ's supremacy over all things in mind, we must ensure that both knowledge and spiritual understanding—both Athens and Jerusalem—work together, not apart. We live in a world where increasingly more is possible thanks to the level of knowledge that science has given us, personifying the extreme power of Athens. For instance, science now allows for the cloning of animals and humans—although the latter is illegal in most countries. But just because we can do something does not always mean we should—even if it is legal. Education in the virtues affords us the wisdom to know the difference between what we should do or not do.

The virtues cannot be heroes all by themselves in the abstract. But we can shine and grow when we are clothed in them, ensuring our maturity as we pursue sanctification in this life.

Recommendations for Further Reading

Mastrangelo, Marc. *Prudentius' Psychomachia*. Routledge, 2022.

Schottenius Cullhed, Sigrid. *Proba the Prophet: The Christian Virgilian Cento of Faltonia Betitia Proba*. Brill, 2015.

Questions for Discussion and Reflection

1. What does Athens stand for, and what does Jerusalem stand for? Why do we need both?
2. What did Prudentius try to achieve with his epic? How do you envision the virtues? Try to draw or sketch a particular virtue—how do you imagine it, and why?
3. Attempt to write a cento of your own, just like Proba did—a patchwork poem from the lines of other poets, whether one or several. What is the topic of your cento? How did you select the poets from whom you borrowed verses for your cento?

CHAPTER

Boethius and the Consolation Philosophy Gives

> She had just finished singing, while the sweetness of her song held me with still attentive ears, struck silent, and eager to listen further. So after a little while I said: "O best of comforters of weary spirits, how well you have revived me with the weight of your arguments and also with the delights of your songs! So well that now I no longer think myself unequal to the blows of fortune."[1]

Of Dungeons and Bookends

Alone in a dark, dank dungeon during the days of the Later Roman Empire, a man pensively leans over a scroll, quill in hand, trying to make do with the meager light available to him. It feels strange to be alone having only one's own words to keep company with for days and months. But someone who has read much is never alone; so it is with this man—the statesman and philosopher Boethius.

Anicius Manlius Severinus Boethius was about as blue blood as it gets in the twilight period of the Roman Empire. He lived a life of political power, wealth, and privilege for the first forty-odd years of his life. And then the spectacular crash came. Falsely accused of conspiring against Theodoric, king

1. Boethius, *The Consolation of Philosophy*, trans. S. J. Tester (Harvard University Press, 1973), III.I.

of the Ostrogoths, in AD 523, Boethius went overnight from power to prison. He was first held in a tiny church baptistery, and then at a remote country estate. After nine months in captivity, he was executed in AD 524. But what he did in this prison excites our interest right now. Put simply, he wrote.

It is striking to consider that captivity or milder forms of rejection—for instance, the loss of prestige or of a political career—were the catalysts for so many great works of literature throughout antiquity. Thucydides started his history before he was exiled from Athens, but his exile allowed him to focus on it in earnest. Sallust turned historian after the premature end of his political career in Rome. Cicero also turned to philosophy after he had lost political influence. Finally, the apostle Paul penned letter after letter to churches around the Roman Empire even in the midst of repeated imprisonments for preaching the gospel.

This brings us back to Boethius. Like all of his frustrated and disappointed predecessors, he wrote in prison—perhaps because he finally had more free time than ever before in his life. No meetings. No letters to respond to. No travel. No visitors begging for his help. Just time alone to manage in any way he wished, within a very confined space and with no amenities. As the literary critic Cynthia L. Haven put it, "Kind of a writer's retreat, without the swag bags."[2] And so, again, Boethius freely scribbled away.

But Boethius didn't write just anything. Rather, bringing together his knowledge of all preceding Greco-Roman literature, Boethius wrote a Platonic dialogue like no other: *The Consolation of Philosophy*, a conversation between himself and Philosophy personified as she consoled him in his time of darkest need. This work, so heartfelt and sorrowful, defies genres—or rather, unabashedly brings them together. This is not necessarily a rare occurrence, by the way. As Andrew Judd notes, "texts are promiscuous"—meaning that the mixing of genres happens. Accordingly, we need to recognize the different elements being mixed so that we can understand the text more fully.[3] Furthermore, the text will only work its full influence upon us when we experience the correct genre correctly.[4] Seasoned educated readers of the sort

2. Cynthia L. Haven, "Consolation in Hard Times: Boethius Knew All About It," *The Book Haven* (blog), Stanford University, October 10, 2020, https://bookhaven.stanford.edu/2020/10/consolation-in-hard-times-boethius-knew-all-about-it/.
3. Andrew Judd, *Modern Genre Theory: An Introduction for Biblical Studies* (Zondervan Academic, 2024), 19.
4. Judd, *Modern Genre Theory*, 167–71.

Boethius is addressing would have experienced this process while reading, which is not so different from the code-switching of polyglots.

Boethius opens with a poetic address to the Muses, just as any pagan poet would have done. Then shifting into prose for much of the work, he will continue to slip into poetry periodically. Boethius also uses the format of the philosophical dialogue—in which he converses with Lady Philosophy. His Socrates figure, she drives the conversation while he is merely the student, responding to her questions. However, we could note that Boethius is also a Socrates figure himself—he is participating in this dialogue while in prison awaiting execution, just as Socrates did in *The Crito*.

There is more to consider. The title of this work reminds us that it is a *consolatio*, a consolation. This genre is intended to bring comfort, such as when Cyprian of Carthage wrote to console his flock during the plague in the mid-third century AD. The purpose of the consolation here is certainly clear: Boethius is seeking solace for himself as he mourns his lost freedom, glory, and imminent execution. Last but not least, this dialogue openly nods to Menippean satire, another genre designed to mock the governing authorities through its most distinctive characteristic: the mixing of poetry and prose.[5]

There is something deeply Homeric about all this. Just as Achilles had to choose between a young death that would bring him immortal glory and a quiet but fameless life into old age, so did Boethius end up earning immortal glory after a young death, all because of this work. He certainly would never have written it otherwise had he not been imprisoned under such tragic conditions. However, his choice was not conscious; left to his own devices, he likely would have chosen a quiet long life instead. This train of thought is condensed into a work that is so deeply personal, timeless, and relatable at a basic level to any writer. Writers do not control their destinies—we write. That is all we can do. And then these words go forth into the world—if we are lucky—and find readers who will love them or hate them. Naturally, we hope to receive adulation rather than disapprobation!

In Boethius's case, *The Consolation of Philosophy* became a well-loved sensation, widely read throughout the Middle Ages. And somehow, somewhere along the way Boethius also became the final glorious bookend of

5. For an overview of this unusual genre, which was revived in Late Antiquity, see Joel Relihan, *Ancient Menippean Satire* (Johns Hopkins University Press, 1993).

Classical literature. Just as Homer is considered the beginning of Classical Greco-Roman literature, so is Boethius its distinguished end. We do not speak of Classical literature after Boethius; we speak of medieval literature. Sure, such bookends seem artificial—but the line must be drawn somewhere.

There are good reasons to draw this line at Boethius. He really is a fitting Janus figure—akin to that old Roman two-faced god who could easily look back at the old and look forward to the new. Boethius, as a good Janus, brings together the old in the many genres and subjects he combines in *The Consolation of Philosophy*. But his innovative creativity—his bold and unapologetic intertwining of all of antiquity to construct his very own creation—seeks to look forward and set a model for the imitative borrowing from the Classical tradition that will become a constant in medieval literature.[6]

Writing in the prologue to her *Lais* during the twelfth century, Marie de France remarked that we are but dwarves standing on the shoulders of giants. The dwarves were the people of her age—and she readily included herself in their number. The giants, by contrast, were the "ancients" from whom Marie and other medieval writers drew so much of their inspiration and their themes, sometimes adapting older stories wholesale. Without literary giants like Ovid, Vergil, and Cicero, there would have been no Marie de France—as Marie would have been the first to admit. But maybe she didn't need to be so hard on herself—the dwarves could always see something the giants couldn't!

Cassiodorus

Born around the same time as Boethius in the AD 480s, Cassiodorus was a prominent statesman who actually became Boethius's direct successor in politics after his arrest and execution. But unlike Boethius, Cassiodorus lived to a ripe old age, reaching close to the century mark.

In his retirement, Cassiodorus founded a monastery, Vivarium, and dedicated his time to learning and writing about

6. See, for instance, Antonio Donato, *Boethius'* Consolation of Philosophy *as a Product of Late Antiquity* (Bloomsbury Academic, 2013) for the view that the figure of Philosophy and the arguments she makes are distinctly sixth century AD—representative of Boethius's age rather than of an earlier time.

religious education. His *Institutions* outlines what will become known as the Trivium (grammar, logic, and rhetoric) and the Quadrivium (arithmetic, music, geometry, and astronomy)—fundamentals of medieval education.

On Life, Liberty, and, Most of All, the Pursuit of Happiness

Boethius would have agreed with Marie de France. He also felt like a dwarf looking back—and up to—the giants, especially the epic poets and philosophers. The question of character, so central to both groups, is foremost on Boethius's mind in his work. This question was, as such things often are, deeply personal and directly relevant to his plight. It is appropriate that the two bookends of Classical literature, Homer and Boethius, were both concerned with the question of character: Who is good? This is, we could note, a timeless question and an admission of our nature as reflecting the *imago Dei*, whether we know it or not. In conversation with the rich young ruler in Luke 18:18–19, Jesus reminds him, "No one is good—except God alone."

Still, human pride and our desire for approval—ultimately, a desire for God to tell us "Well done"—drive us to wonder: Am I good? And—like the rich young ruler—we ask, furthermore: What else do I need to do? What is the minimal checklist for acing this assignment? But we must also consider the related matter of who decides and judges our goodness or our character. By asking Jesus specifically, the young ruler acknowledges a key truth: God genuinely cares about our goodness. Whenever we allow other people to decide on our character, we are opening ourselves up to the possibility of receiving a false judgment—either being judged good when we did evil or (as Boethius learned to his great chagrin) being judged evil even though we did nothing wrong.

Perhaps during his imprisonment Boethius wrestled most with the knowledge that he was actually not guilty of treason against King Theodoric. So, how do people live with such stains on their character and reputation even though they are assured of their innocence? Boethius spends much of the first book of his work tackling this challenge.

Boethius appropriately deals with this question by looking back at Classical literature. After all, such a question is at the heart of the entire tradition. So he opens the work by invoking the Muses—until Philosophy shows up and tells the Muses to get lost. Her response reminds Boethius that the pagan epics could not offer a true answer to his present grief.[7] Or, rather, they themselves could only offer a partial truth, which could at best see the gospel through a mirror dimly.

In the *Iliad*, we saw Achilles and the rest of the heroes struggle with this same question: Who is good? The heroic code ultimately answered: It doesn't matter who is good; it only matters who is best! Thus, all heroes spent the Trojan War competing no less against each other than they did fighting against the enemy. Because their excellence was externally projected and externally judged—you are what others say you are!—it didn't matter if a hero thought that he was good or even best. All that mattered was what everyone else thought.

But through Christ—and also through his conversations with Lady Philosophy, who represents the best of pagan wisdom filtered through biblical principles—Boethius comes to terms with another definition of goodness. In the shifting of categories from epic hero to humble believer, Boethius finds the comfort of Christ, the only one who is truly good. Virtue, he realizes over the course of the meandering conversation with Philosophy in five books of poetry and prose, is not in the eye of the beholder. Rather virtue is something that no false judgment can ever take away from the one who has it. In other words, the world can reject him without shaking his eternal security. His character remains exactly the same in his imprisonment as it was when he was a highly regarded statesman. He has not changed—but, most importantly, God is in control and knows the truth.

In the end, Boethius realizes that although his reasons for writing are personal, this is not a story about him. Rather, it is about God. In Boethius's strange coopting of the Platonic dialogue, Philosophy represents a distinctly Christian wisdom. She exemplifies the good, the true, and the beautiful in a way that pagan philosophy never could. However, Philosophy also paradoxically owes her existence to pagan philosophy and pagan philosophers such as

7. For an analysis of Christian poetry in Late Antiquity, see Timothy E. G. Bartel, *The Poets and the Fathers: Theology and Poetry from Gregory Nazianzus to Scott Cairns* (Wipf and Stock, 2024).

Socrates. She is also not shy about citing Plato, affectionately referring to him as "my Plato" in the process and boldly reconciling his views to her own.[8]

It is fitting that a dialogue between Boethius and Philosophy about happiness takes the prized middle spot in this book—book three out of five. Why discuss happiness over anything else? Philosophy explains:

> The whole concern of men, which the effort of a multitude of pursuits keeps busy, moves by different roads, yet strives to arrive at one and the same end, that of happiness. Now that is the good which, once a man attains it, leaves no room for further desires. And it is the highest of all goods, containing in itself all that is good, for if there were anything lacking to it, it could not be the highest good, since there would remain something outside it which could be desired. So it is clear that happiness is that state which is perfect since all goods are gathered together in it.[9]

All other goals, dreams, and desires are part and parcel of this ultimate goal—the pursuit of happiness. Happiness is "perfect" in the sense of containing all else and lacking nothing.

But is this goal, this happiness, ever achievable in this life? What do we need in order to be fully and undeniably happy? Philosophy's questions to Boethius reveal the imperfections of his previous powerful and wealthy life. He confesses that back then he never had a day when he wasn't worried. But neither power nor money were able to buy his happiness—something else was required. Could it be the Achilles answer—glory? No, not that either, Philosophy asserts: "How deceptive that often is, how base! . . . For too many men have often acquired a great reputation because of the mistaken notions of the mob—and what can be imagined baser than that?"[10] After all, being recognized as the Best of the Achaeans did not bring Achilles happiness—it only led him to an early grave.

And so, Philosophy gently but surely leads Boethius to rule out all other possible sources of happiness. There is no list nor recipe to follow. Instead, the "Sunday school" answer is correct. Philosophy concludes that

8. For example, in Boethius, *The Consolation of Philosophy*, III.VI.
9. Boethius, *The Consolation of Philosophy*, III.II.
10. Boethius, *The Consolation of Philosophy*, III.VI.

happiness can only come from the "Father of all things" before bursting into yet another hymn:

> O you who in perpetual order govern the universe,
> Creator of heaven and earth, who bid time ever move,
> And resting still, grant motion to all else;
> Whom no external causes drove to make
> Your work of flowing matter, but the form
> Within yourself of the highest good, ungrudging.[11]

The psalmist, whom she so readily echoes, was right—the creator of heaven and earth alone is always and perfectly good and all-powerful.[12] We, the children of dust, are none of these things. Most of the time, as Boethius's experience shows, we do not overly dwell much on this reality. However, times of suffering make it impossible to overlook the goodness and sovereignty of God.

The School of Suffering

Perhaps the Psalms wouldn't have first come to mind for many of Boethius's readers. Rather, everyone in Late Antiquity associated another book more closely with such seemingly senseless suffering—Job. After all, Job is the story of a righteous man who suffered much for unfathomable reasons, losing everything he had—all his children, his wealth, his health, and his very reputation. Others blithely assumed that he was experiencing divine judgment as punishment for his wickedness. Stunned by his experiences, Job, while faithful and seeking to trust God through his suffering, is understandably left with questions. In the book's astonishing resolution, he poses all these questions to God.

Similarly to Job, the trajectory of the argument in *The Consolation of Philosophy* moves from sadness at the beginning over the injustice of Boethius's treatment to his ultimate recognition: "Nor vainly are our hopes placed in God, nor our prayers, which when they are right cannot be

11. Boethius, *The Consolation of Philosophy*, III.IX.
12. For example, Psalm 104.

ineffectual. Turn away then from vices, cultivate virtues, lift up your mind to righteous hopes, offer up humble prayers to heaven."[13]

The virtuous Christian, unlike Achilles and his ilk finds much comfort in the awareness of his or her virtues. Even if the ending we experience in this life will not feel like a true reward, God is watching and waiting—and the faithful ones will enjoy eternity with him. Clearly, in the process of writing this work, Boethius came to at least some terms with his excruciating suffering. He recognized that even though his reputation and honor were shredded, he could always trust in God, the only one whose character is ever unchanging, ever good, and ever true.

Let me mention something truly remarkable and easily overlooked about Boethius's writing. Think about his environment. While his prison at a remote country estate was likely better than the darker and crampier baptistery where he was initially held, it was likely far from comfortable. After all, a condemned prisoner's comfort was no one's concern. And so, as we read this rich book, filled with clear references to so much of previous Greco-Roman literature while alternating polished prose with no less polished poetry, we may overlook something obvious: Boethius likely only had access to the most basic writing materials during much or all of his time composing *The Consolation of Philosophy*.

Think about your own writing, whether you are a student or a professional writer. Whenever you sit down to write, if you are anything like me, you are surrounded by a pile of books, notes, more books (perhaps on the floor, since they can't all fit on your desk), and maybe a nice iced coffee. Boethius had none of this. So, how did he write this book without his library? In the same way that anyone who has spent a lifetime reading might: by recalling the books with which he had lived for decades. In particular, Boethius's previous experience of translating Greek authors like Aristotle had likely educated him well for such a time as this.

Indeed, I am presently only slightly younger than Boethius was at the time he wrote his book. And like Boethius I have spent decades reading and rereading many of the texts of the Greco-Roman literary canon. In writing this book, I have been repeatedly surprised at not only how much I was able to remember from books I have read many times over the past three decades

---

13. Boethius, *The Consolation of Philosophy*, V.VI.

but also what I could recall from books that I have not reread over the past decade or more. Put simply, we become what we read. Our reading stays with us a while, and when you need it most you might recall a poem or a passage that perhaps never meant much to you when you had first read it.

A life lived with good books is a life in which we are never alone—even in those times when, like Boethius, we feel abandoned by all earthly friends.

The School of Life

Perhaps the school of suffering is nothing other than the school of life—this process through which we (ideally) keep growing in the virtues. Theologically, this process involves the believer's gradual sanctification. It will not be complete in this life, and yet the school of *this* life certainly matters.

Chances are that Boethius's story does not inspire you to wish for his life trajectory. No one craves this type of suffering. No one desires to be the victim of grave injustice—especially not when this means the loss of one's liberty and life. And yet the nature of the fall of man, at its most basic level, affects all of us by bringing a plethora of miseries into the world. How many of us, even if blessed with a long life, would be able to avoid suffering? Indeed, not even the young are immune to hardship. But since we cannot suffer-proof our lives, we can continue to pursue God and wisdom in the process of everyday life. We know that such pursuits, rooted in deep reading and learning, will prepare us well for inevitable storms.

Recommendations for Further Reading

Boethius, *The Consolation of Philosophy*. Translated by Victor Watts. Penguin Classics, 2000.

Questions for Discussion and Reflection

1. How does Boethius's thinking develop over the course of his dialogue with Lady Philosophy? Why does this transformation take place?
2. If you could speak with Philosophy (and let's say this isn't in prison), what would you like to discuss with her?
3. How do you deal with suffering and sorrow in your life? What gives you comfort in such times?

Conclusion

The Virtues of Rereading

The Joy of Rereading

Perhaps one of my joys in writing this book—and perhaps it will also be one of your joys in reading this book—has been rereading many old friends whom I had first met in my teens. For instance, Homer's *Odyssey* has often been assigned in high school English, but it is one thing to read it as a ninth grader and another thing to read it as a parent, an adult who has experienced a few (or many) of life's knocks.

I come now to the definition that I have neglected to offer so far in this book. Just how do we define the classics? Sure, on the one hand there is the niche academic definition: All of my degrees have come from classics departments, which broadly defined classics as the interdisciplinary study of the Greeks and the Romans. Indeed, I have used this definition to restrict the scope of this book. It is a book about reading the Greco-Roman classics as Christians. You can readily find other guides for reading more recent classics.

But back to that pesky definition problem. If I had to define the classics, perhaps the definition I am the least uncomfortable with is a variation on the customary "they're timeless" retort—which, by the way, is true. They are indeed timeless—but they are more than just that. More specifically, when I say that the books I have considered over these twenty chapters are timeless, I am not simply stating that these books can and should still be read today. Rather, I mean that these books always deserve to be reread. They are repeatedly experienced by a person in a relationship of mutual enrichment over a lifetime. The reader not only gains new insights into the book with each rereading but also feels seen anew by this book in the process.

Let me share my experience with Vergil's *Aeneid*. I first read the *Aeneid* as a high school junior in my AP Latin class. Over the course of that school year, I got to read large portions of the epic in Latin—my first unadapted Latin poetry. It was such a thrill! But I also read through the entire epic in translation just so I could know the story as a whole. I enjoyed it—but much of the joy related to perseverance. I felt indescribably thrilled to read words that a Roman poet had composed over two thousand years earlier!

Fast-forward to a seminar I took in my final semester of college, when I got to read all of the *Aeneid* in Latin in one semester. Needless to say, it was a deeper experience. I had grown in the intervening handful of years, my knowledge of Latin was solid, and I could now relate to Aeneas's fatigue over the unknown: Where will he be? What will he become? Assurances from the gods that he will found a new and great nation meant something to Aeneas, but his life in the meantime felt so stressful in mundane ways. As a college student bound for graduate school, I could feel a hint of such stresses in my own life—this is why we say "Enjoy the journey" rather than focus on the destination. Yet the journey is unavoidably stressful when we're not entirely sure that our desired destination will actually be there when we get to it.

Rereading the *Aeneid* more recently as a mother, I am repeatedly struck by the anguish of the women in this epic. The heroic code exacts a human price, which is too often paid by the women who form the heroes' support staff, also too frequently against their will. I have cried for Creusa, Aeneas's Trojan wife and the mother of his young son Ascanius. She is simply erased from the story after the fall of Troy. And it is difficult not to weep for Dido, who happens to be a convenient tool that the gods could use to get Aeneas a safe stopping place in Carthage for a little while before he could sail on to his true destination. And then there is Lavinia, Aeneas's future Italian wife.

Recently, upon recommendation from a friend, I read Ursula Le Guin's quietly powerful novel *Lavinia*. It is a retelling of the *Aeneid* from Lavinia's perspective, giving words to the shadowy girl who (in the epic) is simply the passive cause of the war between the newly arrived Trojans and some of the native Latins. I realized in reading Le Guin that she also had lived with the *Aeneid* a long time. Only someone intimately familiar with Vergil could have written that book, a modern classic in its own right.

It is right that rereading Vergil over decades had such a powerful effect on Le Guin. Rereading great books shapes us, forming our character in the virtues. Not only does our capacity for mercy and pity to others expand, but so does our ability to bear personal suffering in any scope or intensity. Le Guin is not the only person to have internalized such lessons from Vergil. The first book of Augustine's *City of God*, in which he tells of the sack of Rome by the Goths in AD 410, repeatedly nods to the narrative of the sack of Troy in the second book of the *Aeneid*. The epic gives Augustine the language and inspiration to process the tragedy of his own age and thus feel God's universal provision even in this dark moment.

Indeed, I purposefully selected several Christian writers who read their pagan predecessors with love for the final section of this book. They all had the conviction that Christ offered the wisdom needed for a more complete understanding of the human condition. But more than that, these writers in the dawning age of Christianity share with us a wonder that we might too easily take for granted as we read the pagan classics—that God could love sinful humanity so very much. What a contrast with the pagan gods, who only persecuted people, toyed with them for their own whims, and scorned their very suffering!

Canons and Dilemmas

It seems appropriate here to say a few final words about the "canon." Why did some authors make it into this book but others did not? A canon is a difficult concept to define and is, at least occasionally, subjective. After all, I only had twenty chapters to work with, so I immediately knew that some authors might not get a chapter or section of their own. And while I knew that this book could not claim to be a survey of Greco-Roman classics without a chapter on Homer or Vergil, I could respectfully disagree with other experts about the inclusion of some other authors. Sorry, Polybius and Diodorus—nothing personal. I like you both, but I could discuss only so many historical authors. I feel some more sorrow over not devoting attention to Plautus and Terence, representatives of Roman Republican comedy, as well as the dynamic uncle and nephew duo Pliny the Elder and Younger. As I think about authors—major and minor—who got left out because of limited space, I recall a question from years ago on my PhD exams. I was asked to write an essay about an author whom I would like to add to the canon but who is not currently considered to be a member of it. My answer: Athenaeus. I bet you've never heard of him—and that's okay. We can still be friends.

Sometime ca. AD 200, a group of men gathered for what can only be described as the epic nerd dinner party. Forget Plato's *Symposium*; Athenaeus's *Deipnosophistai* or *Learned Banqueteers* makes Plato's gathering seem like a bunch of irresolute amateurs. To talk just about one topic? For just a few hours? Pfft.

Over the course of Athenaeus's dialogue in fifteen books—and, presumably, at least as many courses—his learned banqueteers discuss diverse topics such as recipes and exotic cuisine, drinking games, obscure science facts, geography, medicine, Greek and Latin grammar, military tactics, history, and a lot of literature of both the well-known and more obscure varieties. They quote from memory a small library of writers—poetry and prose from a wide range of genres. Some of those quoted are otherwise wholly unknown to us today or only known by name. Athenaeus's dialogue is thus a wonderful resource for modern scholars. Years ago, I heard a scholar say that whenever she was looking for ideas for her next project she simply started rereading bits of Athenaeus. She remarked that she would certainly find some obscure detail or a quoted fragment that no one had ever written about, which would inspire her next article or book.

Maybe Athenaeus's dialogue is not everyone's cup of tea—and it does drag at times—but it's still a remarkable work. The thing is, I could mention so many other ancient writers who are not part of the canon but might merit inclusion. On the one hand, we can mourn that only a tiny fraction of ancient literature survived—for instance, a lot more Greek tragedies are lost than the relative few that made it down to our own times. On the other hand, we do still have so much and we should be grateful for this.

And so, not everyone in the canon of Greco-Roman classics made it into this book. Yet some writers I mention are perhaps not uniformly considered part of the canon. My point is: Someone else could have approached this project with a different set of authors or even a different set of themes.

That is okay. My book is not meant to be the final word—but it seeks to encourage you to dig deeper for yourself and find the joy of reading the Greco-Roman classics, just as two millennia of earlier Christians have done.

If reading this book has introduced you to new (and reunited you with very old) friends, I am glad. But even more so, this book is meant to help you see the value of these texts for seeing God. And if reading this book has done that, I rejoice!

Acknowledgments

In one sense, it took ten months to write this book. In another sense, however, this process began in the fall of 1996. At that time I, a new immigrant to the U.S. (and still getting comfortable with English), took my first Latin class as a high school sophomore. All I knew about Latin at that point was what Alice had said about studying it in Lewis Carroll's books. After nearly three decades of studying all things Greek and Roman, I present this book as a testament to the wonderful teachers I was blessed to have at all stages of my education—although I of course emphatically lay claim to all errors as my own.

I find it difficult to imagine how I would have been able to write this book without first encountering Latin in Betsy Dawson's class at East Chapel Hill High School. Then I had incredible experiences at the University of Virginia and at Princeton University—of studying Euripides and Sophocles with David Kovacs, Apuleius with Greg Hays, Vergil and Plautus with John Miller, Roman rhetoric with Robert Kaster, Horace with Denis Feeney, and Thucydides and the Athenian democracy with Josiah Ober, to name just a few. Elizabeth Meyer and J. E. Lendon introduced me to so many Greek and Roman historical writers and taught me to read literary sources with a historian's eye. Sometimes material from classes taken long ago simply floats right back up when needed, such as when I could vividly recall particular readings from Jenny Strauss Clay's *Iliad* seminar and Jon Mikalson's Herodotus seminar, both now over twenty years removed.

I am also grateful for the many students with whom I've had the joy of sharing some of my thoughts on Greek and Roman literature during my own fifteen years as a professor of ancient history and classics. I am now so delighted, finally, to teach Latin and Greek—and Greek and Roman literature—to my own children in our family's homeschool. I am filled with indescribable joy to think that through this book I now get to tell other readers about the texts that I have loved for so long!

Some ideas that made it into this book have appeared in various forms (some more recognizable than others) in *Current*, *Front Porch Republic*, *Christianity Today*, *Providence*, *Religion & Liberty*, and *The Raised Hand*. I am grateful for these and many other publications that have extended lavish intellectual hospitality and allowed me to share ideas in progress.

I was absolutely delighted to work again with the amazing Katya Covrett, whose editorial prowess did much to improve this book. Daniel Saxton's copyediting efforts are worthy of a Pindaric ode, but in the interest of space I can only say: Thank you! And while not an editor for this project, the incomparable Eric Miller, under whose capable leadership I was blessed to work at *Current* until its conclusion in April 2025, was the best friend and mentor any writer could wish for as I was composing this book. I started a new position as Books Editor at Mere Orthodoxy as this project was nearing the finish line, and I am very grateful for the support of Jake Meador and Ian Harber.

The community of saints at Christ Community Church (EFCA) has been a glorious gift for me and my family since our move to Ohio, mere months before I began writing this book. Good friends are a treasure and a true gift from God, and the friends one meets at church are doubly so. I don't make these rules! I am also grateful for mom friends, near and far, who have kept me sane. Their friendship brings as much joy to me as their children's friendship brings to my kids. Forget Plato's *Symposium*—my favorite dinner parties in this season of life involve ten to twenty kids running around while chicken nuggets and chips are set out for the collective enjoyment of kids and adults. I'm especially grateful for the encouragement of Dixie Dillon Lane and Ivana Greco, dear friends and fellow homeschooling mom-writers.

Last but not least, my husband Dan, a gifted historian whose own work I so greatly admire, has been a loving and generous partner in this endeavor, just as in everything else in life. Vergil wrote this phrase in a less pleasant context, but I am happy to redeem it for us: *Omnia vincit amor.*

Glossary

Achaeans: A term used by the Homeric epics to refer to all of the Greeks collectively. Thus the title "Best of the Achaeans," to which every Greek warrior aspired, referred to the best of the collected Greek army. The original Achaea is a region of Greece located just north of Arcadia in the northwestern Peloponnese.

Asia Minor: A region of Greek-speaking colonies located in modern-day Turkey, separated from mainland Greece by the Aegean Sea. The westward expansion of the Persian Empire in the late sixth century BC absorbed the Greek city-states of Asia Minor.

Atlas: A Titan pre-Olympian god, who single-handedly held up the sky in Greek mythology.

Bard: An entertainer who performs epic poetry from memory; typically a traveling profession. Mentioned in the Homeric epics but existed into the Classical period.

Bronze Age: The period of Greek history from ca. 2000 BC to the beginning of the Archaic Period ca. 800 BC. The Trojan War belongs to this period, usually dated ca. 1100 BC. The *polis* (city-state) emerged during this time.

Catapult: A machine used especially in siege warfare, capable of shooting projectiles at great distances. The earliest catapult, resembling a giant bow, was invented in 399 BC.

Catechumen: A new Christian believer in training, who has not yet been baptized into full membership in the church but is preparing to do so.

Classical Period: The period of Greek history from the Persian Wars (499 BC) to the death of Alexander the Great (323 BC). During this time, different city-states vied for control over the Greek-speaking world.

Comedy: A genre of ancient Greek and Roman drama, always done in poetic form. It is characterized by humorous plots and jokes, often involving current events or cultural phenomena.

Consul: The highest elected office in the Roman ladder of offices (*cursus honorum*). Two consuls were elected each year and served as the commanders-in-chief of the Roman army.

Dactylic hexameter: The meter of Greek and Roman epic poetry, which consisted of six units per line of poetry. Each metrical unit could consist of either a dactyl (long syllable followed by two short ones) or spondee (two long syllables).

Democracy: The rule of the people. However, the Athenian democracy—the most famous representative of this form of government in antiquity—did not recognize women as citizens. Likewise excluded were slaves, foreigners, and children not born of legal marriages.

***Deus ex machina*:** At the end of Athenian tragedies, sometimes a god or a goddess would appear on stage, lowered dramatically by a machine device (hence, *ex machina*), and resolve a drama that would otherwise end in the deaths of all the characters.

Didactic: A type of ancient literature that taught its audiences about a particular topic, akin to modern-day handbooks or guides but generally more literary. Could be in prose or poetry.

Epic: The oldest type of ancient literature, originally composed orally by bards—e.g., the Homeric epics. Most often use the dactylic hexameter as the meter.

Etruscans: A flourishing civilization to the north of Rome, which challenged and threatened the early Romans. We read about some of their wars with Rome in the first books of Livy's history.

Genre: A type of literature. A genre is usually recognizable by following particular rules or features. For example, epic poetry is clearly distinct from comedy or didactic medical manuals.

Gilgamesh: A historical king of the Mesopotamian city of Uruk (Warka in modern-day Iraq), who ruled sometime in the first half of the first millennium BC. The fictional *Epic of Gilgamesh*, which survives, displays many of the same features of heroic epic that we see in Homer.

Greece: A land of autonomous independent city-states, each possessing its own government, laws, economy, military, and religious cults. It did not become fully united until the Macedonian conquest in the late fourth century BC.

Hellespont: The narrow strait of water separating Asia Minor (modern-day Turkey) from mainland Greece. During the second Persian invasion of Greece, King Xerxes built a pontoon bridge for his army to cross over from Persian territory into Greece.

Heroic code: The accepted code of conduct by ancient epic heroes. It included the privileging of honor and the pursuit of martial glory and personal excellence over all else.

Hubris: A pride that seeks to rival the gods, consequently inviting their wrath. More than just regular pride, it suggests aspirations to divinity on the doer's part. Example: Xerxes lashing the sea because a storm drowned his ships.

Isis: An Egyptian goddess, whose controversial cult was present in the Roman world.

Meter, poetic: A musical convention characterized in the Greco-Roman era by length of syllables. Syllables can be either long or short, and in different metrical configurations a metrical foot is composed of a number of syllables in particular lengths.

Metic: A resident alien who was not a citizen and thus ineligible to vote. Many residents in Classical Athens fell into this category.

Oligarchy: The rule of the few—as opposed to democracy. For example, ancient Sparta was an oligarchy, although it also had a hereditary monarchy with two kings. In another example, at the end of the Peloponnesian War, Athens was ruled by an oligarchy of the Thirty Tyrants for almost a year.

Pagan: A term that originally in Late Antiquity referred to villagers, as opposed to city dwellers. Because cities were more Christianized than the countryside, the term ultimately came to mean "non-Christian," and that is how I use it in this book.

Panhellenic: Describes a concept or value or institution shared by all the Greeks, as opposed to just one or several city-states. For example, the Olympics were a panhellenic institution, since all Greek city-states were eligible to send participants there.

***Pax Romana*:** The period of relative peace and stability in the Roman

Empire during which the empire reached its greatest geographical extent. This peace lasted from Augustus's consolidation of power in 27 BC to the death of the emperor Marcus Aurelius in AD 180.

Peloponnesian War: The war between Sparta with its allies and Athens with its allies from 431 BC to 404 BC. It engulfed the entire Greek-speaking world, forcing city-states to take sides. While Sparta ultimately won, the war weakened both Athens and Sparta so much that neither ever regained its pre-war prominence. Most of the surviving Athenian tragedies and comedies come from this period.

Pericles: An Athenian politician whose leadership of the democracy transformed the Athenian democracy into an empire. His death from a plague in 429 BC, just two years into the Peloponnesian War, left a leadership void in Athens.

Persian Wars: A series of conflicts between the Persian Empire and its Greek neighbors. These wars, especially the two invasions of Greece (490 BC and 480 BC), form the main subject of Herodotus's *Histories.*

Philippics: Either the Athenian orator Demosthenes's speeches attacking Philip of Macedon in 351–350 BC or Cicero's speeches attacking Mark Antony in 44–43 BC. This term denoting an attack speech has consequently entered the English language.

***Polis* (city-state):** The main type of settlement throughout the ancient Greek-speaking world. A city-state was defined by its autonomy, including its own system of government, laws, military, and more.

Punic: Another term for "Carthaginian"; hence, "Punic Wars" refers to the three wars that the Romans fought against Carthage in the third and second centuries BC.

Roman Empire: The period of Roman history that begins at the assassination of Julius Caesar in 44 BC—or, as some argue, the full consolidation of power by the first emperor Augustus in 27 BC. The Western Roman Empire collapsed in AD 476, but the Eastern Roman Empire—which we know better as the Byzantine Empire—continued until AD 1453.

Roman Republic: The period of Roman history from the expulsion of the kings ca. 510 BC to the assassination of Julius Caesar in 44 BC—or Augustus's full consolidation of power in 27 BC. During this period, the Romans elected annual officeholders who ruled the state together with the Senate.

Siege: A type of warfare that seeks to surround a city and cut it off from all aid, eventually starving the inhabitants into surrender. Sieges before the era of catapults tended to be very long—as the example of the ten-year-long Trojan War reminds us.

***Technê*:** A Greek term for art or skill; origin of the English term "technology." Writing—and literature—are all examples of *technê*, but so is any art done well.

Thirty Tyrants: An oligarchy of thirty rulers installed by Sparta in 404 BC after it defeated Athens in the Peloponnesian War. This extremely cruel government ruled for slightly less than a year before the Athenians were able to expel it and restore the democracy. Several of the Thirty, including their leader Critias, were former students of Socrates.

Tragedy: A genre of ancient Greek and Roman drama, always in poetic form. The plot takes place within a single day, from sunup to sundown. A tragedy is characterized by its ability to make audiences weep over the helpless plight of humanity, and the gods often play a prominent role as the causes of senseless suffering and much death.

Trojan War: A historical but deeply mythologized war during the Greek Bronze Age. It is the subject of the Homeric epics.

Subject Index

Index Locorum

Cultural Christians in the Early Church

Nadya Williams

In the middle of the third century CE, one North African bishop wrote a treatise for the women of his church. He exhorted them to resist culturally normalized yet immodest behaviors in their cosmopolitan Roman city; for instance, mixed public bathing in the nude and wearing excessive amounts of jewelry and makeup. This treatise appears even more striking once we realize that the scandalous women it addressed were single and had dedicated their virginity to Christ.

Stories like this one challenge the general assumption among present-day Christians that the earliest Christians were zealous converts and much more counterculturally devoted to their faith than typical churchgoers today. We also too often think that cultural Christianity is a modern phenomenon generally occurring in areas where Christianity is the majority culture, such as the American "Bible Belt." This book's story refutes both of these misconceptions.

Cultural Christians in the Early Church argues historically and practically that cultural Christians were the rule rather than the exception in the early church. This book uses different categories of sins to consider how culture challenged the earliest converts to Christianity in the Greco-Roman cultural milieu of the Roman Empire. These believers were regular people who blurred and pushed the boundaries of what it meant to be a saint or sinner from the first to the fifth centuries CE. Their stories illuminate difficult timeless questions that stubbornly persist in our own world and churches: When is it a sin to eat or not eat a particular food? Are women inherently more sinful than men? And why is Christian nationalism a problem and, at times, a sin? Ultimately, recognizing that cultural sins are always a part of the story of the church and its people both comforts us and calls us to action in our pursuit of sanctification today.

Available in stores and online!